Lean, Ethical Business Communication

Binod Sundararajan & Linda Macdonald

OXFORD
UNIVERSITY PRESS

OXFORD
UNIVERSITY PRESS

Oxford University Press is a department of the University of Oxford.
It furthers the University's objective of excellence in research, scholarship,
and education by publishing worldwide. Oxford is a registered trade mark of
Oxford University Press in the UK and in certain other countries.

Published in Canada by
Oxford University Press
8 Sampson Mews, Suite 204,
Don Mills, Ontario M3C 0H5 Canada

www.oupcanada.com

Library and Archives Canada Cataloguing in Publication
Sundararajan, Binod, author
Lean, ethical business communication / Binod Sundararajan and Linda
Macdonald.

Includes bibliographical references and index.
ISBN 978-0-19-901121-6 (paperback)

1. Business communication–Textbooks.   2. Business communication–
Moral and ethical aspects–Textbooks.   3. Business ethics–Textbooks.
I. Macdonald, Linda, 1958-, author   II. Title.

HF5718.S86 2016   658.4'5   C2016-905063-7

Oxford University Press is committed to our environment. This book is printed on
Forest Stewardship Council® certified paper and comes from responsible sources.

Printed and bound in the United States of America

1 2 3 4 — 20 19 18 17

Contents

Part Three ◉ Reports and Presentations

Preface

Lean, Ethical Communication for Business is aimed at university and college students enrolled in business or professional communication courses. It is appropriate as an introduction to business communication. We trust that this book will engage, involve, and elevate students and give them much value, not only during the course, but beyond as well.

Basis

The **lean** in the title indicates thinness or, in the context of business communication, a level of preciseness that is required when communicating. This level of preciseness is dictated by the situation, the background, the audience, and the channel to be used for such a communication. The "ethical" in the title indicates the need to have **ethics** at the heart of every business communication effort. Placing ethics front and centre allows the business communicator to display integrity in thought and action.

This book embodies both classical **rhetoric** (ethos, or ethics; logos, or reason; and pathos, or emotion), and modern needs that will empower you to become strategic and ethical communicators familiar with current modes of transmitting messages. We interweave classical rhetoric with modern communication theories to provide a rich, intuitive, case-based, practitioner-oriented approach to becoming lean and ethical business communicators.

We do this by adopting an immersive case study approach coupled with SCOPE (Strategy, Content, Outcome, Presentation, and Ethics), which is a philosophical approach to communication in general and business communication in particular. The following section describes the case study approach. We then describe the SCOPE philosophy and how it will be woven into the **analysis** of the case scenarios we describe throughout the book. At the end of each chapter, we perform a SCOPE analysis of the approaches taken by the actors presented in these scenarios.

The Case Study Approach

Lean, Ethical Communication for Business uses a case study approach to business communication, and presents situations based on real-world examples. In these situations, a problem emerges. Like all problems, a range of solutions is possible. This book reflects some of the options available and provides tools for solving the problem and making a decision. This approach enables us to see the crafting of communication as situational, complex, and strategic.

A case study approach enables us to see the complexities in business communication. A variety of factors influence our approach to any communication. Who is the audience for the communication? Does this audience include supervisors, clients, co-workers, or the general public, or is it a mixed audience with differing needs and expectations? Are there cultural issues to address? What does this audience already know about the situation that prompts the communication? Which communication channel—for example, letter, email, **text** message, or phone call—is best suited for this audience and purpose? What needs to be said? And what strategies are best used to relay this message?

Chapter Flow

You will immediately see a difference between the flow of its chapters and those of most first-year business communication textbooks. We have adopted the route taken by most North American Bachelor of Commerce or business management programs. In many such programs, written and oral business communication are taught together in one course, while other programs separate these two components into two courses: first written and then oral communication or vice versa. Regardless of the order or whether the written and oral components are combined into one course, it is rare for students in their first jobs (whether an internship or a full-time job) to be writing business letters or reports to external **stakeholders**. When they write, it is usually to internal stakeholders. As their managers become confident in their ability to communicate effectively, the interns or new graduates will be allowed to write to external stakeholders.

In undergraduate programs (whether business or engineering) where internships or co-op work terms are part of the experiential learning components, students first learn to assess their skills, craft effective **résumés**, write impactful **cover letters**, and perfect their **networking** and interviewing skills to secure their first internship or co-op work term. Once students have learned the basics of persuasive communication by writing résumés and cover letters, and have acquired the skills to network and successfully interview for jobs, they begin to learn about other forms of business communication, such as letters, memos, emails, and short and long reports. Concurrently, various undergraduate programs also teach students about business presentations to various audiences. All of these concepts are designed to hone students' individual skills as they learn to manage their personal **brand**. Once they secure their first internship, co-op work term, or even their first full-time job, they need to learn how to manage their individual and organizational identities, particularly in the context of continually evolving technologies. This book has been written to support this natural flow as students make their way through curriculum in different courses to finally reach the workplace where they will embark on their individual careers.

Each chapter of this book covers a unique aspect of business communication. To assist with the discussion, each chapter also includes a SCOPE analysis, chapter summary, discussion questions, exercises, and sections on advice and strategic language. Chapter 1 deals with the crafting of résumés and cover letters. Additionally, we address the "elevator pitch" because these short talks, often delivered in front of prospective employers, are a summary of students' skills and abilities and their unique value proposition, and how they will benefit the organization. Chapter 1 follows the cases of Sean McNeill, Lara Leveaux, Maya Chen, and James Patel while they work on their résumés, cover letters, and elevator pitches in their effort to secure internships or co-op work terms.

Chapter 2 follows James Patel and Carrie du Plessis as they attend formal networking sessions and conduct informal networking through **LinkedIn** to look for a work term. The chapter then works through James Patel's preparation for his interview, and documents his actual interview and follow-up note to the interviewer.

Chapter 3 enters the realm of writing with a focus on emails, inter- and intra-office memos, and short reports in **memo** formats. It follows Sean McNeill and Lara Leveaux in their new co-op work terms at APPFORMS and addresses several aspects of writing informational messages, including form, **style**, language, tone of messages (particularly emails), and professionalism.

Chapter 4 discusses analysis and argumentation, subjects not typically found in first-year business communication textbooks. While some of the material is often addressed in other textbooks, none has devoted an entire chapter to the extremely crucial skills that apply not just business communication but to every aspect of life. In this chapter, we detail the various approaches to critical listening, reading, thinking, and reasoning before stepping through the various tools of argumentation, the core skills for every effective business communicator. We do this as we follow Carrie du Plessis, Maya Chen, and James Patel as they face organizational tasks and challenges that require them to think critically about their responses in the **form** of short reports or emails. We discuss processes of analysis, categorization, sorting, and **synthesis** of complex information into manageable chunks, and the construction of readable pieces of business information appropriate to the targeted audience.

Chapter 5 tackles the mechanics and choices involved in writing business letters to external stakeholders. We follow the various actors within and outside APPFORMS, as they correspond with each other regarding business matters. We look at style, fonts, format of business letters, and the choices one has to make as one writes these letters.

Chapters 6 and 7 deal primarily with the writing of reports, both short and long. Most reports are written for internal use; however, there are several instances of reports being written for external audiences as well. In these two chapters, the mechanics and formats remain fairly standard. In Chapter 6, we discuss form and content of reports by following the efforts of Bahram Fonseca, Kirsten Hamed, Dharini Gagnon, and Mithra Charleston as they prepare and write short reports with timelines. In Chapter 7, we follow the cases of Carrie du Plessis, James Patel, and Sean McNeill as they produce long reports.

Chapter 8 addresses the various aspects of making presentations to different audiences using Microsoft PowerPoint, Prezi, or any commonly available presentation application. Form, content, and design elements are discussed as choices the business communicator makes while designing and delivering these presentations. Aspects of delivery, such as style, tone, voice, pitch, and making eye contact with audiences to engage them in the material, are discussed as we follow the cases of Carrie du Plessis and Sean McNeill.

Chapter 9 is also a chapter not typically found in first-year business communication textbooks. While some elements of using social media is discussed in these other textbooks, this chapter informs students, particularly those who are soon to join the workforce in some capacity, about how to manage their individual, social, and organizational identities while at work. The preceding chapters deal with students learning about themselves, developing their skills, and articulating these skills and abilities in written and oral forms. This chapter provides students with the big picture, and how they will fit into the organizations that they will work in. It provides conceptual knowledge about brand, image, identity, and reputation, with a comparison between the individual and the organization, and outlines the distinction between individual, marketing, and corporate communication, with strategies for managing each of them effectively. It follows the cases of Kailee Pereira as she makes a workplace **faux pas** with **Twitter** and **Snapchat** and James Patel as he blogs, and provides clear ways to measure impact on social media sites.

Three things are covered implicitly and explicitly in all the chapters: cross-cultural communication, ethical communication, and diversity. By designing the APPFORMS organization to be diverse, with people from all over the world being represented, much like the pluralistic Canadian society, we have infused **diversity** and cross-cultural communication in every aspect of this textbook. Ethics is central to both the title and the SCOPE philosophy and runs in every choice that the actors make as they design, develop, and produce the various business communication pieces. By taking this approach, concepts like diversity, cross-cultural communication, and ethical communication should become first nature to students as they learn to be effective business communicators.

Acknowledgements

We would like to thank the editors of Oxford University Press for their encouragement and guidance, and the reviewers who helped refine some of the ideas and concepts presented in the book. We would also like to thank Dr. James Barker, Herbert S. Lamb Chair of Business Education at Dalhousie University, for his readings of the initial drafts of this book. We would additionally like to thank three of Dalhousie University's Bachelor of Commerce students, Bryce Cross, Kelly Hawa, and Daksha Gangalaramsamy, who have kindly provided us permission to adapt and present their in-class progress report assignment submissions.

Dedication

Binod Sundararajan dedicates this work to Acharn Sunda, Mom, Debbie, Sharad, Dharini, Lara, and Mithra.

Linda Macdonald dedicates this work to Bob, Joyce, Gary, and especially Jim, Sara, and Felicity.

Introduction

SCOPE

We use the acronym SCOPE to describe the elements that inform business communication: Strategy, Content, Outcome, Presentation, and Ethics. These elements overlap. For example, the communicator must be strategic in the method of communication, with ethics permeating all the decisions being made, and culture influencing the content, outcome, and style of presentation. All five elements must figure in every communication decision the writer or speaker makes.

- Strategy—encompasses choices on form, style, arrangement, flow, context, content, and channel
- Content—encompasses analysis, evaluation and synthesis, argumentation, evidence, and cultural aspects
- Outcome—encompasses choices in audience-centric writing to achieve the desired result
- Presentation—encompasses choices related to formats, structures, delivery, tone, and voice
- Ethics—encompasses ethical choices in both form and content, citations, and truthfulness

These elements comprise the writer's SCOPE, also known as range or vision. SCOPE focuses on the reader or the target audience. Identifying the audience is the writer's first challenge. Then, the writer must decide how best to adapt the content or message to the audience, and must select the form best able to deliver the message and achieve the desired outcome. Throughout this process, the writer must never deviate from a pre-established set of ethical standards. These standards will be derived from the alignment of the organizational values and the writer's own value system. In an era of rapidly developing technology, writers must move agilely between communication tools. Choosing a method of communication, like all other writing choices, depends on the targeted audience. The iterative process of analysis, evaluation, and synthesis with the SCOPE philosophy may be envisioned as an ever-expanding spiral. The spiral emanates from the creator of the text/message to reach either an individual receiver or a broad audience. The word *text* indicates all created forms of communication (documents, videos, tweets, memos, emails, letters, reports, presentations, graphics, etc.). Feedback keeps the creator/writer constantly aware of the "fitness for the occasion" (the Greek word *kairos*) and ethical considerations.

Strategy

Successful business communication, like successful business, requires strategic and deliberate decision-making. Writing strategy refers to the choices made in crafting communications. The choices you make will determine whether or not your message is successful in achieving its goal. The purpose and audience of your message determine your strategy.

The purpose of your message must first be identified. What is its goal? What do you hope to achieve by delivering this message? As long as the purpose of your message is unclear to you, you are unlikely to be successful. For example, a report without a clear purpose may wander and, with no clear direction, the reader is soon lost. Clarity in identifying purpose strengthens the delivery of the message because only after a clear goal is established can the writer then select the best method for delivery, from the most appropriate channel (memo, report, email, social media, etc.) to sentence structure and individual word choice.

Writers must also identify the audience and the audience's needs. This too requires strategy. Assessment of your potential audience involves careful consideration. Who is the target audience? What characteristics of the audience must you consider? Will cultural **attributes** influence the way your message is delivered? What level of formality will the audience expect? Will age, position, or situation affect this level of formality? Will the message require a particular sensitivity? If the audience is not clearly identified, how should you approach the subject? What form of writing is appropriate for this audience? In developing your strategy, you must also consider the audience's potential response and design messages that carefully balance the needs of the audience with the purpose of the message.

The audience dictates the style and form for the message. If the audience lacks familiarity with or access to the Internet, email communication is clearly an inappropriate form of transmission. If you must communicate particularly sensitive information—for example, the inability of a business to satisfy a customer's request—you must choose words and sentence structures that demonstrate attention to the audience's potential response. For some audiences, beginning a letter by establishing your social connection may be the best approach, while in other situations beginning with a direct statement of purpose is best.

The writer or speaker must also be strategic when constructing the message. You must seek to find evidence for any claims you want to put forward, and anticipate possible objections or counterclaims from the audience to be able to prepare and present a meaningful, evidence-based rebuttal. This strategy allows you to reduce any objections from the audience and have the message received in the manner intended.

Successful business communication does not happen accidentally or spontaneously. Rather, it is formed from the series of strategic choices the writer or speaker makes. Every decision you make, from the placement of a comma to the selection of a greeting to the identity of the audience and the purpose of the message, determines your success. Strategy in communication is the art and science of leading a reader or listener to a pre-determined goal.

Content

As a writer, it is essential to understand what makes the content of a message important to the reader. Once you have analyzed a situation, you need to know how to synthesize your information and present it in a manner that is intuitively understandable by your audience. You need to consider the cultural norms and expectations that influence both you and your reader. In an increasingly global world, cultures have, to a certain extent, converged. The widespread uses of Standard English, BELF (Business English as Lingua Franca, a common language used for the conducting of business), and Globish (a simplified form of English described by Jean-Paul Nerriere) have confirmed English as the language of modern business.

Shared language does not equate with shared culture or understanding. In a rapidly changing world, cultural boundaries are in a constant state of flux. Assumptions about culture may be outdated quickly. For example, the supposed preference for indirect forms of communication in some Asian countries has ceded, to some extent, to a preference for direct communication, which requires the effective use of both language and non-verbal communication.

Communicators, then, must consider the audience's needs and choose language appropriately. As a writer, you must develop sensitivity to the cultural situation of your audience. A lack of sensitivity can result in a failure to communicate. For example, the use of casual language that might be intended as a way of establishing relationships may be interpreted as a lack of professionalism in some cultures. Non-verbal communication also can convey messages. Sitting on a table during a presentation in New Zealand may be intended as a method of relaxing the audience, but may be interpreted as highly offensive by that population.

Culture can also be specific to an organization and to how people within the organization operate. For example, the level of informality in a small start-up differs from more policy-driven procedures in small to medium enterprises or larger organizations. Reports written for an internal audience may incorporate language or acronyms that would not be appropriate for an external audience. In business communications, you must be aware of cultural factors both inside and outside the organization.

In a global world, cultural elements can shift or blend, and can be fluid or fixed. It is increasingly unlikely that any organization can target only audiences with a shared cultural background. Even within a local market, businesses cannot assume that the cultural attributes of their audiences are uniform and static. Thus, you need to include appropriate evidence in support of your argument and in a style that considers cultural norms and expectations of your audience. The choices you make in communications must consider cultural influences as a central element of your strategy.

Outcome

What do you expect the receiver of your communication to do with your communication? What is the intended result? The reader or listener must know what it is you are trying to achieve. Your success will be demonstrated by their reaction.

If, for example, you are writing a cover letter and résumé, your desired outcome is a job. Your aim is to get the recruiter or hiring manager to call you for an interview. To obtain this desired outcome, you must create documents that convince the reader that you can bring value to the organization. Merely describing your training and previous experience will not be enough to achieve this; keeping the outcome in mind as you compose these documents will help you refine your approach. Strong action verbs that demonstrate what you achieved and anecdotal evidence citing a situation in which you overcame adversity to achieve organizational objectives will highlight which aspects of your abilities will benefit the organization. Once you obtain an interview, you can emphasize how you meet or exceed the needs of the hiring organization and convince the recruiter (ethically, by not inflating achievements or making up stories) how you can benefit the organization.

In delivering some messages, the desired outcome may contain opposing elements. For example, you may want to convey that you no longer wish to patronize a business, but do not wish to cultivate bad feelings. Or, you may refuse a request to provide a refund, but wish to retain customer loyalty. The desired outcomes, then, may sometimes be complex. A clear understanding of the message's purposes will enable you to achieve multiple goals.

Presentation

The method of presentation requires strategy based on audience and desired outcome. Today, multiple means of presentation exist. Forms and accessibility of communication have evolved rapidly in the past two decades and promise to develop still further in the future. Once primarily produced through hard-copy memos and letters, flipcharts, and written reports, communications now may include Skype, text messages, Twitter, email, **Facebook**, and presentation aids like PowerPoint. Face-to-face meetings rely increasingly less on physical proximity and more on teleconferencing, which involves different strategies for maximum effect.

With so many options available, the selection of an appropriate communication channel is difficult, but contributes greatly to the ultimate success of the message. The short form of a Twitter message requires careful and deliberate selection of words and may not be appropriate for all messages. Email may be appropriate to target certain audiences, but may entirely miss a younger audience more familiar with Facebook, **Xing**, or **QQ**. Audiences accustomed to immediately accessible information may now rely on more direct and shorter forms of communication.

To be adept in business communication, then, you need to be familiar with a wide variety of communication techniques, and be able to manipulate these techniques strategically and agilely toward your intended goal. You also need to be constantly alert to changes in audiences' preferred modes of receiving communications. The presentation choices you make contribute significantly to the result. Furthermore, the tone and style of the written or spoken presentation can also have specific effects on the intended audience and, if done incorrectly, the audience is not likely to receive the presentation well.

Agility in choosing from available communication channels and the ability to adapt to changing business and consumer needs will allow the lean and effective communicator to respond to new technologies that are likely to mediate communications between senders and receivers, writers and audiences.

Ethics

Ethics is a system of moral principles that governs the actions of the individual or culture and pervades all decision-making. Derived from the Greek word "ethos," meaning character, it refers to the trustworthiness or credibility of an individual. The key to effective business communication is the credibility of the writer or speaker. To stress the role of ethics in all communication, we apply ancient Isocratean rhetoric, which essentially defines rhetoric as the art of ethical choice in all human public and private decision-making. The lean and ethical business communicator constantly seeks to have credibility in the words that he or she writes or speaks.

The elements of the SCOPE philosophy are applied in this book through case studies. These case studies offer you an opportunity to analyze the issues that prompt the communication, identify the audience for the response, assess the available methods of transmittal, and craft the message to achieve the desired outcome. They are drawn from actual events or are fictional accounts that reflect actual events. In the early chapters, the case studies focus on a multicultural Canadian environment; as you work through the book and progress to external communications, they broaden to include national and international scenarios. The case studies reflect the complexities inherent in communication and allow you to apply your decision-making skills. This approach reflects the same decision-making process of communication in the business world where employees face daily choices in how and what to communicate, and to whom.

Throughout this book, the cases are based in one organization: APPFORMS. We present business scenarios in which actors within and outside the organization must respond to certain events using written or verbal communication or both. We follow the fates and fortunes of these actors as they face business problems and learn from their experiences.

APPFORMS—The Organization

APPFORMS Inc.—Applications for Mobile Computing and Smartphones

APPFORMS creates various practical, functional, and recreational applications for mobile computing and smartphones, including Apple iPhones, Android phones, BlackBerry OS phones, Windows Mobile phones, and a host of tablet and convertible computers. It is a growing organization, having started with 3 people, but with 45 full-time employees currently. APPFORMS is a technology company where decision-making is left to the individual product groups and only strategic decisions are pushed up to senior management. Each group thus works as independent profit centres within the larger organization and is accountable for every aspect of the business. Such an organization is typically referred to as an adaptive organization, as they are able to respond quickly to changes in the environment and the market. The organizational culture is built on open communication, and trust is critical to overcome miscommunication and errors in processes and products. APPFORMS also uses incentives and programs to reward successes, but the drive for employees is to build products that enhance peoples' technology experiences. The opportunity for innovation is the key motivator of the people who work at APPFORMS.

APPFORMS Inc.—The Story

Goran Duro stared out the window at the ferry from Dartmouth crossing the harbour to Halifax. His eighteenth-floor office in Purdy's Wharf Tower 2 afforded him such a view and he made it a point to spend the first 10 to 15 minutes of every morning enjoying and appreciating the magnificent view. Not only did it give him time to think and reflect, it often took him down memory lane; his daily commute from the Eastern Passage to the Dartmouth Ferry terminal, the crossing over to Halifax, and the hopping onto the number 10 bus to take him to his graduate computer science and business classes at the university. That was not too long ago, and he felt a sense of achievement each time he realized where he started and how far he had come. He and his partners, Alvira Cairns and Abdul Hamza, had been able to skillfully nurture their start-up through the growing pains and initial financing troubles into a successful and profitable organization. They were not just business partners managing a technology company; they were extremely good friends and trusted one another implicitly. Goran felt that he had the best associates.

Goran walked over to study the APPFORMS's organization chart that hung on the wall. Alvira and Abdul and the company directors were due shortly for the regular morning meeting and they were going to discuss the chart. He looked at each member of each team and smiled to himself as he remembered the early days. They had decided to keep the organization lean and focused from inception, and felt that keeping a team-based structure would serve them best. They had learned about this type of structure from one of the case studies covered in class about a company called Yammer (Amin, 2012). Each team was built around an operating system, so there were teams for the Android phones, the BlackBerry phones, the iPhones, and the Windows Mobile phones. Alvira, Abdul, and Goran had had a discussion about creating applications (**apps**) for tablets and personal laptops that converted to tablets (convertibles), and decided to create a separate team for that. There was some cross-over in functionalities between the tablet team and the other teams, but Alvira, Abdul, and Goran were all convinced that the convertible/tablet team would stay as a separate group and issues could be dealt with as they came up.

APPFORMS ORGANIZATION & COMMUNICATIONS CHART

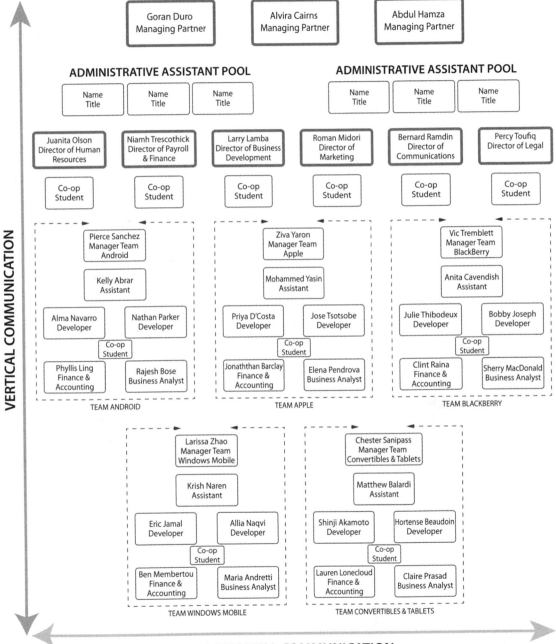

They had done well and had a great organization with people committed to both the organization and their work. APPFORMS also had a good team of directors who oversaw some of the strategic and functional areas in the organization. Juanita Olson was the dynamite head of Human Relations & Resources with a passion for ensuring that every employee was well taken care of by way of compensation and benefits. She also was amazing at spotting talent. With news from the Nova Scotia Business Inc. saying that "world leaders in ICT (Information and Communication Technology) choose Nova Scotia as a location for growth" (NSBI, n.d.), many smart people would be looking for an opportunity and he would need Juanita to head the team to recruit some new talent. He reminded himself to tweet about it. Goran also wanted to chat with Alvira, Abdul, and Juanita about participating in a networking event at the universities. He had always been keen that their organization be headquartered in a university town so that they would have access to a talented pool of graduating students. Halifax had three universities and there were many more in the province, as well as the rest of the country. He would send out a memo (horizontal communication to his partners and vertical communication to the director of HR) about this later.

Goran walked back to his desk and saw the Outlook Calendar beeping a reminder about his morning meeting that was about to start. He glanced at his sales **BI dashboard**, which showed sales and download figures of the various apps that APPFORMS produced. The Windows Mobile apps had a slow **uptake** but they were picking up. The iPhone apps downloads were steady, although they had a serious issue with the new Apple iOS when it would not sync the calendar. Several other apps had sync issues as a result, but everything was sorted out when Apple sent in the updates. The BlackBerry OS10 was definitely an improvement over the previous BlackBerry OS, and sales of apps for the BlackBerry smartphones was also increasing. With the possibility of BlackBerry partnering with Android and BlackBerry devices using the Android platform, sales were bound to increase. Anyway, things looked good, and Goran was ready for the meeting. They met daily, and they made it a point to record the minutes of each meeting so that they could track their decision-making process, learn, and constantly improve.

Goran looked at the four smartphones on his desk (he had one for each operating system), picked up his BlackBerry, logged into his Twitter account, and tweeted the following: "NSBI forecasts growth in ICT sector. Contact #APPFORMS." It was 9:12 a.m. and Goran scanned the **agenda** for the morning meeting. He had a minute or two to go.

APPFORMS Inc.

DAILY MORNING PARTNERS' MEETING

Wednesday, December 9, 2015
9:15 a.m.–10:30 a.m.
Conference Room

Standard business meeting agenda format provides information about the nature of the meeting, the participants, the time and date, and the location

Agenda

1. Approval of Agenda
2. Minutes of December 7, 2015 (attached)
   a) Review and approval
   b) Matters arising (Alvira Cairns and Abdul Hamza)

Most formal meetings start with the approval of the agenda, followed by a review and approval of the minutes of the previous meeting

SUBSTANTIVE ISSUES

3. Review of second quarter forecasts (Larry Lamba/Roman Midori)
4. New products and business (Larry Lamba/Roman Midori)
5. Hiring—experienced talent and co-op/students/interns (Juanita Olson)
   a) Job ads
   b) Networking events at universities
6. Cultural sensitivity training (Juanita Olson)

Substantive issues are those that require considerable thought before any action is taken

OTHER TOPICS

7. Employee Retreat (Juanita Olson)
8. Takeover offer—legal aspects (Percy Toufiq)
9. Internal and external communication (Bernard Ramdin)
10. Holiday bonus and packages (Niamh Trescothick)
11. Holiday party
12. Other business

Other items and routine organizational events/issues are also discussed

Exercises

1. Define the elements of SCOPE.
2. What is an adaptive organization?
3. What is the purpose of having **substantive** issues in a meeting agenda?
4. Why is ethics important for effective business communication?
5. Looking at the organization chart of APPFORMS Inc., define and explain horizontal and vertical communication.

CHAPTER ONE

The Career Portfolio: The Résumé, Cover Letter, and Elevator Pitch

Learning Objectives

A. **Identify** options in creating a résumé, cover letter, and elevator pitch.
B. **Assess** a job description and company to identify relevant and transferable skills.
C. **Select** the most appropriate language for you, the audience, and the message.
D. **Focus** on the employer's needs.
E. **Consider** the role of ethics in decision-making.
F. **Create** a strategic approach for crafting a résumé, cover letter, and elevator pitch.

The Story So Far

In the introduction, we described the philosophy, the five elements that comprise the approach, and how each element is a critical factor to effective business communication. We also looked at the story of APPFORMS and read how one of its managing partners, Goran Duro, went about preparing for his daily meeting with APPFORMS's senior management. We learned what an adaptive organization is and what goes into creating a typical business meeting agenda. The agenda items have a direct relevance to many situations and tasks that interns and co-op students are likely to encounter in their placements.

Chapter 1 follows four students as they create effective career portfolios to give them success in their job search. These students and others will all eventually secure positions at APPFORMS, and we will follow their progress as they learn and grow in their positions.

Introduction

Businesses today are heavily dependent on the analysis, storage, and exchange of knowledge. The Organisation for Economic Co-operation and Development (OECD), of which Canada is a member, defines a **knowledge-based economy** as one that depends on knowledge, information, and high skill levels, and relies on the exchange of intellectual capital. The knowledge-intensive industries of high-tech manufacturing, telecommunications, education, health, finance, and business services require effective communication for the successful understanding and exchange of knowledge. According to the OECD Science, Technology and Industry Scoreboard (2001), "the ability to create, distribute, and exploit knowledge is increasingly central to competitive advantage, wealth creation, and better standards of living" (p. 7).

Successful communication of knowledge is key to success in business. In addition, communication creates and sustains the relationships that are central to all business practice. The quality of these communications impacts success.

When you apply for a position in an organization, you must demonstrate an ability to create, apply, analyze, and share knowledge. You also need to demonstrate an ability to establish relationships with co-workers, management, and clients. How you construct your application package indicates your potential for effective knowledge-sharing and relationship-building. Because your application reveals so much about you and your potential, creating a strong application requires strategy.

Strategy is the art of designing and implementing tactics to achieve a desirable outcome. To be successful, a strategy must be responsive to the conditions. Today's businesses exist in an ever-changing global marketplace where technological advances continually shift how we work. In such a fluid environment, a successful strategy must be responsive and continuously revised. The strategy you create now for applying to a particular organization will not be the same strategy you use two weeks from now for another employer. Your success depends on being proactive in anticipating changes brought about by your learning progress, shifting focuses in a dynamic environment, and cultural differences. No two employers are alike, even within the same industry, and no two applicants are alike in experience and skill, so there is no one-size-fits-all résumé, cover letter, or elevator pitch.

In this chapter, we look at the strategies of prospective employees of APPFORMS, a company in the knowledge-intensive industry of mobile applications. The company is rapidly expanding and seeks to build its human resources by hiring a co-op student in marketing and at least one full-time employee in finance.

Résumés and Cover Letters

Résumés and cover letters require strategic decision-making. Some decisions concern highly visible elements, such as the ordering of categories and the selection of elements to include on résumés, while smaller details, such as the use of bold or underline or what verbs to use, can have equally powerful effect. The key to strategy is awareness of audience—in this case, the organization that is hiring. As you develop your résumé and cover letter, you should keep the organization's needs at the forefront. After all, the organization would not post a job if there was not a need to be met.

A résumé and cover letter are written summaries of your achievements and skills, while the **elevator pitch** encapsulates your attributes verbally. To create an effective elevator pitch, you need to determine your audience's needs, select elements of your experiences to highlight how you can address those needs, and create a structure of delivery appropriate for the situation.

Sean McNeill, Lara Leveaux, and Maya Chen have each identified APPFORMS as an ideal employer and need to craft a suitable résumé and cover letter. James Patel has already designed his basic documents and wants to present his strongest attributes in an elevator pitch.

The Case of Sean McNeill

Sean McNeill, a second-year university student seeking a co-op position in marketing, has been drawn to APPFORMS ever since he attended a job fair hosted by the university. At the fair, a recruiter told him how APPFORMS relies on **cross-functional teams** to facilitate its growth in the emerging application technology sector. As a marketing assistant, Sean would work on a project with a team that includes technology experts, communications experts, and account managers.

The job description appearing on his university's Career Services Centre website increases Sean's interest in the company.

APPFORMSCanada

JOB TITLE: Marketing Assistant (co-op work term)

COMPANY: APPFORMS Canada

CONTACT PERSON: Juanita Olson, Director of Human Resources

JOB DESCRIPTION

The Marketing Assistant works with the other members of the Marketing Department as well as with members of other departments toward creation, development and sales of new technology applications. The assistant will be an active member in establishing a plan to achieve financial goals. The assistant will also work with the Director of Communications in maintaining the company websites, producing material for external stakeholders, and researching media outlets

TASKS/DUTIES

- Assist in maintaining the company website and Facebook, Twitter, and blog accounts
- Support the Marketing team at special events
- Compile media analyses
- Conduct product research as required
- Work in a collaborative team environment

JOB REQUIREMENTS

- Co-op student in any year of university
- Enthusiastic, self-starting and dynamic individual
- Ability to work in a collaborative team environment
- Strong work ethic
- Strong interpersonal communication skills
- Strong written and oral communication skills
- Ability to use both Microsoft Office (Word, Excel, PowerPoint) and Apple software packages; knowledge of other computer applications like MS Access, MS Visio, and SAP are a plus
- Ability to work outside normal business hours at special events

As with all applications submitted through the university's Career Services Centre, Sean must submit a résumé, cover letter, and transcript.

Sean analyzes the job description to assess his suitability for the position. He circles words that show the strongest connections between his skills and experience and the description: *co-op student, self-starter, team,* **work ethic**, *communication,* and *computer applications.* The duties of maintaining websites and social media accounts, of researching, and of collaborating with a team all interest him, and he believes that his academic background has provided him with the skills and experience necessary for the job.

He also wants to ensure that the company's mission, values, and focus coincide with his own. Sean's research on the company reveals that the organization celebrates its diverse population and its team structure. The homepage of APPFORMS's website prominently features a photo of an ethnically diverse group of well-dressed young adults around a desk in a modern-looking, brightly lit room. He clicks the About Us tab.

APPFORMSCanada

ABOUT US: OUR VALUES

APPFORMS dares to be different. Our company is founded on the belief that our difference leads us to innovative design and practice. We apply our energy, our spirit of innovation, and our commitment to excellence in our products. We dare to redefine who we are every day, an effort that keeps us moving forward and succeeding in a highly competitive environment.

Sean proceeds to Careers. He scans the pages and notes several key words and phrases: *challenging, daring, team, collaborative, high achievers, fulfilling career, exciting opportunities,* and *creative potential.* He notes that APPFORMS has a training program to help employees develop technical as well as interpersonal and management skills and that he will be placed with a coach who will guide him through projects and provide information and feedback.

In looking through the company website, Sean worries about his experience. He has limited work experience and no volunteer experience. His summer job for the past three years was on his family's farm, where he separated produce for shipment from produce to sell at the local farmers' market. He and his younger brother then sold the produce at the market every day during the summer and on weekends in the fall. The money Sean earned allowed him to pay a substantial portion of the costs of his university education.

He wonders how he can create a résumé given his limited background. He has never written a résumé and begins his search for a model. He finds a variety of Microsoft Word templates suited to various levels of experience. Although Sean would like his résumé to be noticed, he chooses to avoid complicated templates and colour to attract attention. He will be submitting his documents online rather than in person and some colours would appear grey or the contrast between colours will be lost if his document is printed in black and white.

After surveying a range of templates and selecting some of the features that appeal to him, Sean chooses not to use a **template** but to create his own format. Noting what he sees as the best elements of each template, he decides to format his résumé in a simple style more suited to his personality than the Microsoft Word templates.

However, without the flashy template filling up space in the header or margins, Sean worries that his lack of experience will stand out. He envisions his résumé as consisting of mostly white space.

Sean then explores the headings in résumés in the Microsoft Word templates, the résumé samples provided by Career Services Centre, and various job-seeking and university websites. These headings will categorize his information.

Name and Contact Information

Sean notes that the same type of information is always contained in the name and contact information section, although the placement on the page and the font size and type vary tremendously. He opts for a font size that will make his name stand out. He also includes his physical mailing address. He chooses to provide his parents' address as well as his address during the school year since the university residence is not permanent. He chooses, however, not to include the phone number at his parents' address but instead includes his cellphone number. He then changes the message on his cellphone from "Yo, bro" to a more professional message. To enhance his professionalism, he also provide his university email address rather than his Gmail address. The university system has an option for personalizing the address, so he changes the address to something memorable: Sean.McNeill@myuni.ca.

Objective Statement

Some résumés include an objective statement that identifies the candidate's goal. These can appeal to a broad audience, for example, "Junior Communications Assistant" or "To obtain a position in a marketing firm that can benefit from my technology background." Other statements are directed at a particular employer, such as "Marketing Assistant position in which my expertise in research, design, and innovative implementation strategies will be employed." In his online research, however, Sean notes conflicting opinions on the value of an objective statement. An objective statement would briefly summarize the type of position he wants and would provide an opportunity to link his skill set to APPFORMS's needs. It has the added benefit of filling space on his sparse résumé. On the other hand, if it is not well written or merely repeats information that would be better placed in his cover letter, he will have attracted negative attention. Sean decides to omit the objective statement since his university's Career Services Centre's guidelines advise against them.

Profile/Summary of Qualifications

Sean's research indicates that a profile or summary of qualifications section places the main attributes in bullet points at the top of the page in a place of prominence. The summary should highlight the skills or attributes most attractive to the particular employer. He notes that the structure and content of this summary varies. One summary, for example, includes the item "Fluent in English and French," while another states "Achieved French Immersion Certificate," and yet another states "Recipient of French Student Excellence Award by Canadian Parents for French in recognition of bilingual ability and academic distinction." Sean's survey of sample résumés tells him that the best summaries of qualifications contain bullet points that are neither too general nor too long and detailed. The weakest bullet points list attributes that most candidates could claim and that do not contain supporting evidence, for example, "possess strong communication skills." He concludes that the best approach is to highlight, with evidence, the attributes most relevant for the position and the employer.

Education

Sean's sample résumés include information about the candidate's educational background. The university, program studied, and location are featured prominently, with the university and degree program often in bold. In some résumés, the degree program follows the university name and in others the degree program is first. He decides to include his major and his current GPA, which is especially high, and his entrance scholarship as well as his Dean's List status. He also includes the location of his university.

Some of Sean's research suggests that high school education should not be listed, and the sample résumés vary in whether or not it is included. Sean decides that because he went to a small school in a rural community, including the name and location of his high school, as well as his status as valedictorian, might add a point of interest.

Work and Volunteer Experience

Sean feels daunted by the sections on work and volunteer experience. The guidelines of his university's Career Services Centre state that he should use a reverse chronological order. They also indicate that Sean should describe his activities using strong active verbs and refer him to one of the many online lists of useful terms. These lists provide options for replacing weaker verbs like *do* and *have* with words like *calculate*, *handle*, *research*, and *collaborate*. Sean does not know how to approach this section. The guidelines generally indicate that for each position he should identify his job title, the name and location of the organizations, and a bulleted list of what he did. This section will be the focus of the potential employer's attention.

Awards and Achievements

Sean has a few items he could include in the section on awards and achievements. He has been on the university's Dean's List, he is the captain of his rugby team, and he has received a scholarship. He is not sure how to arrange these disparate activities on the page, however, especially since he already included the scholarship and his Dean's List status under Education.

References

The Career Services Centre says it is no longer customary to include references on the résumé unless the employer has specifically asked for them and recommends that Sean take a copy of his references to the interview should he get one. Writing "References available upon request" at the bottom of the résumé, as shown in several of the samples, seems pointless to Sean, and he chooses to leave out this phrase.

Sean's lack of work experience other than on his family's farm means he does not have a previous employer to use as a reference. He considers who might know about his character, work ethic, and achievements and might be willing to write a letter or receive a phone call about him. After much thought, he decides he needs someone who can attest to his technical and marketing knowledge, such as one of his professors. The manager of the farmers' market where he sells produce might also be willing to act as a reference since she has observed his customer service style and sales success for the past three summers.

Since APPFORMS's focus on teamwork was made apparent in his meeting with the recruiter at the university job fair and by the company website, Sean would like to have a reference who can affirm his teamwork skills, but most of his teams have been composed of peers. He knows that selecting a friend to act as a reference may compromise his credibility.

Finally, Sean notices that some sample résumés include relevant courses, activities, publications, technical skills, and other categories. Having reviewed the major categories, he applies these other categories to his own experience. He crafts the following document.

SEAN McNEILL

Manderson Hall, Rm 12   **42 Sun Drive**
Halifax, NS A1B 20Z   **Long Trail, Nova Scotia D1E 2F3**

Sean.McNeill@myuni.ca

555-4321

SUMMARY OF QUALIFICATIONS

☐ Proficient in Microsoft
☐ Experienced in teamwork through multiple group presentations at university and through sports activities that resulted in provincial championships in three successive years
☐ Creative and innovative, which is evident in how I changed the ways I marketed produce at the summer and weekend markets

EDUCATION

☐ **Nova Scotia University, Bachelors of Commerce Program (Co-op program), Major in Marketing, Halifax, Nova Scotia**
Will graduate 2018
Dean's List, Fall term
Entrance Scholarship

☐ **Long Trail Rural All-grade School, Long Trail, Nova Scotia, High School Diploma**
Valedictorian

ACTVITIES

Rugby, Captain, Regional Rugby League, 2012–14
Farmer's Market produce sales, 2011-2014

Sean is not entirely pleased with the result. The résumé lacks the professional polish he wants and he does not know how to use some of his experience or where he should place it in the résumé. He visits the Career Services Centre for advice. The advisor's comments are noted on the draft.

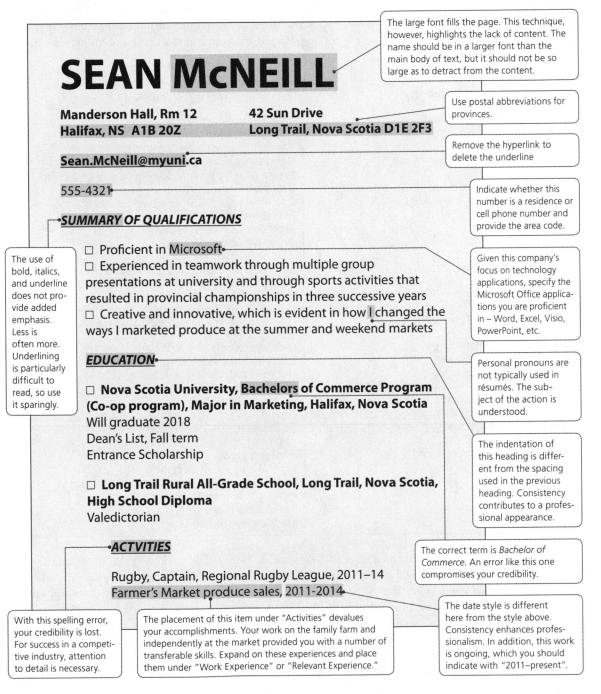

SEAN McNEILL

Manderson Hall, Rm 12   42 Sun Drive
Halifax, NS A1B 20Z   Long Trail, Nova Scotia D1E 2F3

Sean.McNeill@myuni.ca

555-4321

SUMMARY OF QUALIFICATIONS

☐ Proficient in Microsoft
☐ Experienced in teamwork through multiple group presentations at university and through sports activities that resulted in provincial championships in three successive years
☐ Creative and innovative, which is evident in how I changed the ways I marketed produce at the summer and weekend markets

EDUCATION

☐ **Nova Scotia University, Bachelors of Commerce Program (Co-op program), Major in Marketing, Halifax, Nova Scotia**
Will graduate 2018
Dean's List, Fall term
Entrance Scholarship

☐ **Long Trail Rural All-Grade School, Long Trail, Nova Scotia, High School Diploma**
Valedictorian

ACTVITIES

Rugby, Captain, Regional Rugby League, 2011–14
Farmer's Market produce sales, 2011-2014

The large font fills the page. This technique, however, highlights the lack of content. The name should be in a larger font than the main body of text, but it should not be so large as to detract from the content.

Use postal abbreviations for provinces.

Remove the hyperlink to delete the underline

Indicate whether this number is a residence or cell phone number and provide the area code.

The use of bold, italics, and underline does not provide added emphasis. Less is often more. Underlining is particularly difficult to read, so use it sparingly.

Given this company's focus on technology applications, specify the Microsoft Office applications you are proficient in – Word, Excel, Visio, PowerPoint, etc.

Personal pronouns are not typically used in résumés. The subject of the action is understood.

The indentation of this heading is different from the spacing used in the previous heading. Consistency contributes to a professional appearance.

The correct term is *Bachelor of Commerce*. An error like this one compromises your credibility.

With this spelling error, your credibility is lost. For success in a competitive industry, attention to detail is necessary.

The placement of this item under "Activities" devalues your accomplishments. Your work on the family farm and independently at the market provided you with a number of transferable skills. Expand on these experiences and place them under "Work Experience" or "Relevant Experience."

The date style is different here from the style above. Consistency enhances professionalism. In addition, this work is ongoing, which you should indicate with "2011–present".

Sean critically assesses the format, style, and professional appearance of his résumé, and reflects on the transferable skills he would bring to APPFORMS. The advisor points out the value of his experience on the farm. He did, after all, earn enough to pay many of his school expenses.

He thinks about his experience and brainstorms a list of what he did in each role. He doesn't worry about correct word use or about whether or not what he did was relevant to the position he is seeking. He just tries to capture as much of his experiences as he can.

(1) Student	(2) Rugby Player/Captain
Submit assignments on time Attend classes Do group projects Attention to details in assignments Participate in class Speeches and presentations Research for reports online, library Essays, reports, business letters High GPA Scholarship Manage complex data Word, Excel, Visio, SAP, Publisher School sports Party party party	Attend all training sessions Organize training sessions Keep players motivated and on-task Help team to championship 3 years Create training sessions to help fitness, team work Support other players Coordinate plays with coach and players Represent team to ref during game Represent team at school events Act as liaison between team and coaches Won MVP 2015 Maintained personal fitness schedule over summer Recorded personal fitness and eating habits Make sure locker room is left neat
(3) Farm Labourer	(4) Produce Sales/Stall Owner
Drive farm equipment Organize team of labourers Harvest crop Make sure labourers safe around equipment Separate produce by grade Record produce weights, amounts, dates of harvest Check quality of produce Assign labourers to shifts Clean equipment (trucks, tools) Check organic quality	Maintain records of goods sold Select and track inventory Use cash and credit machine Help customers find correct products Friendly to customers Present stall to attract and keep customers Find ways to sell goods—free samples, buy one/ get one Transport produce Maintain regular store hours Good relationships with other market vendors Identify customers' needs Sweep, clean area Made money for university

Next, Sean categorizes the information. He starts by reviewing the job description and identifying five general skill categories. Then he sorts his activities by category with numbers indicating the position in which he performed these skills. Some items appear in more than one category. He decides to create a separate category called Additional Responsibilities for those activities that do not fit somewhere else. That way he can determine if these additional responsibilities should be grouped in another category or if he should omit them. He decides that being self-starting and having initiative are elements of leadership, so he includes these activities together in one category.

Research Skills	Communication Skills
Research for reports online, library (1) Manage complex data (1) Word, Excel, Visio, SAP, Publisher (1) Attention to details in assignments (1) High GPA (1) Organize training sessions (2) Recorded personal fitness and eating habits (2) Record produce weights, amounts, dates of harvest (3) Maintain records of goods sold (4) Select and track inventory (4)	Do group projects (1) Participate in class (1) Speeches and presentations (1) Word, Excel, Visio, SAP, Publisher (1) Essays, reports, business letters (1) High GPA (1) Party party party (1) Keep players motivated and on-task (2)Help team to championship 3 years (2) Support other players (2) Coordinate plays with coach and players (2) Organize team of labourers (3) Friendly to customers (4) Present stall to attract and keep customers (4) Find ways to sell goods—free samples, buy one/ get one (4) Help customers find correct products (4) Good relationships with other market vendors (4) Identify customers' needs (4)
Team Skills	Self-Start/Initiative/Leadership
Party party party (1) Help team to championship 3 years (2) Keep players motivated and on-task (2) Create training sessions to help fitness, team work (2) Support other players (2) Coordinate plays with coach and players (2)	Scholarship (1) School sports (1) Attend all training sessions (2) Create training sessions to help fitness, team work (2) Coordinate plays with coach and players (2) Keep players motivated and on-task (2) Help team to championship 3 years (2) Represent team to ref during game (2) Represent team at school events (2) Act as liaison between team and coaches (2) Won MVP 2015 (2) Maintained personal fitness schedule over summer (2) Make sure locker room is left neat (2) Organize team of labourers (3) Make sure labourers safe around equipment (3) Check quality of produce (3) Assign labourers to shifts (3) Maintain regular store hours (4) Made money for university (4)
Tech Skills	Additional Responsibilities
Manage complex data (1) Word, Excel, Visio, SAP, Publisher (1) High GPA (1)	Drive farm equipment (3) Harvest crop (3) Separate produce by grade (3) Clean equipment (trucks, tools) (3) Check organic quality (3) Use cash and credit machine (4) Friendly to customers (4) Transport produce (4) Sweep, clean area (4)

The chart shows Sean how his skills match the job description and the company's values as described on the company website. He finds that his communication and leadership skills are particularly evident and would be strong selling points for APPFORMS. Sean uses this chart to draft a new résumé that highlights the attributes the company seeks.

Sean McNeill

42 Sun Drive
Long Trail, Nova Scotia D1E 2F3
Manderson Hall, Room 12
Halifax, NS A1B 20Z
email: Sean.McNeill@myuni.ca   cell: (999) 555-4321

SUMMARY OF QUALIFICATIONS

☐ Excellent teamwork and leadership skills evidenced through sports activities resulting in provincial championships in three successive years
☐ Creativity in marketing demonstrated through produce sales of $800 per day
☐ Technical skills in Microsoft Office, Visio, and SAP

EDUCATION

Bachelor of Commerce, Co-op Program   Candidate 2018
Nova Scotia University, Halifax, Nova Scotia
    Dean's List Fall 2014
    Renewable Entrance Scholarship $5000

High School Diploma   2014
Long Trail Rural All-Grade School, Long Trail, Nova Scotia
    Valedictorian

WORK EXPERIENCE

Green Trail Farms, Farmers' Market Vendor Long Trail, Nova Scotia   2011–present
    ☐ Founded and developed produce stall at regional farmers' market
    ☐ Created effective marketing campaign to attract consumers to organic produce
    ☐ Currently net an average of $800 per weekend

Green Trail Farms, Farm Labourer Long Trail, Nova Scotia   2010–2014
    ☐ Coordinated a team of labourers in efficiently harvesting produce
    ☐ Demonstrated attention to detail in sorting and labelling produce for shipping
    ☐ Maintained accurate records of harvested areas, produce weights, and soil conditions

RELEVANT EXPERIENCE

Regional Rugby League, Captain   2012–2014
    ☐ Led team through three successive provincial championships
    ☐ Developed training schedule and exercises for 25 players
    ☐ Recognized by teammates as "Most Valuable Player 2015"

Satisfied with the résumé, Sean now turns to creating his cover letter. He has never written a cover letter before. He starts by looking at the letter templates available in Microsoft Word. He sees a range of options, including templates for cover letters with salary expectations, cover letters in response to ads, and cover letters for both **chronological and functional résumés**. Some templates use bulleted lists, others use short paragraphs, and all use a **block style** in which every section begins on the left margin and line spaces separate paragraphs. The range of possibilities in length and structure is confusing, so Sean looks for guidance on the website of his university's Career Services Centre. He notices that some of the differences between cover letters may be attributed to the targeted industry.

Sean decides that he will use a block style. He chooses a bulleted list because it will fill a page more easily and because he will have less chance of making errors if he writes less. He also reasons that since he will have to submit several applications throughout his job search in addition to the one for APPFORMS, he should write a cover letter that he can use for several employers.

> You could demonstrate your understanding of business style if you follow a traditional business letter format in the return and recipient address.

> Your audience might want to know where you saw the ad. In addition, your educational background contributes to your story.

42 Sun Drive
Long Trail, NS

> You will make a stronger connection with your audience if you personalize the letter. Here you could use the name that appears on the ad.

> Using the company name personalizes the letter for the employer and establishes a connection between you and your audience.

December 2, 2015

Dear Recruiting Officer,

I have heard through my university that you are looking for a co-op student for the winter term. I would like to develop my skills in a reputable company like yours. Although I have no job experience in a company, I am well qualified for the job.

> "I have" is used four times in the text, three times at the start of a sentence. This emphasis on "I" indicates that your focus is on satisfying your needs, not the needs of the company. You must demonstrate to the employer that hiring you will be mutually advantageous.

I have been attending Dalhousie University for one year. I have developed the following skills at university:

1. Ability to work in a team
2. Ability to analyze data and record information on spreadsheets
3. Ability to take initiative
4. Ability to use interpersonal skills
5. Ability to use oral and written communications skills

> This list is ineffective. The repetition of "ability to" detracts from focus on the action. In addition, you neglect to provide evidence of these skills. You could use the STAR technique, in which the Situation and Task, Action, and Result are addressed. By stating the context, your actions, and the results of these actions, you could provide effective details to support your claim.

I believe these skills along with my experience working at the farmers' market will make me a great addition.

If you think that I am the right person for the job, you can contact me on my cell phone any time of the day or night.

> The "I believe" weakens the effectiveness of the sentence and does nothing to enhance the meaning or move the sentence forward. If you begin the sentence with "these skills," the sentence will have more impact.

Cheers,
Sean

> You should end with a more confident statement of your suitability for the position and with a stronger call to action.

> Although APPFORMS is a young and progressive company, do not assume informality. You can increase the level of formality by using a more formal closing and providing both your first (or given) name and your last (or family) name.

The advisor at the Career Services Centre looks over Sean's letter and suggests that he reread it from the employer's perspective. What does APPFORMS need, and how can Sean best meet that need? The company wants an employee whose skills match the job description, but they also want an employee who understands the industry and organizational culture. He suggests that Sean find a way to communicate the benefits he brings to the company.

The advisor also points out that the cover letter is another opportunity to tell his story. In the cover letter, Sean can use his story to demonstrate his fit with the company. The advisor points out that a significant number of Sean's sentences begin with "I." Rather than focus so heavily on the benefits he will receive, Sean should focus on the value he brings to the organization by discussing how his skills in identifying, assessing, and addressing the consumers' needs at the farmers' market could be used in delivering appropriate services to APPFORMS's clients. Because the cover letter will address Sean's fit with APPFORMS, he now realizes it cannot be used again with another job application.

Sean revises the letter and shares it with his friends and family, a university writing centre advisor, and a former teaching assistant in his business communication course. After receiving their feedback, he incorporates the advice he finds most useful and appropriate for his situation (see revised letter on p. 15).

Sean's cover letter now effectively connects his experience and values to the needs and values of APPFORMS.

The Case of Lara Leveaux

The job application that Sean submits was **solicited**—APPFORMS advertised the position on the university's Career Services Centre website. Lara Leveaux seeks an accounting position for a summer internship. She has learned that APPFORMS hires four interns each summer, one in accounting, from a friend of her mother's who suggested she contact the company. Lara's job application is **unsolicited**—APPFORMS has not advertised an intern position in accounting. She hopes, however, that her skills and experience make her an attractive candidate to APPFORMS.

Lara seeks to intern during the summer before her final year at university. She hopes the experience she gains will enable her to return to work for the company after graduation. She knows from living in the Atlantic region that APPFORMS has a strong record of corporate social responsibility. She researches APPFORMS Canada by visiting the company website. Looking at the career page, she sees references to the company's search for "excellence" and to "challenging" opportunities. She also learns that the company treats its interns as an investment in its future by grooming them for possible hire after graduation.

During the school year, Lara works part-time as a marker for first-year finance and accounting courses and as a research assistant for a professor in her program. She is an active member in the university's Commerce Society, participates in case study competitions, and has volunteer experience as a student tax consultant and student orientation leader. Lara has also had a variety of summer jobs. Her latest résumé was aimed at a front-desk position during the tourist season at an Ontario hotel. The résumé focused on her customer service skills, and her cover letter emphasized the energy and enthusiasm she would bring to the job.

Sean McNeill

42 Sun Drive
Long Trail, Nova Scotia D1E 2F3
email: Sean.McNeill@myuni.ca   cell: (999) 555–4321

November 15, 2015

Juanita Olson
APPFORMS Canada
1600 White Horse Way
Halifax, NS A1B 2C3

RE: Marketing Assistant Co-op Position

Dear Ms. Asad:

Please accept my application for the Marketing Assistant co-op position advertised on Nova Scotia University's career services website. My innovative and enterprising spirit and team skills suit this position well.

APPFORMS prides itself on its innovative designs and practices; I, too, am proud of my innovative spirit. As a labourer on the family farm, I realized that some of the produce unsuitable for commercial sale could be sold at a local farmers' market. Our produce is organic and therefore highly marketable to today's consumers. I began to sell this produce on weekends. Over the years, my stall at the market has expanded. I have a loyal customer base and earn on average $800 per weekend, money I am using to fund my education. This enterprising spirit ideally suits APPFORMS' focus on innovation.

In addition, I offer the company an ability to work effectively in a team. This ability comes from my work on the farm and was further developed through sports and through coursework at university. As the team captain of the Regional Rugby League, I helped turn a collection of individual athletes into a unified team. Our success as a team is evident in our winning successive provincial championships. My university education has provided me with further opportunities to work with groups on various projects. My success in these groups is shown in my marks, which are consistently high. My team skills would enable me to contribute to the team at APPFORMS.

I also offer APPFORMS strong technological skills, as indicated in the attached resumé, and flexibility in my work schedule, as required in the job description. I look forward to further discussing my contributions to your company in an interview.

Regards,

Sean McNeill

Sean uses a subject line and bold here so that the reader can quickly identify the position for which he is applying.

He clearly identifies the position and the source of the job information.

This sentence links to the job description and the website and provides an overview and projected organization of the following paragraphs.

Sean extracts this phrase from the company website. This technique indicates that he is familiar with the company. It also enables him to show that his values and the company's values are aligned.

In an earlier draft of this letter, Sean had written "the focus on innovation at APPFORMS." This wording resulted in "APPFORMS" appearing at the start of the line, which looked odd with "APPFORMS" at the start of the first line of the paragraph. With the rewording, Sean not only avoids this awkwardness, he also highlights the word *innovation*, which now sits in a visually prominent position at the end of the sentence.

LARA LEVEAUX
5240 Gooseberry Street
Halifax, NS   Z9Y 8X7
cell: (999) 555-4213   LLeveaux@myuni.ca

Profile

- Enthusiastic customer service demonstrated in leading high-energy orientation activities
- Fluency in English, French, and German
- Strong presentation skills developed through case competition

Education

Canadian University, Halifax, NS
Bachelor of Commerce, Accounting   Expected May 2015
- Accounting GPA: 4.0/4.3, Cumulative GPA: 3.8/4.3
- Dean's List 2012–2015

Selected Work Experience

Canadian University, School of Business, Halifax, NS   September 2014–present
Accounting and Finance Marker, Research Assistant
- Maintain confidentiality in managing student records
- Create spreadsheets and accurately record student marks
- Evaluate student work while ensuring fairness and accuracy
- Conduct focus groups on behalf of the lead researcher
- Enter and code data

Trendy Tandoori Restaurant, Halifax, NS   May–September 2014
Server, Cashier, Host
- Utilized time-management and problem-solving skills to provide efficient food service
- Prepared nightly bank deposit
- Hosted and served at special catered events, including business retreats and weddings

Slap Happy Bar, Antigonish, NS   May–September 2013
Server, Cashier
- Provided efficient customer service to weekend crowd
- Handled cash and credit transactions

Camp Carysbrook, Riner, Virginia, USA   June–August 2011, 2012
Camp Counsellor
- Utilized leadership skills in managing a cabin of 10 girls
- Coordinated evening activities with a team
- Provided regular updates to parents through Facebook and Twitter

Extracurricular Activities

- Ethics Case Competition, 2nd place, 2015
- Canadian University Commerce Society Council, Commerce Representative, 2014–2015
- Student Orientation Team Leader, 2012–2015
- Student Tax Preparer, 2013–2015
- KPMG Finance Case Competition, 2014
- Feed the Province Volunteer, 2013
- Residence Hall Intramural Hockey Captain, 2013

Lara crafts a new résumé for APPFORMS that shifts the focus from customer service to accounting and finance. She also wants to lessen the emphasis on her interpersonal skills and elevate the importance of her experiences managing information and handling money. Because her application is unsolicited, she decides to include an objective statement so that her purpose is clear.

Lara changes the points in her profile to highlight attributes relevant to an accounting position and to the organization as she understands it through her network, information available through the Internet, and the company website.

The skills used in this position as a marker are transferable to a position as a summer accounting intern so she chooses to leave this section as written in the original.

LARA LEVEAUX

5240 Gooseberry Street
Halifax, NS   Z9Y 8X7
cell: (999) 555-4213   LLeveaux@myuni.ca

Objective   To obtain an accounting internship at APPFORMS

Profile

- Efficiency and accuracy in data collection demonstrated through accounting and research experience
- Fluency in English, French, and German
- Proficiency in Microsoft Word, Excel, and PowerPoint, SAP, and Visio

Selected Work Experience

Canadian University, School of Business, Halifax, NS   September 2014–present
Accounting and Finance Marker, Research Assistant

- Maintain confidentiality in managing student records
- Create spreadsheets and accurately record student marks on Learning Management System
- Evaluate student work while ensuring fairness and accuracy
- Conduct focus groups on behalf of the lead researcher
- Enter and code data

Trendy Tandoori Restaurant, Halifax, NS   May–September 2014
Server, Cashier, Host

- Utilized time-management and problem-solving skills to provide efficient food service
- Handled cash and credit transactions in a fast-paced environment
- Prepared nightly bank deposit
- Hosted and served at special catered events, including business retreats and weddings

Slap Happy Bar, Antigonish, NS   May–September 2013
Server, Cashier

- Provided clientele with prompt service while maintaining a casual atmosphere
- Efficiently managed cash and credit transactions

Camp Carysbrook, Riner, Virginia, USA
Camp Counsellor
  • Utilized leadership skills in managing a cabin of 10 girls
  • Coordinated evening activities with a team
  • Provided regular updates to parents through Facebook and Twitter

Relevant Volunteer Experience

Canadian University, School of Business, Halifax, NS   Seasonal 2013-2015
Tax preparer
  • Completed training through Canada Revenue Agency's Community Volunteer Tax Program
  • Assisted community members in comprehending and preparing tax forms

Education

Canadian University, Halifax, NS
Bachelor of Commerce, Accounting   Expected May 2015
  • Accounting GPA: 4.0/4.3, Cumulative GPA: 3.8/4.3
  • Dean's List 2012–2015

Extracurricular Activities

  • Ethics Case Competition, 2nd place, 2015
  • Canadian University Commerce Society Council, Commerce Representative, 2014–2015
  • Student Orientation Team Leader, 2012–2015
  • KPMG Finance Case Competition, 2014
  • Feed the Province Volunteer, 2013
  • Residence Hall Intramural Hockey Captain, 2013

> This heading initially appeared on the previous page, but Lara moves it down so that the heading is not separated from the job information and bullets.

> Lara expands on this volunteer position in the résumé for APPFORMS to highlight her relevant experience and transferable skills.

> Lara drops the "Education" section to below the "Work Experience" to give her work experience a position of greater prominence.

In a cover letter, Lara hopes to attract her reader's attention. Through her mother's connections, she gets the name of the head of accounting. After confirming the identity and the spelling through LinkedIn, Lara addresses the letter to this individual, which will help attract attention as well as demonstrate her knowledge of the company. There is no job description, but Lara can predict some of the qualifications APPFORMS might be looking for through her knowledge of the industry, the company website, and media reports about APPFORMS.

Lara places her return address in the traditional business letter format. Although she could have opted to use a personal letterhead instead, she prefers the simplicity of this style. In addition, the name and contact information block on the résumé does not look as effective here; it seems to make the page appear imbalanced.

5240 Gooseberry Street
Halifax, NS Z9Y 8X7

April 2, 2014

Mr. Abdul Li
Head of Accounting
APPFORMS Canada
1600 White Horse Way
Halifax, NS A1B 2C3

With this phrase, Lara seeks to emphasize her commitment since she has heard that APPFORMS invests and trains new hires with hopes of retaining them.

Dear Mr. Li:

Here Lara links her values with the values of the company.

I seek a summer internship in Accounting with APPFORMS, a role I hope will lead to full-time employment after my graduation in May 2015. As a resident of the Halifax Regional Municipality, I am aware of APPFORMS' reputation as an industry leader with a dedication to excellence and a strong sense of corporate social responsibility, and I long to be a part of the company.

With this sentence, Lara begins providing evidence of her pursuit of excellence.

Like APPFORMS, I pursue a high standard of excellence. This standard is reflected in my GPA. I earned the top mark in both my Financial Accounting and Accounting II courses. Based on my academic performance, I was selected to be a course marker and research assistant. The promotions I have earned with various employers further demonstrate my standard of excellence. I plan to continue this pursuit of excellence through the CPA Professional Education Program, which will enable me to earn CPA certification while working for APPFORMS.

This sentence indicates several things to the employer—her desire for continued learning, her goal-setting, and her commitment to the industry.

APPFORMS' community involvement strongly appeals to me. As a child, I benefited from the company's support of technology in schools and participated in your O-Snapp competition, which challenged me to create an original mobile application aimed at Maritime youth. I actively engage in the community through my volunteer tax preparation for low-income families and my efforts for Feed the Province. I also dedicate my time to the university's Commerce Society and to the student orientation program. Through a position at APPFORMS, I can inspire others to engage in the community while representing the company that inspired me.

On the one hand, the repetition and placement of "APPFORMS" at the end of this line and the start of the following line have a slightly negative impact. On the other hand, this repetition and placement highlight the focus on the company and its needs rather than Lara.

I look forward to discussing a summer internship with you. I will contact you in two weeks to discuss the possibilities and to arrange an interview. I have enclosed my résumé and an unofficial transcript. Please let me know through email to LLeveaux@myuni.ca if you require any additional information.

Thank you for your consideration.

Regards,

Lara Leveaux

Lara has made full use of the page. The paragraph breaks provide white space and lessen the visual weightiness of the text.

Lara chooses to be proactive and indicates when she will be making contact.

Lara mails her job application and plans to follow it up with a phone call requesting an informational interview with someone in accounting at APPFORMS.

The Case of Maya Chen

Maya Chen has just graduated in finance from the university. She sees the following advertisement posted by APPFORMS to her university's Career Services Centre website.

APPFORMSCanada

JOB TITLE: Financial Assistant

COMPANY: APPFORMS Canada

CONTACT PERSON: Birgit Asad, Recruiting Officer

JOB DESCRIPTION

Reporting to the Finance Team Leaders on a rotational basis, the successful candidate will work as an active member of the Finance Department.

TASKS/DUTIES

- Perform financial analysis
- Assist in financial statement preparation
- Prepare analytical reports
- Lease and contract assignments
- Contract and procure assignments
- Perform ad hoc assignments

JOB REQUIREMENTS

This opportunity is ideal for a hard-working self-starter who values the importance of teamwork and demonstrates excellent oral and written communication skills. You must be proficient with MS Office software with particular focus on MS Excel and MS Word. You should be comfortable learning and using business software applications. Applicants must hold a degree in Accounting or Finance. Previous experience working in an office environment would be an asset.

APPLICATION PROCEDURES

Please send a cover letter, résumé, unofficial transcript, and any other appropriate supporting documents (such as letters of reference and copies of certifications) to Birgit Asad, Recruitment Officer at Birgit.Asad@APPFORMS.com.

She knows that employers prefer that finance résumés be limited to a single page, a convention confirmed by the university Career Services Centre. Maya, then, must select her details strategically. She reviews the job description and the company website to identify areas in which she is a good fit for the company.

Maya carefully selects from her experiences the information relevant to a position in Finance for APPFORMS. She omits her experience working in a restaurant of a family friend when she first arrived in Canada because this work was conducted prior to her receiving a work permit. Although the experience was useful in developing her language abilities and customer service skills, it does not qualify as legitimate work experience. She also decides to limit her list of extracurricular experiences. She decides to include her experiences as a group leader to illustrate her leadership ability, her experience with peer support to illustrate her leadership and her communication abilities, and her experience as an event emcee to illustrate her confidence and presentation skills. She leaves out her participation in intramural volleyball. Although her participation in sport demonstrates her ability to work effectively with a team, which would be of interest to a company like APPFORMS, she can address teamwork in the Work Experience section. She wants to emphasize her ability to communicate cross-culturally and sees this skill as an essential component of the teamwork valued by the company. She decides to refer to this ability a couple of times in the document.

MAYA CHEN

2000 University Way, Toronto, ON G3H 4R2

999-555-1234 | Maya.Chen@myuni.ca

PROFILE

- Strong ability to work effectively and efficiently under pressure demonstrated during peak tax season at Ernst & Young
- Excellent analytical abilities and strong grounding in mathematics developed through formal education
- Proficient in both Apple and Microsoft computer applications, including Google Docs, Firefox, Safari, and Microsoft Publisher
- Comfortable with cross-cultural communication and diverse workplaces

EDUCATION

Bachelor of Commerce in Accounting   Candidate 2015

Ontario University, Toronto, Ontario

Recipient, Dalhousie Entrance Scholarship

High School Certificate   2011

No. 22 Beijing High School, Beijing, China

WORK EXPERIENCE

Ernst & Young, Finance Co-op   May–August 2014

Toronto, Ontario

- Demonstrated ability to work well under pressure during peak tax season to meet filing deadlines
- Exercised teamwork and collaboration skills in support and assistance of team members
- Displayed professionalism and effective communication skills with stakeholders through interactions to clarify and solve issues
- Extracted financial information to assist in preparation and amendments of tax computations, tax forms, worksheets, and letters
- Conducted a research project on taxation treatments of initial public offerings

Ernst & Young, IT, Risk and Assurance Co-op   September–December 2013

Waitomo, Ontario

- Utilized technical expertise to analyze financial data and assist managers in addressing risks
- Identified opportunities in the banking industry to improve performance and mitigate risks
- Produced an internal audit report with project team

continued

Ontario University, Communication Assistant, Co-op   January–April 2013
Toronto, Ontario
- Developed a marketing strategy for a new program aimed at international students
- Established a working relationship with student societies to facilitate interactions between domestic and international students
- Produced a written report on the international student experience for the director of the School of Business

VOLUNTEER EXPERIENCE

Student Group Leader for Ontario University Open House   September 2014
- Demonstrated strong leadership skills by leading a group of prospective students to their organized sessions and programs
- Responded to queries by relating and sharing relevant experiences

School of Business Peer Support for   September–December 2013
International Students
- Provided support with English communication by offering a comfortable medium for students to practise speaking
- Engaged in conversation groups with culturally diverse students to facilitate their transition into university

Chinese Students and Scholars Association, Volunteer   February 2013
- Emceed Chinese spring festival gala for an audience of over 850

Like Sean and Lara, Maya includes a cover letter with the résumé in her job application. However, because she is sending her documents by email, Maya also needs to write a message identifying the position for which she is applying and the documents included as attachments. In her cover letter, Maya addressed the benefits her unique background brings to APPFORMS. In discussing her decision to leave China and pursue a career in Canada, she invokes the words *dare* and *different* that are used on APPFORMS's website. She briefly introduces these themes in her email as well, and provides her contact information.

Date:	Tuesday, 21 May 2015, 6:11 PM
From:	Maya Chen <Maya.Chen@myuni.ca>
To:	Birgit Asad <Birgit.Asad@APPFORMS.com>
Subject:	Financial Assistant position

Dear Ms. Asad:

Please find attached my materials in application for the Financial Assistant position advertised through Ontario University Career Services.

I bring to APPFORMS an ability to see things from multiple perspectives, an attribute attained through my experiences as an international student and through my work experiences in organizations that utilize diversity in teams. Like APPFORMS, I dare to be different.

Please let me know if you require additional materials to complete my application.

Regards,

Maya Chen
2000 University Way
Toronto ON G3H 4R2
Email: Maya.Chen@myuni.ca
Cell: 999-555-1234

The Elevator Pitch

The Case of James Patel

James Patel, an international business major at the University of Saskatoon, seeks a position for a co-op work term. His first work term was with his university, where he assisted with student recruitment strategies in South American markets. He is not sure what position he wants for his second work term, or where, but he is interested in working for a growing company that encourages environmentally sustainable practices and provides opportunities for learning both within his field and in other areas of the business.

Identifying and Understanding Stakeholders

James hears that a number of employers will be attending a job fair at his university, including APPFORMS and DonnaLee Exports, and plans to attend. Although he has a small social network and a few business contacts established through his summer work as a house painter and his first co-op work term, he has never attended a formal networking event like a job fair.

He asks a more experienced fourth-year student, Yiwei Trent, for some guidance. Yiwei recommends that James take a copy of his résumé and a prepared elevator pitch to the networking event. James has already completed his résumé, but he has no idea what an elevator pitch is or how to prepare one. Yiwei explains that the elevator pitch is a brief personal introduction that tells who he is and the benefit he can bring to an organization—his value proposition. It also provides an opportunity to display his passions. The pitch's goal is to move to the next stage of a relationship by prompting further contact—a business card, an exchange of email addresses, an interview, or an information meeting. The elevator pitch will be the recruiter's first impression of James, so Yiwei recommends that James manage this impression carefully.

Choices and Alternatives

James's initial online explorations reveal a range of uses for a personal elevator pitch. It can be used as part of a cover letter in telling the candidate's story. It can also address the request "Tell me about yourself" or the question "Why should we hire you?" in an interview. The elevator pitch can also be used, as its name implies, as a way to introduce yourself during a chance encounter or at a more formal networking event or job fair.

In each of these situations, the elevator pitch changes to reflect the context and the differing needs of the audience. James will need to plan the elements of his pitch but remain flexible in his approach. Even though the situation, and therefore the pitch, may change, dedicating time to preparing an elevator pitch provides an opportunity for him to reflect on the attributes he most wants to convey to an audience unfamiliar with him. Preparation will help him to avoid rambling in response to "Tell me about yourself" and avoid being at a loss for words in an unexpected encounter with his ideal employer.

James gathers ideas about what to include in an elevator pitch through his research and by consulting with the Career Services Centre, his friends, and his former instructors. According to several sources, the pitch should reveal his interest in the organization and indicate the attributes that would make him a successful employee. It should answer the following four questions:

1. Who is he?
2. What can he do?
3. What value would he bring to the organization?
4. How can he be contacted?

James also discovers an alternative approach to the elevator pitch that focuses on the following four questions:

1. Who is he?
2. What does he do?
3. What uniquely defines him?
4. What does he hope to achieve?

Selecting Material: Claims and Evidence

James decides that the best approach in speaking to the APPFORMS and DonnaLee Exports representatives at the networking event is a combination of strategies. Obviously he needs to say his name and, at this point in his career, he should mention his affiliation with the university and his degree program. He would like to highlight one or two of the key attributes he can bring to the company. James wants to be clear about what he is looking for from the prospective employer (a co-op position), and he wants to ensure he can maintain contact by asking for a business card so that he can send a follow-up letter after the job fair.

James decides that for him the best way to structure his pitch is to address the following questions:

1. Who is he?
2. What does he do?
3. What evidence of his experience can he provide?
4. What evidence of his success can he provide?
5. What does he hope to bring to the company?
6. How can he reach the person he is speaking with?

James decides to spend most of his time on sections 3 and 4, the most difficult sections. He begins by researching APPFORMS to determine what experiences he has that would be of benefit to this company. He discovers that APPFORMS is a rapidly growing company specializing in mobile applications. From his work in student recruitment in South American markets for his university, James knows that Brazil, in particular, has a high per capita Internet and mobile phone use. He believes his experience using various technologies when recruiting in South America makes him uniquely qualified to provide the company with insights into that market. If he has time, he would like to mention that he follows APPFORMS's Managing Partner Goran Duro on Twitter. He believes that a comment on Duro's Twitter updates will make him more memorable to the recruiter.

Style, Arrangement, and Design

James records his answers to his selected questions:

1. James Patel
2. Bachelor of Management in International Business

3. Student recruitment in South America through Internet and mobile applications (Twitter, Facebook, **Vostu**, and Orkut).
4. Worked with a team to increase South American applicants by 28%
5. Co-op work term in which he can develop his knowledge of the industry further
6. Request for a business card

He uses his answers to create the following elevator pitch. The numbers in parentheses correlate with the list above.

> Hello. My name is James Patel (1). APPFORMS appeals to me because of its expanding global business. As part of my international business co-op program at the University of Saskatoon (2), I worked on recruiting South American students to the university. This opportunity provided me with an understanding of how South Americans, particularly Brazilians, currently use technology (3) and how we might use this understanding in our marketing strategy. By using Orkut, Twitter, Vostu, and Facebook to connect with this market, my team and I contributed to an increase in applicants of over 28% (4). I've noticed Goran Duro's recent tweets on the importance of global connections. This mutual interest in expanding global markets makes working at APPFORMS very appealing to me. I would be happy to send you a copy of my résumé. May I have your business card? (6)

Next, James researches DonnaLee Exports. This company offers financial and risk management solutions to assist exporters in expanding their international business. DonnaLee's website emphasizes its innovative strategies and creative teamwork. The company typically hires three co-op students per term, evidence of its dedication to developing young talent. DonnaLee also boasts a corporate social responsibility program that provides financing to small enterprises in developing countries. Although the program does not involve the environmental sustainability James is interested in, he finds the idea of working with small businesses in developing countries intriguing.

James does not have a particular interest in accounting or finance, but he appreciates the international business aspect of the company. He decides to create an elevator pitch for this company in which he focuses on the company's innovative spirit.

> Hello. I'm James Patel (1). DonnaLee Exports' focus on innovation appeals to me. As part of my international business co-op program at the University of Saskatoon (2), I worked on recruiting South American students to the university. This opportunity challenged me to understand how South Americans, particularly Brazilians, currently use technology (3) and to identify how we might use this understanding in our marketing strategy. My team and I developed a marketing strategy using Orkut, Twitter, Vostu, and Facebook. Our innovative efforts contributed to an increase in applicants to our university of over 28% (4). I would like to bring my creative spirit to DonnaLee (5). Can we arrange a meeting at your convenience so we can discuss further what I can contribute? (6)

Tone, Voice, and Pace

James writes out the elevator pitches so that he can see the words on the page and think through what he can cover in a short amount of time. But the reality is that although he can prepare a pitch, the opportunities to deliver it will be more spontaneous. In a conversational situation, it is unlikely he will deliver a 60-second pitch without interruption or without feeling as if he is dominating the conversation. If he delivers the pitch as a speech, he may compromise the relationship he seeks to establish with the representative of the company; it is essential that he appear natural and confident. If he attempts to deliver a memorized pitch, his focus will be on remembering his lines rather than on his audience. In addition, a memorized speech negates the conversational pace and language of a more impromptu speech. Because the purpose of the pitch is to establish a relationship with the audience, James needs to appear as his genuine self, not as a crafted product. The solution, he decides, is to practise the pitch over and over again with various audiences until it becomes natural. He also records his pitch using his laptop camera, plays it back to review it, and makes some revisions.

◉ SCOPE

As we look at the experiences of Sean, Lara, Maya, and James, we can identify elements of SCOPE: strategy, content, outcome, presentation, and ethics.

Strategy involves making deliberate choices to attain a goal. In developing a clear strategy, each candidate must first determine the audience and purpose of the message. In the case of résumés, cover letters, and elevator pitches, the candidates are addressing a prospective employer with the goal of attaining an interview with the company. Each candidate develops a strategy based on the job description, the organization's values, current events, and personal networks and then creates applications and presentations that show how his or her individual characteristics match the job requirements and the mission and values of the organization.

In crafting their documents, the candidates make choices that move them toward their goals. While the form of a résumé and cover letter are largely determined by industry standards, there are a number of options within that form—from the selection of font to the details of layout and the choice of language—that can be individualized and adapted. Furthermore, techniques in résumé and cover-letter writing shift with current trends. How the candidates manoeuvre within the form and how they manipulate these trends distinguish them from each other. This manoeuvring is similar to a marketing campaign; the candidate has a product to offer and seeks to motivate the prospective employer to offer an interview. For example, Sean's strategy is to demonstrate professionalism by adhering to traditional forms. He uses a standard block style in his letter and formal language without slang or contractions. Within this traditional form, he aims for simplicity. These choices contribute to his personal brand.

Part of the candidates' strategies involves the selection of information. Lara's deliberate selection of what information to include is evident when she adapts an old résumé to use with a new audience. While her work in customer service was of great appeal for work in the hotel industry, her technical skills and cash-handling experiences are more relevant for APPFORMS. Lara develops a body of evidence to support her presentation as a candidate suited to the particular position. Maya, too, carefully selects her *content*. Limited to a single page, she strategically chooses evidence from her experience that addresses requirements in the job description and matches the culture of the organization as revealed on its website. If an elevator pitch is intended to last only 60 seconds or so, what can candidates include and what can they omit? James chooses six to use in creating his elevator pitch. He adapts his pitch to two different audiences to illustrate how his experiences in recruiting South American students to his university would enable him to contribute to each organization.

To achieve the desired *outcome*, the candidates focus on the audience's needs. The desired outcome or result from a résumé, cover letter, or elevator pitch is always an interview. To achieve the desired outcome, the candidates must carefully analyze the audience, select the best approach for this audience, and address the audience's needs. Sean's first cover letter focused too heavily on himself with the majority of his sentences beginning with the pronoun *I*. Sean wants the company to see the benefits his experience and training offer them. His analyses of the job description and the company's website help him to identify the benefits his experience and training bring to the company. He can then refocus his letter on his audience. Maya understands that APPFORMS relies heavily on teamwork and needs employees who can communicate effectively cross-culturally. She crafts her document to address this need of her audience.

The candidates use the standards of formal written English in *presentation*. Although APPFORMS is a progressive young company, Sean chooses a formal tone in a traditional block style for his cover letter. Given his youth, he decides that this formality will be more effective. If he opted for a more casual tone and an informal approach, his audience might perceive him as ignorant of professional standards. Sean also recognizes that APPFORMS's multicultural environment means that a heavy use of slang may be difficult for some readers.

Ethics guide the candidates' decisions. Each candidate has established his or her own ethical standards derived from personal, familial, and cultural values as well as the ethics of the industry. Although the candidates want to earn a position in the company, this goal does not supersede the desire to present themselves genuinely. In marketing themselves to the potential employer, the candidates adhere to the Canadian Marketing Association's *Code of Ethics and Standards of Practice* (2015) in maintaining "the highest standards of honesty, truth, accuracy, fairness, and professionalism" (p. 6).

Crafting successful résumés, cover letters, and elevator pitches requires carefully considered decisions. From the font choice to the selection of content to the construction of paragraphs, the writer must make a series of decisions. There is no one right way to craft these documents, and each one is different depending on the job description, the organization, the mode of delivery, and the relevant qualities of the applicant.

Chapter Summary

This chapter focused on the strategies of creating effective résumés, cover letters, and elevator pitches. Varied approaches for each were revealed through the examples of Sean, Lara, Maya, and James. First, the candidates researched the company and conducted an inventory of their skills and attributes. Second, they aligned their personal skills and attributes with the job requirements, as revealed in the job description, and the company's culture, as revealed on the company website. Third, the candidates reviewed current practices in résumés and cover letters through online research and their university's career services centres and to determine what aspects to include. Fourth, based on personal preferences and needs, audience, and content, they crafted and revised their documents while maintaining professional standards, which include considerations about formal language and formats, ethical standards, and cultural expectations.

Discussion Questions

1. Infographic résumés represent information visually in graphic form. Should any of the candidates consider submitting an infographic as a supplement or a replacement for the traditional résumé? Consider the following:
   a) Who is the audience for the infographic, and what characteristics of this audience should be considered in crafting a visual résumé?
   b) What would be the benefit of submitting an infographic résumé to a company like APPFORMS? What aspects of a company or industry make it a suitable audience for this form? Do these benefits apply equally to the departments of marketing, accounting, finance, and international business, and to management?
   c) What technical skills are required to create an effective infographic?
   d) What elements of the résumé lend themselves to the infographic form? Brainstorm possible ways to visualize the information contained in each category.
   e) What are the potential negative effects of using an infographic for APPFORMS?

2. If you were applying to APPFORMS, what skills would you focus on to demonstrate your suitability for the position? What aspects of the company's mission, values, and structure would indicate that you are a good match for the company's culture?

3. Résumé templates are available through Microsoft Word or Apple Pages, but using them carries risks. Trained recruiters can easily identify a template by its graphics and layout and may dismiss your résumé as a quick-and-easy, cut-and-paste résumé. The quality of the templates varies tremendously. On the other hand, a template provides a form, enabling you to focus instead on the content. In what, if any, circumstances might a template be appropriate for a résumé?

4. Consider the following cases and determine whether the decisions are ethical.
   a) Angus Tinibu, a first-year student applying for a co-op work term, has little work experience to include on his résumé. His summer job is fixing bikes for a local bike rental business. He decides that writing "June–August 2013" on his résumé minimizes the job and would make a potential employer wonder about his long-term commitment even though the position was only for the summer. He considers writing "Summer 2013" to make it clear that the work was seasonal, but decides instead to write just "2013." He thinks that writing the date in this way avoids highlighting the short term of the experience. Is his decision ethical? Explain.
   b) Philippa Barbier has worked hard at her university studies in the past two years. Her first year, however, she invested more time in the social scene than in textbooks. As a result, she has an overall GPA of 3.1/4.3, but in her major she has a 3.8/4.3. She decides to use the GPA in her major on her résumé and not her overall GPA. Is decision ethical? Explain.
   c) In his cover letter, Miguel Gorshkov refers to his computer abilities as "exceptional." He uses this word to emphasize his skills with computer graphics. In a business applications course, he received a B+, but he believes that this mark was unjust and that he deserved a higher mark. He lacks evidence of his exceptional skill but uses the word anyway. Is his decision ethical? Explain.
   d) Last term, Steve Abeyta worked on a group project in which the team conducted an analysis of the strengths, weaknesses, opportunities, and threats (SWOT) of a proposed restaurant location. As part of

the project, the team conducted interviews with various restaurant owners, researched and mapped available real estate in the downtown area, and determined costs. Steve's role was to complete the industry analysis for the literature review while other team members worked on interviews and data presentation. In the cover letter, Steve states, "Last term, my team conducted an analysis of restaurant locations in Greater Winnipeg. We completed a thorough report that included sophisticated tables and graphics using Visio." Because it was a group project and decisions were made with the team, Steve feels justified in taking credit for the entire product even if he did not work on all the individual components. Is his decision ethical? Explain.

e) During the summer, Franklin Choudhry worked for a bank. The bank manager asked each employee to volunteer at the Bluenose Marathon. Each employee received a T-shirt and could use paid company time to participate. Franklin discusses the experience as an illustration of voluntary community involvement in his cover letter even though the activity was sponsored by the employer and he would not have attended if he had not been paid and if the event had been scheduled after hours. Is his decision ethical? Explain.

5. Sixty seconds is a long time for a monologue. In what scenarios would delivering a 60-second elevator pitch be appropriate? In what scenarios might speaking for 60 seconds be inappropriate?

Exercises

1. Using an actual job description obtained online or through a career centre, create charts similar to Sean's. Assess and then categorize your experience according to the key points listed in the job description and on the company's website. Consider all types of experiences from which you have developed skills that can be transferred to the workplace, including volunteer positions, and travel or study abroad.

2. Create a résumé and cover letter for two different positions in two different companies. Describe how you have altered the documents to adjust them to different audiences.

3. You have been invited to attend a leadership conference sponsored by one of the top firms in your field and asked to prepare a short introduction of yourself. Create your pitch.

Good Advice or Bad?

1. Jörgen Sundberg, the Undercover Recruiter, recommends that résumé templates not be used because they fail to distinguish your résumé from that of other candidates, and the recruiter may view it as a mere cut-and-paste résumé. Good advice or bad? Why?

2. *Business Insider* reported on LinkedIn's list of the 10 most overused terms on résumés in 2011. LinkedIn's list includes the words *creative, organizational, effective, extensive experience, track record, motivated, innovative, problem* *solving, communication skills,* and *dynamic*. LinkedIn advocates omitting these words from your résumé. Good advice or bad? Why?

3. *Business Insider* reports that some companies, particularly large ones, use computer scanners to identify qualified candidates through a keyword search of résumés. To make it past the scanner, *Business Insider* recommends that candidates use the exact words used in the job description, instead of other, more creative language. Good advice or bad? Why?

4. Since scanners may be used to filter candidates not qualified for a position, candidates who do not have the basic qualifications may try to find ways to get their résumés past this initial scan. One way is to insert keywords randomly using a white font that is invisible to the reader but will get the résumé past the automated scanner and into the hands of a recruiter. Good advice or bad? Why?

5. In a 2013 article in the *Globe and Mail* entitled "Paper résumés headed for extinction," journalist Wallace Immen reports that some career development specialists recommend that job applicants develop an online portfolio through LinkedIn, Facebook, and a personal website instead of printed résumés, which are out of date. The article quotes one source as saying that big high-tech companies will discount an applicant who submits a paper résumé. Good advice or bad? Why?

6. Some career specialists recommend discussing in the cover letter only those skills listed in the job posting. Because young candidates in particular do not know what knowledge or experience would be most valuable to an employer, they should avoid mentioning any other skills, even if they think they could be valuable in the role. Good advice or bad? Why?

7. Katie has to present an elevator pitch in her business communication course, and she is terrified. Her roommate suggests that she memorize the pitch word-for-word. Good advice or bad? Why?

8. Jin has prepared an elevator pitch he plans to use when he meets people at corporate events. He wants to make his pitch unique and memorable. He decides to use humour while introducing himself by stating, "Hi, my name is Jin—like a bottle of gin," and conclude his pitch with "So let's meet—perhaps over a gin?" His friends think this approach is sure to engage his listeners, and they encourage him to use it. Good advice or bad? Why?

Strategic Language: Powerful Verbs and Parallelism

The reader of your résumé and cover letter will focus particularly on your choice of verbs. Prospective employers want to know what you did in your previous jobs. The verbs describe what you did, or the actions you took, and help you tell your story.

One strong verb can be more effective than a string of weak words. For example, in his cover letter, Sean writes, "I have experience working at the farmers' market and took responsibility for talking with customers and for the money." *Have*, along with *do*, *be* (*am*, *are*, *is*, *was*, *were*), and *make* are weak verbs. In Sean's sentence a better verb (*talking*) is buried in the middle of the sentence. The sentence would be more effective if he moved the verb forward and added another describing his actions, for example, "In working at the farmers' market, I talked with customers and handled cash transactions." Instead of writing, "There was a conflict I resolved between the team members," an applicant could say, "I resolved a conflict between team members."

Nominalization occurs when a verb is changed into a noun, for example, *observe* to *observation*. However, because résumés and cover letters tell the reader about your actions on the job, it is essential to identify strong verbs and avoid nominalization. Helen Sword (2012) refers to verbs converted to nouns as "zombie nouns" because they "cannibalize active verbs." If you worked as a summer intern and "did research on the industry standards," your action would be better showcased if you wrote "researched industry standards." "He made a reference to the job posting" would be better as "he referred to the job posting."

1. Identify the verb cannibalized by the following nouns:

clarification	participation
development	decision
accomplishment	identification
improvement	documentation
collaboration	negotiation

2. Identify the weak or nominalized verbs in the following sentences and phrases and consider alternative ways of expressing the action:

    a) I made several accomplishments as a Communications Assistant.
    b) As a counsellor at Camp Waitomo, I was responsible for the development of the evening camp program.
    c) The decision was made by the volunteers to extend the weekend hours.
    d) The proposal was created in collaboration with the team.
    e) I gave clients clarification on the tax procedures.
    f) My participation in the student society was active.
    g) Provided identification of resources for the research group
    h) Was responsible for accurate documentation of the event planning stages
    i) Involved in negotiation of contracts for the rental agency
    j) My improvement throughout the work term was great.

To reduce length and enhance readability, résumés often use lists. The Work Experience section, for example, provides a list of bulleted and relevant activities and accomplishments. These lists must be parallel in structure, which means they must use the same grammatical form throughout. For example, when describing your work as a marketing assistant, you wouldn't say "prepared, write, and delivered a presentation on human resource sustainability." The verb *write* is in the present tense while the other two are past tense. The correct phrase would be "prepared, wrote, and delivered."

Sean's revised résumé includes the following bulleted list of his activities. The verb phrases are parallel.

•   Coordinated a team of labourers in efficiently harvesting produce
•   Demonstrated attention to detail in sorting and labelling produce for shipping
•   Maintained accurate records of harvested areas, product weights, and soil conditions

Revise the following lists for verb use and parallelism. Consider how to strengthen the items to create an effective résumé by using active verbs in the present tense for positions that are ongoing and in the past tense for jobs that have ended.

1. English Language Tutor, Seoul School of Language, Seoul, Korea   2013–2014
    •   Taught beginning and intermediate English
    •   Communications skills and leadership skills
    •   Ability to identify issues and problems

2. Office Assistant, Oakville Insurance, Moncton, NB   2015–present
   - Administer medical, dental, and pension plan for over 10,000 members
   - Responding to member inquiries, creating formal letters, and reporting remittances
   - Collaborate with members in both official languages
   - Analyzed and improved department database using Microsoft Word and Excel
   - Utilize persuasive written and oral skills in internal and external professional communications

3. Research Assistant, Dalhousie University, Halifax, NS   Sept 2013–Jan 2014
   - Record large amounts of data on Microsoft Excel
   - Sorting, number, and organize data accurately and in a timely manner
   - Collaborate with research team to develop and deliver survey results
   - Coding of data

Additional Resources

Twitter

Harvard Biz Review @HarvardBiz
   Management tips, daily statistics, and links to blog posts that address communication and employment issues, as well as trends in human resource management, from Boston, MA–based *Harvard Business Review*
The Globe and Mail @globeandmail
   News and features from Canada's Toronto-based national newspaper
Undercover Recruiter @UndercoverRec
   Links to relevant news and websites from a London, UK–based career and recruitment blog

Websites

Harvard Business Review. Retrieved from blogs .hbr.org/.
Infographic Visual Resumés. Retrieved from pinter-est.com/rtkrum/infographic-visual-resumes/.
International Association of Business Com-municators Code of Ethics for Professional Communicators. Retrieved from www .iabc.com/about-us/governance/code-of-ethics/.
Purdue Online Writing Lab: Résumés and Vitas. Retrieved from owl.english.purdue.edu/owl/ section/6/23/.
Services for Youth. Retrieved from www.youth .gc.ca/eng/topics/jobs/index.shtml.

Grammar and Language Links

Language Portal of Canada: Gateway to English. Retrieved from www.noslangues-our languages.gc.ca/fss-gte/fss-gte-eng.php.
Purdue Online Writing Lab: Categorized List of Action Verbs. Retrieved from owl.english .purdue.edu/owl/resource/543/02/.
Purdue Online Writing Lab: Parallel Structure in Professional Writing. Retrieved from owl.english.purdue.edu/owl/resource/ 644/1/.
Boston College: Action Verbs & Keywords. Retrieved from www.bc.edu/offices/careers/ jobs/resumes/verbs.html.

CHAPTER TWO

Networking, Job Interviews, and Follow-Up

David Paul Morris/Bloomberg via Getty Images

Learning Objectives

A. **Develop** strategies for formal and informal networking.
B. **Consider** the employer's goal in the interview process.
C. **Focus** on employer's needs.
D. **Understand** the importance in establishing a relationship with interviewers.
E. **Consider** the role of ethics in interviewing.
F. **Create** a strategic approach for answering common interview questions.
G. **Use** anecdotes, examples, and stories to demonstrate strengths, motivation, and fit.
H. **Understand** the effect of body language in interviews.

The Story So Far

Chapter 1 introduced you to four prospective employees of APPFORMS. Sean McNeill, a second-year student, responded to an advertisement for a co-op position in marketing. He researched the company and determined how his skills and interests aligned with the values and mission of APPFORMS . He constructed a résumé and cover letter and revised them until they effectively displayed how he could meet the company's needs. Lara Leveaux heard about APPFORMS through a family friend and submitted an unsolicited application for an internship position. She adjusted her documents to appeal to her targeted employer. Maya Chen sought a position in finance. She produced application documents that reflected the standards of her field and the benefits she offered the company through her international experience. James Patel plans to attend a networking event and prepared an elevator pitch he hoped would initiate a relationship with the company.

Introduction

Chapter 1 focused on preparing résumés, cover letters, and elevator pitches to initiate a relationship with an industry representative or organization. Chapter 2 focuses on further developing the relationship between potential employee or intern and an industry or company representative through networking and interviews. We continue with the story of James Patel as he attends a university-sponsored formal networking event and are introduced to Carrie du Plessis, who does informal networking through LinkedIn and her high school contacts. We then follow James as he interviews at APPFORMS.

Whether the position is full-time or part-time, a co-op work term placement, or an internship, searching for a job is time-consuming and requires focus. You need to study the job market and the job requirements, and analyze your skill sets before crafting a résumé that matches the needs of the job. You could wait until a job is formally advertised, but finding a position through your network can be more effective. Recruiters, career services centres, professors, and job websites all advise new and experienced job seekers that networking can yield good opportunities.

Networking is the process of creating or activating relationships in which information and services can be shared. While networking, you need to both present yourself in the best possible manner and indicate to your potential employer that you have something to offer (**the "give"**) that will benefit the organization. During the networking process, you can highlight your skills, resourcefulness, eagerness to share and learn, and willingness to grow with the organization. You are offering your knowledge, ability to research, and ability to do the job. In return, you can expect to receive an offer, good remuneration, benefits, growth, and most importantly, experience (**the "get"**). Networking is about giving and getting and doing so in a way that leaves a favourable and lasting impression.

If your résumé and cover letter or your networking skills demonstrate your ability and desire to do the job, you may be invited to an interview. For the interviewer, the purpose of an interview is to select the best candidate for the position. While skills and experiences are listed in the résumé, the interview reveals much more about the candidate's motivation for seeking the position and the candidate's fit with the organization's values, goals, and culture. For you, the candidate, the interview is an opportunity to tell the stories behind the details of the résumé and cover letter, to develop a relationship with the employer, and to determine whether the organization suits your goals and preferred working style.

Interviews can be held with individuals or small groups and can be held either face-to-face or by phone or video call. Each type may require slightly different preparation, but all types require you to prepare stories that illustrate each of the requirements in the job description; that demonstrate knowledge of and fit with the position, organization, and industry; and that address the most common interview questions.

Formal and Informal Networking to Create, Build, and Maintain Business Relationships

The Case of James Patel: Formal Networking

A networking event has been organized by James's career services department in the atrium of his faculty's building. About 10 companies are scheduled to be there, and while it is one of the smaller events, the companies in attendance include large ones and a few start-ups. The networking event starts in the morning, followed by lunch and information sessions.

James has taken the time to prepare for the event. He practised his elevator pitch in front of the mirror and a couple of friends and is feeling confident. He is dressed in a charcoal-grey three-button suit, a light-blue plain shirt, and a smart-looking light-red tie to provide contrast. He shaved and bathed and feels fresh. His shoes are polished. He has practised his handshake so that it is brief, with a firm grip (not too hard, not too limp) and one or two shakes before letting go. He knows that body language and non-verbal communication are as important as verbal communication. He also remembers that making eye contact, nodding, and leaning forward all indicate engagement with what the speaker is saying.

James carries 10 copies of his two-page résumé in a nice black leather portfolio that has a pen and a note pad. This portfolio also has a slot for his tablet computer in which he has saved the electronic version of his résumé. The computer will allow him to research a company while he is waiting for his turn to speak to its representatives. He can also easily record their contact information and email them a quick thank-you note after his interaction.

As James walks into the networking event, he is both nervous and excited. It is 10:45 a.m., and the buzz in the atrium is quite thrilling. He feels ready and walks toward the DonnaLee Exports' booth and stands in line. James counts about six students ahead of him and pauses to look around the room. He recalls his pitch to DonnaLee. He wants it to be free flowing, and he does not want to sound too rehearsed. As he approaches the booth, he decides he will start with some small talk. It is an impulsive decision, but he feels if he says something interesting, he will be memorable and he will also ease some of the tension he is feeling. Three students are now in front of him, and he is able to hear some of the conversation. He studies the two DonnaLee representatives. They are dressed smartly and in full business attire. He is not sure who will be free to speak to him when he reaches the front of the line. He decides to quickly prepare two opening sentences that will serve as both a greeting and informative statement. Now only one student is in front of him, and that student goes to speak to the male representative from DonnaLee. James knows he will be speaking with the woman and decides on his opening remarks.

As he approaches her, she smiles and extends her hand. James steps forward, smiles and says, "Hi, I am James Patel." The woman replies, "Hi, James, I am Cynthia Hwang, pleased to meet you." The Chinese name "Hwang" is typically pronounced as Wong and in his eagerness to say something unrehearsed, and in the excitement of his first formal networking encounter with a company representative, James hears Won, which he knows to be a distinctly South Korean name. To say something interesting, and to be remembered as somebody up-to-date on current events, James remarks, "So glad for South Korea that the Sea of Japan will be renamed the East Sea." To his horror, James sees Cynthia wince, but being the professional that she is, she smiles and urges James to tell her about himself.

James realizes that he has made a serious error and that he should not have uttered that statement. Somehow he manages to go through most of his prepared pitch without stumbling. At the end of the conversation, Cynthia takes James's résumé and says they will contact him if he is selected for an interview. He asks for and receives her business card.

James leaves thinking that he needs to sit down somewhere and reflect on his first encounter with a company representative. He realizes that making an impromptu statement is not a bad idea, but he made a couple of incorrect assumptions that could cost him a job opportunity. Her business card says Cynthia's last name is Hwang. He did not hear her correctly. He should have clarified and politely asked her to repeat her name.

From her business card, James now knows Cynthia is of Chinese origin and would have been offended by his comment. He slowly regains his composure and tries to stay focused. He decides to immediately email Cynthia Hwang and thank her for her time and the conversation. He decides to apologize to her for unknowingly causing her discomfort with his statement. He feels that he may not get an interview call from DonnaLee Exports, but sending the email is the right thing to do.

James feels better after sending the email. He is now in a clear frame of mind and confidently walks toward the APPFORMS's booth and waits in the line. When his turn finally comes to talk to the APPFORMS company representative, whom he learns is the director of human resources, he delivers a flawless pitch and has a great conversation. He leaves feeling good about the experience. James continues to walk around the atrium and stops at a couple of other booths. At the end of the evening, he feels that he has emerged from his first formal networking event with many gains.

The Case of Carrie du Plessis: Informal Networking

Carrie du Plessis, a first-year commerce student at Northern Canada University, has avoided information and networking sessions. Such events are quite intimidating for her. A friend recommends that she begin where she is comfortable—with her current network. Carrie belongs to several organizations that might provide her with contacts, including her sports club and her high school alumni association. Her friend encourages her to reach out to these contacts.

Carrie writes down the names of people she knows in these organizations. In her sports club, she can talk to her coach, Eleanor Saunders; the team manager, Kareem Larson; the team physiotherapist, Amy Brown; and of course her teammates. From her high school alumni association, she could talk to the president, Huma Alvarez; the treasurer, Kiran David; and Lenny Barua, who holds the title of member-at-large. She follows the association on Twitter and Instagram and knows a few of the other members. She got along well with them and decides to contact them via Facebook. Carrie's business communication professor had emphasized that networking establishes mutually beneficial relationships. Carrie wants to "give" as well as "get."

She then sets out to write to her contacts and starts with an email to Huma Alvarez. Carrie identifies herself as an alumna of the high school and a first-year commerce student considering a major in accounting at Northern Canada University and explains that she is looking for a co-op opportunity. She asks if Huma would provide her with some contacts. Carrie is amazed when Huma quickly replies and says she would be happy to help Carrie in her search, but suggests that Carrie connect with her on LinkedIn. Huma says that LinkedIn is an easy way for her to make introductions to potential hiring managers.

Carrie thanks Huma and by the end of the day has created a LinkedIn profile. It is rich in information about her academic and non-academic activities, including her sports achievements and volunteer work. She realizes that she could add many more pieces of information about herself on the profile than in a standard two-page résumé. She connects with Huma on LinkedIn and then starts looking for others she might know as well as possible co-op/internship opportunities through the LinkedIn job search feature.

Carrie finds Kareem Larson on LinkedIn. She had intended to send him an email as well but decides to send a LinkedIn Invitation instead. She adds a personal message and asks if he has contacts in the accounting field. It is a couple of days before Kareem accepts her connection, but he replies that although he has a lot of connections, only a few are in the accounting field. However, he adds, he will introduce Carrie to Niamh Trescothick, director of payroll and finance at APPFORMS, a tech company located in Halifax, Nova Scotia. He also adds that Niamh is pronounced NEEV and that she is a woman. Carrie promptly thanks Kareem for both the valuable information and the introduction.

Soon, Kareem sends a message on LinkedIn introducing Carrie to Niamh Trescothick. Carrie then composes a message of her own. She decides to update her profile on LinkedIn and knows that her message to Niamh Trescothick should be professional and brief, yet informative. She copies Kareem on the message. The comments on the side of Carrie's message indicate the ways in which she establishes herself as a memorable contact.

Date:	April 21, 2016
To:	Niamh Trescothick; Kareem Larson
From:	Carrie du Plessis
Subject:	RE: Introducing Carrie du Plessis—Co-op Opportunity

Dear Ms. Trescothick,

> Carrie begins with a professional salutation. Kareem had already indicated to Carrie that Niamh Trescothick is a woman

> Here she refers to the introduction by Kareem Larson and also graciously acknowledging his gesture

Kareem Larson, my varsity team manager, was kind enough to provide this introduction. I am writing to introduce myself and direct you to my LinkedIn profile. I am a first-year commerce student at Northern Canada University. While my major is as yet undeclared, I have strong interests in technology, marketing, and international business. In my spare time, I have created several apps for Android phones and have a basic understanding of the process of submitting newly developed apps for approval in the online smartphone stores. I have researched APPFORMS and learned that it is a technology company that creates apps for mobile devices.

> Carries directs the reader to a place where there is more information

> This statement is truthful, but she then provides clear information about interests

> This sentence highlights verifiable skills and how they can benefit the organization. Again, she is being truthful about her abilities in app development

Kareem indicated that your organization may be looking for co-op students with backgrounds similar to mine. I would love to discuss with you, at your convenience, how I can contribute to your organization.

Sincerely,

> The email closes professionally

> Carrie shows initiative in researching the organization

> Carrie's closing sentence asks for action leaving the choice of communication channel—phone or otherwise—to the reader, while acknowledging the receiver's busy schedule

Carrie

On 30/01/16 6:48 AM, Kareem Larson wrote:

Hi Niamh,

> The message is brought back to the reason for the introduction and this message

Trust things are well in Halifax. You had mentioned that your company was planning to hire some co-op students. I wanted to introduce one of my volleyball players to you. Carrie du Plessis is a first-year commerce student at Northern Canada U and is my star spiker and someone I am very happy to recommend. I will let Carrie write and introduce herself to you. Talk to you soon.

Best,

Kareem

In a separate message to Kareem, Carrie thanks him again for his gesture. She realizes that this action is one of the ways to maintain network relationships. Carrie feels good about her networking start.

Interviewing—The Employers' Perspective

Both formal advertisements and formal and informal networking can lead to the next stage of the hiring process: an interview. The following section presents this stage from the interviewers' perspective.

Selecting the Candidates

Juanita Olson, APPFORMS's director of human resources, and Roman Midori from the marketing group will select a short list of candidates and conduct the interviews for the co-op Marketing Assistant. They review the job description and have a quick look through the cover letters and résumés of the 42 applicants to remove any that obviously do not meet the job requirements.

APPFORMSCanada

JOB TITLE: Marketing Assistant (co-op work term)

COMPANY: APPFORMS Canada

CONTACT PERSON: Juanita Olson, Director of Human Resources

JOB DESCRIPTION

The Marketing Assistant works with the other members of the Marketing Department as well as with members of other departments toward creation, development and sales of new technology applications. The assistant will be an active member in establishing a plan to achieve financial goals. The assistant will also work with the Director of Communications in maintaining the company websites, producing material for external stakeholders, and researching media outlets.

TASKS/DUTIES:

- Assist in maintaining the company website and Facebook, Twitter, and blog accounts
- Support the Marketing team at special events
- Compile media analyses
- Conduct product research as required
- Work in a collaborative team environment

JOB REQUIREMENTS:

- Co-op student in any year of university
- Enthusiastic, self-starting and dynamic individual
- Ability to work in a collaborative team environment
- Strong work ethic
- Strong interpersonal communication skills
- Strong written and oral communication skills
- Ability to use both Microsoft Office (Word, Excel, PowerPoint) and Apple software packages; knowledge of other computer applications like MS Access, MS Visio, and SAP are a plus
- Ability to work outside normal business hours at special events

Juanita and Roman immediately remove two applicants who are not enrolled in a co-op program and therefore do not meet the job requirement. Since even minor errors can affect the company's image and reputation, they also remove three applicants whose résumés contain errors or misjudgements in use of language. One applicant wrote *form* rather than *from* in the cover letter, referred to marketing *expierience* (Juanita notes this as a spelling error), and had multiple sentence structure errors. Another applicant began all but one sentence in the cover letter with *I*, which indicates to Juanita and Roman that first, the applicant is unaware of the stylistic effect of this repetition and, second, the applicant has limited knowledge of or interest in APPFORMS and can therefore only address qualifications rather than fit. Another applicant is clearly sending only slightly modified cover letters to each organization to which she is applying. She refers to the position of marketing assistant and then proceeds to outline her accounting skills and refers in the final paragraph to her desire to obtain an accounting position at a local property company. The job description identifies strong communication skills as a requirement, and while the applicants claim these skills, their documents reveal otherwise.

The formatting of some of the documents also reveals a lack of professionalism. APPFORMS needs workers who are adept at communicating with various stakeholders. Poor formatting indicates poor understanding of audience and medium. One applicant submitted a résumé using an excessive amount of bold, italics, and underlining. The document was difficult to read, though perhaps not as difficult to read as the résumé from a candidate who used 6-point font to squeeze in all the information, some of which was redundant or insignificant, onto a single page. Another applicant demonstrated a lack of awareness of standard business letter form. The cover letter had no date or recipient address block, used *Juanita* instead of *Ms. Olson* in the greeting, and used 1.5 line spacing. Both Juanita and Roman consider themselves receptive to modern forms of communication, but these candidates selected formatting that inhibited easy reading and revealed ignorance of professional standards. They end up rejecting a quarter of the applicants because of lack of attention to detail, lack of expertise in written communication, or lack of professionalism.

Next, Juanita and Roman take a closer look at the cover letters. They identify 20 applicants who have demonstrated their skills by describing experiences and transferable skills such as leadership, creativity, and teamwork. Then they look at each of the 20 for indications that the candidate would be a good fit. Five of the candidates show little knowledge of the company's history, values, and focus, and provide no indication that they are familiar with the organization. The remaining 15 illustrate their match to APPFORMS's commitment to diversity, entrepreneurial spirit and innovation, or team orientation. Their résumés and cover letters persuade Juanita and Roman that they have the skills for the job, that they have the motivation to succeed in the position and the industry, and that they would be a good fit with the company's culture.

Juanita and Roman independently select 5 candidates from the remaining 15, and end up with a short list of 8, of which Juanita has already met 3: 1 at a job fair, another on a corporate tour who later connected with her on LinkedIn, and the last who came in for an informational interview. They decide that they will include these 3 in their short list. Of the remaining 5, they choose 2. One offers an especially interesting background, having contributed significantly to the production of a promotional video for a local private school. Another candidate wrote an especially interesting cover letter. She relates APPFORMS's use of coaches to train new hires to her own experiences as a student and a coach at a local sailing club.

Juanita calls the five applicants who made it onto the short list and makes note of her exchanges with each one. The first candidate she calls is Mohamed Anderson, the candidate she met at the job fair. On the phone, he strikes her as polite and enthusiastic. She finds the same enthusiasm in the second candidate, Sean McNeill. She reaches the voice mail of the next candidate, Sabine Goldman. Sabine's voice message states that she is sorry to have missed the call but will finish classes at 4:00 and will be happy to return a message then. Juanita notes that her message demonstrates organizational ability, attention to detail, and awareness of the caller's needs. The fourth candidate takes her call in a crowded shopping mall. Juanita is distracted by the background noise and offers to call back in a few minutes, but the candidate insists on arranging the interview right away. The fifth candidate answers the call and accepts the invitation to interview, but Juanita can barely hear her and is taken aback by her lack of enthusiasm. She is not sure if she just woke her up or if she really doesn't care. Juanita also calls James Patel in Saskatoon. James says he will be in Halifax for a case competition on the date of the interview and asks for a late afternoon time slot. Juanita is impressed by James's involvement in the case competition.

Selecting the Interview Questions

After connecting with the all the candidates and arranging the interviews for the next two weeks, Juanita and Roman next meet to plan the format of the interview and the questions they will ask. They agree that each candidate will be interviewed for 30 minutes and be asked to complete a writing sample afterwards. Because they have conducted many interviews, Juanita and Roman and have a set of questions they typically ask. They already know from their résumés and cover letters that the selected candidates have the basic skills to do the job. The interviews will now confirm these skills and give each candidate a chance to explain why they want to work for APPFORMS. They also want to determine if the candidate is a good fit. They want to find someone that they can connect with and would enjoy working with every day.

Juanita and Roman like to start the interview with the most common interview request: "Tell us about yourself." The responses reveal character and personality and provide an opportunity for Juanita and Roman to adjust to the candidate's volume, accent, and pace before they get to the main part of the interview. The first impression matters. Juanita and Roman will gain their first sense of the candidate's likely fit with the company. Most candidates expect this question or a similar one, so Juanita and Roman see it as a question that will relax the candidates.

They tend to follow the introductory question with two other standard questions: What are your strengths, and what is your greatest weakness? Juanita and Roman are looking for strengths that satisfy their current needs, in this case, for example, experience with updating a website and blog. They also look for strengths that ensure fit with the organization. The question can be asked in various ways, such as: What assets will you bring to the organization? Tell me what your last employer would say is your greatest strength. Why do you think you would be successful in this position?

By asking about weaknesses, Juanita and Roman hope to discover if the candidate is self-aware. They also want to know how the candidate has overcome obstacles. The question presents an opportunity to determine the candidate's honesty and sincerity. In Juanita's experience, the question on weaknesses is always revealing. Some candidates follow standard advice to present a weakness on a quality that is not essential for completing the job. Juanita thinks that to a certain extent this approach makes sense; if a job requirement is managing a social media campaign, the candidate should not identify a lack of familiarity with social media as a weakness. But some candidates take this advice too far and select a weakness that is far removed from work at APPFORMS, such as the one who said her greatest weakness was her fear of snakes.

Some candidates take a positive quality and present it as a weakness. This approach drives Juanita crazy. She does not want to hear the candidate say she works too hard or that he is a perfectionist. These answers seem insincere. Everyone has weaknesses. She also doesn't want to hear from a candidate that can't say "no." She's heard that too many times. She wants an honest answer. Juanita's own weakness is a tendency to interrupt. She anticipates what is coming and cuts in. This behaviour can have a negative effect on her employees. She has made an effort to correct this weakness by remembering that the speaker will be more engaged if she feels heard and by nodding in response. She wants the candidate to be equally sincere. This sincerity is a step toward developing a strong, trusting working relationship. Being too real is also undesirable. In a recent interview, a candidate for an accounting position said she had problems with punctuality and meeting deadlines. She did not address how she was working to correct the problem. One candidate for a finance position actually said he was bad with numbers. This answer indicated he did not meet the basic job requirement.

Juanita and Roman ask the question about weaknesses in different ways, such as: What have you learned from a mistake you have made in the past? What would your previous employer tell me you should work to improve? They sometimes ask what characteristics the candidate is currently developing, what the candidate would change about herself if she could change one thing, or what the candidate sees as one characteristic he must change to be successful in the industry. For this interview, they decide to ask the candidates: Describe a weakness that you have worked to overcome.

Juanita and Roman then devise questions that illustrate how a candidate has reacted in a given situation or reveal how the candidate might react in the future. Juanita and Roman consider the current marketing group. One staff member will be going on paternity leave in six weeks, and another is taking extended sick leave. The best supervisor and coach for the new co-op student is Christiane Xue. Christiane had issues with the last co-op student, whom she found lacking in initiative. If Christiane or another senior member of the marketing team was not providing constant supervision and direction, the co-op student was focused on her personal social media accounts and taking selfies. Because Christiane places great importance on initiative, they create a question to assess this quality and determine the candidate's fit with Christiane. They consider asking the following questions:

- Tell us about a time when you showed initiative.
- Tell us what motivates you to do a good job.

- Tell us about a time when you took the lead on a project.
- Tell us about a time when you identified a problem, and talk me through the steps you took to solve it.

In the end, they decide to ask: Sometimes we have down time between projects. What would you do to make the most of this time? Juanita and Roman also decide to ask three separate questions to help them determine the candidate's communication skills, analytical and research skills, and knowledge of the organization.

Questions to assess communication skills can focus on a range of abilities including cross-cultural communication, team communication, written communication, presentation, or public relations. In the past they have asked candidates to describe a challenging writing assignment, explain what made it challenging, and discuss how they accomplished the task. They have previously asked candidates to explain how they have dealt with a difficult team member, give an example of a time when listening skills helped in overcoming a problem, and describe how they have communicated with a client with limited English skills. Since the successful candidate will be assisting with online messages, they also decide to ask a situational question related to external communication: Your co-worker has asked you to review a blog post he has written for immediate release. You notice errors with both language use and content. How would you approach the co-worker?

To address research skills, Juanita and Roman choose to ask: You have been asked to conduct research on apps that provide information on metro bus routes and schedules. How would you go about conducting this research? They hope the question will reveal how the candidate approaches a problem and any skills in marketing research. To determine the candidate's knowledge of the organization, they decide to ask: Why do you want to work for APPFORMS? The answer to this question will reveal the candidate's motivation and knowledge of the company's values and mission.

Their last question will be: Do you have any questions? If the answer is no, they may consider the candidate unprepared or disengaged. Juanita and Roman are also a bit sick of some of the more common questions such as, "What training will you provide?" These questions focus on the candidate's needs, not those of the organization. Juanita and Roman are looking for questions that demonstrate familiarity with the organization and reveal something about the candidate's sincere interests.

Interviewing—The Candidate's Perspective

As we saw in the previous section, the employer's focus is on selecting the candidate with the skills, motivation, and fit for the position. Candidates prepare for interviews by reviewing stories that illustrate these key items.

The Case of James Patel: Face-to-Face Interview

James receives a phone call from Juanita Olson, and they arrange an interview for after the case competition before he returns to Saskatoon.

Preparing for the Interview

James begins his preparation by reviewing the job description. He lists each of the elements of the job description and requirements. Next to each skill or requirement, he makes notes of an experience from his résumé or a story he can tell to illustrate that skill. For example, he notes his experience working as part of a team during his marketing course, his experiences on soccer teams, his case competition team, and his work with various community groups. He really likes to talk about his blog, so he thinks of various ways this experience fits with the job description. In thinking of a story for each item, he considers stories about himself, stories that illustrate his interests and passions, and stories that demonstrate attributes relevant for APPFORMS. The best stories will combine all three.

James then visits the APPFORMS website and reads about their activities, product lines, and key people. He reviews the About Us section, which contains a brief history of the organization as well as their mission and values. Another page is dedicated to community action, which he revisits. He also visits the Careers page since it indicates the type of person APPFORMS seeks. He then goes to the News section of the website. After reviewing the website, he looks at his Twitter feed. He already follows Goran Duro, one of APPFORMS's managing partners. In addition, James researches the organization through his university's databases, beginning with MarketLine, a database that provides information on companies and industries from around the world.

Next, James goes online to search for common interview questions. As he looks at the questions he finds, he considers how he might answer each one and thinks of appropriate examples for the top 10 questions. James's research tells him that all interviews essentially focus on three questions (Bradt, 2011):

1. Can you do the job?
2. Will you love the job?
3. Can we tolerate working with you?

He looks back at the lists of questions. His answers to questions about time management, problem-solving skills, computer skills, work and volunteer experiences, strengths, weaknesses, and education will determine whether he can do the job. Questions about why he has applied for the position, what he knows about the company and industry, where he sees himself in 5 or 10 years, and what experiences he has found most rewarding will assess his motivation for working in this position for this company in this industry. Questions that employers might ask about team skills, previous interpersonal challenges in the workplace, or examples of showing initiative or reacting to conflict address his fit with the organization and whether his future employees will tolerate working with him.

James also prepares responses to situational or behavioural questions. A **situational question** asks candidates to tell how they would deal with a hypothetical situation. His university hosts an interview competition every year, and he recalls a situational question from the last competition, when the interviewer handed the candidate an old cellphone and asked her to sell it to him. **Behavioural questions** ask candidates to tell stories from their experiences. These stories might be about a time the candidate handled a team conflict or a difficult customer, solved a complex problem, or dealt with an ethical dilemma. The best responses use the **STAR** technique to describe situation, task, action, and results. For practice, James considers his answer to a question asking him to describe a time when he worked effectively under pressure. In his case, the situation involved managing six courses while working part-time. His task was to complete an analytical report and prepare for two midterms while working extra shifts to cover for a hospitalized co-worker. James's action was to clarify exactly what needed to be done, then listing and prioritizing the work by importance and deadline. He created a schedule and kept to it. The results were high marks on the report and midterms and a supervisor who was impressed by his loyalty and dedication.

His research tells him that an opportunity to ask questions is presented at nearly every interview and is his chance to leave the interview with a strong impression. He prepares a short list of questions, including a couple questions that focus on key areas he would like to address during the interview. If, for example, he does not have an opportunity to discuss his blog writing, he will say: *I have managed my own blog for three years and have a special interest in this area. The job description mentioned working on blogs. Can you tell me more about what work I might do in this area?*

James wants to use his questions to confirm his knowledge of the position, his fit with the organization, and his interest in the job. His research revealed that, in addition to many other community service ventures, the company provides volunteers for a kids' triathlon. To demonstrate that he shares the company's values, he will write the question, *I noticed on your website that you support the kids' triathlon. I am really interested in supporting youth, as you can see from my work with Big Brothers and Big Sisters. Will there be opportunities for me to work with this program or other community projects?*

He reviews the questions he finds online and adapts them to himself, the job, and the company. For example, one question asks about the company's culture. He can adapt this question to show his knowledge about the organization by asking: *In the job description and on your website, I see that the word team appears often. Can you tell me about the team culture at APPFORMS?*

Finally, James organizes his documents. He puts an extra copy of his résumé and a sheet with full contact details of four references in his smart black leather portfolio. He also takes his list of questions.

An hour before the interview, James gets ready. He chooses to wear a blue suit, which is a conservative business colour and will demonstrate his professionalism. He matches it with a solid-coloured shirt and a bright tie. While he wants to balance his obvious youth with a polished appearance, he also wants to appear modern, so his shirt and tie, while not too hipster or wild, are current in design and colour choice. He is freshly shaved and checks to see if his fingernails are clipped and trim. He ensures that his shoes are polished and his socks match his shirt. He also ensures that his tie falls just over his belt buckle. He buttons the top two buttons of his three-button jacket and checks himself over in the mirror. He feels ready. He turns off his cellphone to ensure it does not ring during the interview.

After getting dressed, James takes a few minutes to prepare mentally. In university he watched Amy Cuddy's TED talk on the ways in which "power posing" can change the brain. He wants to appear confident and self-assured, but his anxiety about the interview makes him want to run and hide. He knows from the Cuddy video that closing his body up and making himself small diminishes his feeling of power. He stands and places his hands on his hips, taking up physical space as Cuddy suggests. He doesn't want his great enthusiasm for the position to overwhelm him, so he tries to relax his neck and shoulders, arms, and hands. He works at steadying his breathing, and he warms up his voice by humming.

When he is ready, James makes his way to the APPFORMS offices a block away. He greets the receptionist and introduces himself. Although the receptionist will not be interviewing him, James knows that it is important to make a good impression on everyone he meets in the company. The receptionist leads James to a conference room where Juanita and Roman are waiting. He enters and shakes each interviewer's hand. Juanita indicates where he should sit. James sits down and places his leather portfolio in front of him. He sits up straight and keeps his hands and arms on the table. This posture makes him appear confident, and keeping his arms on the table helps him to lean slightly forward toward the interviewers—an effective way to establish credibility, confidence, and rapport.

The Face-to-Face Interview

JUANITA: Hi, James. Good afternoon. I am Juanita Olson from human resources and this is Roman Midori, director of marketing at APPFORMS. How are you? How was the case competition?

JAMES: Hi, Juanita. Hi, Roman. Good afternoon. Thank you for inviting me to participate in this interview. The case competition was a fantastic experience. We came in second to Dalhousie!

Juanita and Roman laugh, as does James. This reference to the home team lightens the mood and relaxes James.

JUANITA: James, I will quickly outline the agenda for the next 30 minutes. We will start by asking you a few questions about yourself, then move on to your work experiences, and other things related to this position so that we can learn a little more about you. At the end, we will have some time for you to ask us any questions you may have. Okay?

JAMES: Yes!

JUANITA: Great! We would like to start by having you introduce yourself. Can you tell us a little bit about yourself?

James had already decided to use his elevator pitch as an introduction and to answer such a question. He has modified it to make it appropriate for an interview setting.

JAMES: I am a second-year Bachelor of Commerce student at the University of Saskatoon, majoring in marketing and international business. I completed my first co-op work term at the University of Saskatoon where I assisted in recruiting South American students to the university. This opportunity provided me with an understanding of the way South Americans, particularly Brazilians, currently use technology and how we at the university might use this understanding in our marketing strategy. By using Orkut, Twitter, Vostu, and Facebook to connect with this market, my team and I contributed to an increase in applicants of over 28%. I am also an avid blogger and blog about technology trends and student experiences. I tweet about these trends and point people in my network to my blog posts. I have had many retweets. I also follow business leaders on Twitter. I have noticed Goran Duro's recent tweets on the importance of global connections. This mutual interest in expanding global markets makes working at APPFORMS very appealing to me. I am an active Big Brother at the Big Brothers and Big Sisters organization and I play soccer on weekends.

After delivering his introduction, James feels he has accurately summarized his recent co-op work experience, his passion for blogging (by choosing to use the word *avid* to qualify the activity), his interest in the company and industry through his presence on social media and following of APPFORMS's CEO and other business leaders on Twitter, his volunteerism, and his team sports activity. He can see from the appreciative nods from both Juanita and Roman that they seem to like what they have heard. It is a good start to the interview, and James feels confident.

Although Roman has a second question ready, he wants to find out more about James's blogging activities and decides to ask a follow-up question.

ROMAN: James, that is very interesting. It appears that you have a wide range of activities that you are involved in. Can you tell us a little bit more about your blogging?

JAMES: Sure! I started blogging about three years ago when I was in high school. I was always interested in technology, as most teenagers are, and was an early adopter of smartphones and tablet computers. This hobby can be expensive, so I would save money from my summer jobs doing painting or yard work in my neighbourhood and working as a grocery store clerk to buy these products. I researched each product extensively. I would look at product user boards to read reviews from users and then make my purchases. Through this process, I learned a lot about not just the products, but also about how people, especially teenagers and young people around the world, use smartphones, online chat, and other applications. I was surprised to learn that both high school and university students, regardless of where they were from, use these devices in a similar manner. I thought that I should share my new-found knowledge about these trends and user experiences so that others could benefit from it, which resulted in my blog posts. I now blog regularly. It gets difficult sometimes to find time, with class assignments and other activities, but I try to manage my time so that I have at least a few hours a week to research some trends and write about them. The blog has really helped me improve my writing skills. I've learned to say a lot in a small space and provide convincing evidence for my points. I believe this approach has made my blog posts believable and honest, and from the number of tweets and retweets and likes to my posts, I think my readers enjoy the content and style and look forward to new blog posts.

James's answer provides specific information about one of his activities. He also demonstrates his work ethic, his methodical approach to research, and his communication skills. He supports his claims with verifiable evidence. In his introductory answer, he was able to tie his response to APPFORMS. Here he does not do so specifically; however, the skills he lists are transferable skills—skills that he will bring with him to his position at APPFORMS.

JUANITA: Great! The next question is then quite appropriate. Suppose your co-worker has asked you to review a blog post she has written for immediate release. You notice some errors in the document in both language use and content. How would you approach the co-worker?

JAMES: That is a great question! I think this situation would be a wonderful opportunity for me to not just learn about my co-worker's approach to writing, but also how she approaches her work. The situation also offers a chance for my co-worker to learn about my abilities. I would prefer that we sit together and go through the blog post so we can share our ideas for improving it for our audience. I would not criticize her writing, but would offer suggestions for making the piece even better. If my co-worker has errors in sentence construction, I can suggest alternative sentences that would convey the message more effectively. If the errors relate to the formatting and structure of the entire post, then I can show examples where different ways of arranging the information can be more effective. If the content has factual errors, I can show her sources where she can collect verifiable information. I hope to come away from this experience with the knowledge that I earned the respect of my co-worker and also with new appreciation of her work.

This question is situational. In his answer, James demonstrates his ability to review and critique a document from several perspectives. His approach indicates patience and the ability to critically analyze information. He also demonstrates that he wishes to build a good working relationship with a co-worker.

ROMAN: Very good, James. You have already described some of your skills and the areas about which you are passionate. Can you now tell us about some of your strengths, and describe a weakness that you have worked to overcome?

JAMES: I can answer both questions together. I have always been good at organizing my thoughts, and that has helped me organize my work. However, at times I have not been good at managing my time. As a first-year student, I used to leave assignments until the last minute and realized it was affecting my performance and my morale. I attended a time-management course and became better at learning how to schedule my time effectively. Organizing and time management have now became my strengths. I learned to reduce stress while working toward deadlines by clearly outlining the work that needs to be done, sharing and delegating where necessary, and planning ahead.

My greatest strength is my ability to connect with people. Whenever I meet new people or I am part of a new group for a class project, I quickly try and find out about the interests the others may have and try and relate to them. I take time to listen, which I feel is an extremely useful skill. Listening not only helps me understand and relate to people; listening also helps me learn from everyone I meet.

I'm also a creative thinker and explore alternative options to problems and try not to rush to conclusions. This process allows me to analyze a particular problem by evaluating multiple scenarios before arriving at conclusions and recommendations.

While choosing to answer both questions, James has been able to mention one weakness and many strengths. Even the weakness was tied to an ongoing effort by him to improve and integrate his skill set. He describes the weakness and shows how he has worked to overcome it. He then describes his ability to work well in teams and his ability to think and analyze problems critically before presenting recommendations. He ends his answer with the strengths so that he concludes on a positive note.

JUANITA: Tell me what your last employer would say is your greatest strength.

JAMES: My last employer would say that my greatest strengths were my organization skills, my unique ability to spot technology trends, and my excellent written and oral communication skills. Another strength my last employer would mention is my ability to connect with people in Brazil by using their preferred social media platforms and to engage with prospective students and build relationships.

ROMAN: What assets would you bring to our organization?

JAMES: I bring several assets to the organization. In addition to my ability to manage my time well, which allows me to take on multiple tasks, I am also organized, and have successfully completed every assignment or project for class or at work on time. I also take the initiative to plan well so that my tasks are completed ahead of schedule so that I can revise and review my work. Planning allows me to help my teammates and take on other tasks when doing group work. Also, as I mentioned earlier, my blogging and active presence on social media have given me a network. If I am offered the co-op Marketing Assistant position at APPFORMS, I will be most happy to tap into this network to test the efficacy and need for apps created by the APPFORMS's development teams. My network consists of users of iPhones, Android phones, BlackBerry phones, and even Windows Mobile phones. I know you have development teams for each of these platforms, and my experience in following and tracking trends will help identify customers for current as well as future apps that your teams may be developing.

James knows from his preparation that the question really addresses "Can you do the job?" In his answer, he highlights transferable skills such as planning, managing time, working well in teams, taking initiative, and meeting deadlines. He then proceeds to outline some specific attributes like his network and social media activities and ties them to APPFORMS's product lines, showing not only his awareness of APPFORMS's line of work, but also how his skills and network can benefit their marketing and product development activities. James successfully uses his answer to show both his ability to do the job and his fit with the organization.

JUANITA: Tell us what motivates you to do a good job.

JAMES: Every time I return from a Big Brothers and Big Sisters event, I am supercharged with purpose and determination. The children in the group are bright and smart, but sometimes lack the resources or the access to many things we regard as standard. I feel extremely fortunate for the breaks I have gotten in life. I am enormously motivated to produce high-quality work so that I can get to a position where I can do more for these children by showing them how to work hard, teaching them transferable skills, and giving them a good start. I have also learned how to face obstacles by watching these children deal with their situations.

In answering this question James brings into the conversation his volunteer activities and how that motivates him to do well in all aspects of his work.

ROMAN: How have you successfully overcome obstacles while at work or at school?

JAMES: During my last co-op work term, I needed access to some university enrolment figures. However, the people working in the registrar's office were obviously busy and could not immediately respond to my email requests. I needed these numbers in order to proceed with my work so I decided to walk over and wait until I could meet with the person who would be able to help me. When she was free to talk to me, I introduced myself and told her my need. I said I understood how busy she was but that the data would not only help me with my work, but help the registrar with potential new enrolments from South America. She listened to my request again and was kind enough to provide me with the figures I needed. I stayed in touch with her throughout my co-op work term and was able to provide the registrar with some new and relevant information that helped them in their processes.

James again uses the STAR approach. He first presents the situation—his co-op position and research—and the task—the need to access data from the registrar's office. He then describes his actions persuading someone to spend time helping him. He explained his need and how, by helping him, the registrar would also benefit. He shows how he used a patient and respectful approach. He then demonstrates the results: he received the information he needed and established and maintained an effective working relationship.

JUANITA: Tell us about a time when you identified a problem. Talk us through the steps you took to solve it.

JAMES: I can think of a recent event that occurred when I was taking an introduction to marketing course. We were working in groups and each group was tasked with choosing a brand and creating a comprehensive marketing plan for it. We had to create strategies to promote the product, come up with pricing options for a diverse market, and develop product placement strategies for different outlets, such as brick-and-mortar and online stores. Then we had to produce a full-length written report and cite our sources. Our team decided to pick a consumer product because social media outlets could form part of our marketing and promotion plan. We agreed on the SoBe® brand of energy drinks from Pepsico®. We were excited about this product because all the team members had active lifestyles and had consumed this product at one time or another.

We assigned each other tasks to collect market data and research the product and began coming up with strategies for promotion and product placement. I was fortunate to be in a team in which everyone was engaged in the project. Soon we began to deliver our individual pieces. I volunteered to put the whole report together, edit and proofread it, and prepare it for submission. When I received a segment from one of my group members, I was really impressed with the nearly flawless writing and extensive research that this person had done. But soon I started to get seriously worried. Judging by some of his other work, this teammate did not have superior writing skills. I called and asked him about it. Initially he insisted he had written it, but when I gently asked him again, referring to some of his other work, he confessed that he had been running behind and could not deliver his part on time. Since he did not want to delay the project, he found a website where professional writers would do the work for him for a fee.

I was shocked at my teammate's confession. I told him that we could not use this material for our report, and I had to tell the rest of the team. First, it was wrong; it was cheating. Second, the rest of the team had done a lot of work, and we should not jeopardize our reputation for a few marks. Even if no one ever found out, it would bother my conscience. I don't produce my work this way. I explained to him that he should have told the team he was having trouble meeting his deadline, and together we could have divided up the work to ensure both quality and timeliness.

As a team, we came up with a new plan and task allocation and took on extra work to finish the project on time. We only got a B+ for the project, because in the final rush to submit on time, we had made some errors, both in content and in editing. But as a team we held our heads high and were happy with the outcome.

James's answer has all the elements of tension caused by working toward a deadline, feeling pressure to complete tasks, and resorting to alternative means to finish the assignment. Team consultation determined his course of action in resolving an ethical situation. Given time, the team could have produced work deserving of an A, but they were happy with the B+ because they remained true to their ethical and moral principles. James was able to use this story to demonstrate his integrity to Juanita and Roman.

> ROMAN: Sometimes we have gaps between projects—what we often refer to as down time. What would you do to make the most of this time?

> JAMES: Down time is the perfect opportunity to develop my skills. I could use the time to familiarize myself further with APPFORMS's products and perhaps test a few of them. I could read business and technology news, not just from Canada but from around the world, to stay current and to see what opportunities are out there for development. I could use the time to learn new app programming skills. I would also use the time to develop working relationships with people in other departments and learn more about the company and how it operates. I would certainly use my down time productively.

> JUANITA: Excellent, James! We have asked all of the questions we wanted to ask. Do you have any questions for us?

James takes a moment to review the questions he had prepared. He has already told stories about his blogging and his volunteer work. He believes he has demonstrated his strengths, his motivation, and his fit with the organization. James knows the interview is an opportunity not just for the employer to evaluate him but also a way for him to evaluate the organization. If the organization is not a good fit for him, he should consider other options. He decides to ask his question about the team culture at APPFORMS. James's personal preference is for a balance of independence and team work; he wants to ensure that the corporate culture at APPFORMS is ideal for him. Juanita and Roman have not said what will happen next in the hiring process, so he asks when he might hear from them. Once Juanita and Roman answer James's questions, the interview ends. Before he leaves, James asks for their business cards so that he can send a follow-up email. On his way out, James thanks the receptionist again.

Interview Follow-Up

When he returns to his hotel, James makes a few notes about the interview. He records the names of all the people he met so he does not forget them. He also writes down as many of the interview questions as he can remember so that he can use them to prepare for future interviews. He then sends an email to his references telling them they might be contacted by Juanita Olson or Roman Midori from APPFORMS. He briefly describes the company and the position for which he applied to them.

He then sends a thank-you email to Juanita and one to Roman.

To:	Juanita Olson
From:	James.Patel@usask.ca
Date:	January 29, 2016
Subject:	Thank you

> James states clearly and directly the purpose of the message. He states the date of the interview. He does not know when Juanita will check her mail, so he does not say "today."

Dear Ms. Olson:

Thank you for the opportunity to interview with you on Friday, January 29, for the position of Marketing Assistant. I enjoyed meeting you and Mr. Midori and hearing about the team culture and mentoring approach at APPFORMS.

> He summarizes his key skills.

> James refers to Juanita and Roman's answer to his question about the team environment. This reference links to the corporate culture at the company.

My visit to your offices confirmed my desire to work for APPFORMS. My experience with social media, my technical skills, and my interpersonal and written communication skills can contribute effectively to your team. As we discussed in the interview, I have the ability to approach problems in new ways, as evidenced by work on my blog and in my success in case competitions. I welcome the opportunity to contribute this ability to APPFORMS's "spirit of innovation."

> He refers to Juanita and Roman's answer to his question about the team environment. This reference links to the corporate culture at the company.

I look forward to hearing from you soon about the position. Please let me know if you need any additional information from me.

Regards,

James Patel, Second-Year Co-op student

Bachelor of Commerce Program
University of Saskatoon School of Business

> Juanita and Roman knew James was in Halifax for the case competition, but other than the opening comments in the interview, James did not have an opportunity to discuss the case competition or his relevant skills as part of a successful team. He mentions the competition here to remind his audience of his analytical and presentation skills.

⦿ SCOPE

As we look at the experiences of James Patel and Carrie du Plessis, we can identify the elements of SCOPE: strategy, content, outcome, presentation, and ethics.

Strategy is about selecting from available choices. James develops a *strategy* for the formal networking event. He analyzes his situation and makes decisions based on the situation, but carries out his strategy poorly, leading to a serious error. On the other hand, James performs effectively in his interview with APPFORMS. When responding to interview questions, he revealed as many relevant elements of his story as possible by talking about his experiences from his previous co-op work term or his volunteer work. Candidates who secure a position successfully communicate to the interviewers their strengths; their fit with the position, organization, and industry; and their desire for the position. Success in securing a position depends on making strategic choices of what to present and how. Each response is a strategic choice. The most effective responses answer the question directly, provide relevant examples or anecdotes, and either address an organizational need or establish a fit.

Interviewers similarly employ a strategy when they choose questions to ask of candidates. Skilled interviewers strategically select questions that will reveal the talents, goals, and appropriate fit of candidates. The goal is not to fill a position with just anyone, but to find the most suitable candidate for the position. To determine fit, they look at all aspects of a candidate's responses, starting with body language, attention to detail, presence, dress, and, of course, actual content. For the candidate, a job offer is the *outcome* of a long period of preparation and the start of a potentially exciting period of work or career.

Even when the content of responses at a networking event or during an interview is strategically enacted, *presentation* of the candidates can affect the outcome. Candidates must demonstrate familiarity with business standards. Those candidates who appear too casually dressed may show a lack of understanding of industry standards or the client-base. Body language can indicate a level of discomfort that prevents the interviewers from seeing the candidate's genuine character. The manner of presentation can reveal flaws that, were the candidate hired, might reveal themselves in unprofessional behaviour.

Throughout the interview process, interviewers and candidates must maintain a high standard of *ethics*. Interviewers must avoid illegal or unfair questions and candidates must always strive to answer truthfully. Candidates should also strive to demonstrate their integrity by providing verifiable anecdotes from their own experiences. Ethics encompasses all aspects of communication and human actions.

Chapter Summary

Successful job candidates carefully consider their audience when preparing for a networking event or interview. The job description outlines what skills are needed to complete the job. Candidates prepare by determining how their achievements, training, and experience have provided them with the skills necessary for the position. To demonstrate fit with the workplace culture, candidates familiarize themselves with the values, goals, and history that guide the organization, as presented on the company's website and social media posts. Employers seek a candidate who has the skills to do the job; is passionate about the work, the company, and the industry; and is a good match for the organization and current employees. To illustrate these qualities in a networking event or interview, candidates explore their own experiences, identify examples, and craft stories. Stories that use the STAR approach effectively explain the background, describe the candidate's actions, and, most importantly, tell the results of the actions. Following the networking opportunity or interview, the candidate makes notes, contacts references, and composes a thank-you message.

Discussion Questions

1. Mackenzie Goldman seeks a summer job. It is already April, and many positions have already been filled. To get her name out quickly, she decides to use her social media network. She has 812 friends on Facebook. Some of these people are university friends and others are friends she made in previous jobs. She posts the following:

   Hi, everybody! I am looking for a summer job. I am willing to do just about anything anywhere! Waitressing, camp counselling, tour guiding. . . I'll go anywhere from Whitehorse to Winterpeg to PEI. Let me know if you hear about anything! THANKS!!!

Is this post likely to be successful? Why or why not? What would you recommend to Mackenzie?

2. To expand his network, Tristan Hanna decides to subscribe to e-newsletters and follow local business owners on Twitter. Some of these business owners have followed him back. Tristan decides that since the relationship is now reciprocal, he is in a position to send a sales pitch asking for help in getting a co-op placement. What positive or negative issues might Tristan experience as a result of this approach?

3. Joe Mann would like to attend a networking session hosted by his university's career centre, but he is very shy. He considered attending the event with a friend, but he knows that if he takes this approach, he is likely to spend more time talking with his friend than meeting new people. What strategies might Joe use to approach people at the event given his shyness? If large events are too uncomfortable for him, what alternative networking strategies should Joe use?

4. Yuan Ding is an international student in marketing. She considers herself very proficient in English, but the idea of making "small talk" terrifies her. She is afraid that she will not understand the people she is speaking with because of their accents and that her own accent will prevent her audience from understanding her. Yuan also worries that her proficiency in formal spoken English will not be sufficient in a casual social situation where cultural references are more likely to appear in conversation. What would you recommend Yuan do to make herself feel more comfortable at networking events?

5. To prepare for interviews, candidates typically turn to company websites, social media posts, and annual reports to learn about a company's history, mission, values, and current activities. If no or limited information is publicly available, what sources could a candidate turn to instead?

6. To what extent does appropriate dress and body language affect the outcome of the interview?

7. Sometimes interviewers ask oddball or tricky questions, such as: What dish would you bring to a potluck lunch? If you were an animal, what would you be? We unplugged that clock on the wall—why did we do that? Why would an employer ask a difficult or unusual question?

8. Juanita has issues with some of the common responses to questions on weaknesses. In his response, James discusses his lack of organization in his first year of university. Is this answer likely to please or displease Juanita?

9. In his interview, James is asked to identify a problem he had and how he solved it. Review his response and explain how he used the STAR approach.

10. What do you understand by the word *fit*? What do employers mean when they look for a fit?

Exercises

1. Conduct an online investigation of networking groups in your city or region. Identify the types of professionals that attend each group, what benefits membership in the group offers, when and where the group meets, and the group's contact information. Organize this information into a table. Then write a paragraph discussing which group you might consider joining as a student and why.

2. Create a list of your contacts and their affiliations. Ask people who know you well if there are additional contacts you may have overlooked.

3. Ryerson University's Career Centre recommends that students create a business card to distribute to contacts. This card acts as a "mini-résumé." The centre suggests including your name, a description of your career interest (for example, database specialist or seeking systems analyst position), and your physical and electronic addresses. Ryerson also recommends using the back of the card to list your top skills. Explore the samples and templates available in Microsoft Word and design a business card for yourself.

4. Imagine that recruiters from your ideal employer are coming to your university next week to hold an information session and networking event. Create a 60-second elevator pitch aimed at acquiring a job at this organization.

5. Explore the website of an organization for which you really want to work. What skills do you have that coincide with the goals of the organization? What values do you have that coincide with its values? Are there words that are highlighted or repeated on the website? Create an answer to the interview question: Why should we hire you? In your answer, incorporate some of the language from the website to demonstrate your fit with the organization.

6. Search online for common interview questions. Look at your list of the 10 most common ones and determine how each question addresses strength, motivation, or fit.

7. Respond to each of the following behavioural questions using the STAR approach:
   a) Tell about a time when you had to handle multiple tasks with close deadlines.
   b) Describe a time when you had to resolve a conflict between team members.
   c) Give me an example of a time when you set a goal for yourself. What steps did you take to meet the goal and how successful were you in achieving it?
   d) Tell me about a time when you received negative feedback from a co-worker.
   e) Describe a time when you persuaded someone to accept one of your ideas.

8. Respond to each of the following situational questions:
   a) You have discovered that a co-worker has made an error in a written communication and inadvertently promised a customer delivery in two days rather than two weeks. How would you address this miscommunication?
   b) Here is a floppy disk. Sell it to me.
   c) You work in a leading department store. The store has donated coats to a local charity serving the homeless. A recipient of one of the coats brings it to the store and asks for an exchange. Exchanges without a receipt are not permitted. Your supervisor refuses to consider the exchange and tells you to refuse the request. How would you respond?
   d) Your company holds an orientation session for all new hires. The session includes important information, but you cannot understand the heavy accent of the orientation leader, and you are missing most of the information. What do you do?
   e) Your co-worker is putting handfuls of company stationery in his backpack as he prepares to leave for the day. What do you do?

Good Advice or Bad?

1. In "Business Is Personal: 5 Common Networking Mistakes" (http://janefriedman.com/2013/09/11/business-is-personal/), Christina Katz (2013) advocates avoiding networking behaviour that may appear too aggressive. She writes that "relationship building is not guerilla marketing" and recommends that "when you legitimately need a favor (whether of an old friend or a new one), ask for it in a humble, straightforward manner." Good advice or bad? Why?

2. In "Mix & Mingle Like the World's 100 Most Powerful People" (www.networkingtoday.com/article/Mix Mingle Like the World's 100 Most Powerful People-1479), Jeff Beals (2014) writes that when networking, "You should leave discussion partners with an item of value but this is nothing you can see, taste or touch. It's intangible —something like a joke, piece of trivia, or a bit of interesting insider information. These intangible leave-behinds make you and your message more memorable." Good advice or bad? Why?

3. In an interview posted on YouTube, Natalie Cooper, editor of Career Sparkle, talked to author Devora Zack, about effective networking. Zack says that networking is "building meaningful, lasting, mutually beneficial relationships one person at a time." Real networking, she says, is about connections. She provides an example of a networking event in her industry for which she researched the attendees, focused on the one she believed was the perfect fit for her, and approached that person. Her targeted audience was impressed by both her knowledge of the organization and her passion. Zack explains that although the common belief is that the goal of attending an event is to meet as many people as possible, the goal instead should be to focus on a single audience and establish one strong connection. Good advice or bad? Why?

4. In "Why Networking Is the Wrong Way to Succeed in Business: Or, If It Happened in the Government, We Would Call It 'Corruption,'" William Tapscott (2010) states, "If there is one consistent theme in popular business books, it is that networking is the best way to succeed in business, but the conventional wisdom is wrong. Networking itself is wrong." He goes on to say that networking creates "phony relationships" in which people are wrongly used to achieve a goal. He argues that with networking, jobs are earned through who you know, not what you know. Tapscott concludes that "it is still possible to succeed on one's own merits. And even if you don't succeed (due to your lack of networking), at least you can enjoy real relationships with your family and friends. That is something networkers cannot do, because once you see people as tools, it is hard to see them as anything else." Networking, according to Tapscott, should be discouraged. Good advice or bad? Why?

5. Brenan has an interview tomorrow for an on-campus, part-time position. He doesn't have time to go home and change clothes after the interview and has an afternoon full of classes. His girlfriend suggests that he wear black jeans and a nice sweater over a T-shirt to the interview, so he can take the sweater off in the

afternoon and feel comfortable both during the interview and the rest of the day. Good advice or bad? Why?

6. A common interview question is: What is your greatest weakness? Many career advisors recommend presenting a strength as a weakness. For example, Laura DeCarlo, in "What's Your Greatest Weakness?" (www.careercast.com/career-news/whats-your-greatest-weakness), recommends presenting a "weakness that is really a strength in disguise." She provides an example in which a candidate claims to be a "workaholic." Good advice or bad? Why?

7. Career Corner's "Phone Interview: Tips and Tricks" www.pongoresume.com/articles/43/phone-interviews.cfm) suggests that you stand up and walk around during a phone interview because the technique improves both projection and vocal quality. Good advice or bad? Why?

8. You have just finished an exam in microeconomics and realize too late that you answered a question worth 20% incorrectly. Your confidence is low, and you are tired after staying up most of the night to study. You have a job interview scheduled for that afternoon, but you don't believe you can do well given your exhaustion and low spirits. Your friend recommends that you cancel the interview by email and ask to reschedule. Good advice or bad? Why?

9. Juan Pablo has a **Skype** interview with his ideal employer. He is extremely nervous. His mother suggests that he wear a dress shirt, tie, and jacket with pajama bottoms. The part his audience will see will be formally dressed, but he will feel relaxed and comfortable in casual bottoms. Good advice or bad? Why?

10. Naren Smith has a phone interview with a potential employer. Phone interviews are typically screening interviews and successful candidates often get invited for face-to-face interviews. Naren decides to take the phone interview in his dorm room. His friends suggest that he could prepare well, but for the fun of it take the phone call in his underwear. Good advice or bad? Why?

Strategic Language: Word Choice

Your credibility in an interview depends on an accurate depiction of your assets. Anything that diminishes credibility affects the relationship you are trying to establish with the organization.

In "The One Word That Can Basically Ruin Your Credibility" (www.workopolis.com/content/advice/article/the-one-word-that-can-basically-ruin-your-credibility/), Peter Harris (2015) presents a scenario in which he interviewed a candidate for a position and the candidate "proceeded to undercut all of his alleged accomplishments by saying that he had 'basically' done them." When asked about his experiences, the candidate repeatedly used the word *basically*, stating he "basically" launched a website and "basically" updated the content. Harris states, "Saying that you 'basically' managed something or were 'basically responsible' for the results will always diminish (or even destroy) your credibility."

The word *just* can have a similar effect because it can be interpreted as meaning "only." If you are asked in an interview what responsibilities you had in your position as a summer camp counsellor, you should not reply, "I just managed a cabin of eight boys and helped out with the evening activities." Such a statement negates the importance of your leadership and the responsibilities involved in maintaining the safety and happiness of your clients. When asked about the hours you worked at the café, stating that you "just" worked the lunch shift diminishes the value of working at the busiest time of the day. Although you might intend to convey the meaning of *just* as "precisely," the word might be interpreted as "only."

Nor should you use inflated or exaggerated language to demonstrate your attributes. If you are asked to discuss the assets you bring to the organization, you should not begin by saying, "I am the best candidate for the position because I bring great customer service skills and experience working in two branches of the Bank of China." You do not know if you are the "best" candidate because you do not know who the other candidates are. Rather than use *best*, which makes you appear arrogant and indicates that you make unfounded claims, you could say that you are an "ideal" candidate. The word *ideal* sounds confident and is a claim you can prove.

Identify the words or phrases that may diminish credibility if used in an interview and revise the sentence to enhance the speaker's credibility:

1. At the Toronto Waterfront Marathon, I basically just recorded runner times as a volunteer.
2. I've only done volunteer work and don't have any paid work experience.
3. I am the best candidate for the position because I bring exceptional skills with a lot of computer software as well as some experience repairing hardware.
4. I can probably help the company with the skills in research that I developed as part of the risk and assurance team during my summer internship.
5. As an undergraduate co-op student, I have extensive training in financial accounting and statement analysis.
6. My greatest weakness is my inability to say "no."
7. Besides my experience selling electronics on weekends in my parents' store, I have no work experience.
8. My superior skills in communication can help your company grow.

Additional Resources

Twitter

The Hired Guns @TheHiredGuns
LinkedIn @LinkedIn
    A professional network based in Mountain
    View, CA, that offers links to blogs, videos,
    and other professional resources
The Canadian Chamber of Commerce
@CdnChamberofCom
    "The voice of Canadian business. A network of
    over 450 chambers of commerce representing
    200,000 businesses."

Blogs and Blog Posts

The Hired Guns. Retrieved from www.thehired
    guns.com/blogs/
Joshua Waldman's Career Enlightenment. Retrieved
    from http://careerenlightenment.com/
PwC. (2012, August 17). The art of networking—
    How to network successfully! Retrieved from
    http://pwc.typepad.com/pwcconnect/2012/08/
    the-art-of-networking-how-to-network-
    successfuly.html
Ruparelia, Sital. *Sital's Blog.* Retrieved from
    http://sitalruparelia.com/

Additional Internet Sources

CareersNZ. (n.d.) Tips for answering interview
    questions. Retrieved from www.careers
    .govt.nz/how-to-get-a-job/interviews/
    tips-for-answering-interview-questions/
Green, A. (2014, February 24) The most common
    job interview questions—and how to answer
    them. *Money.* Retrieved from http://money
    .usnews.com/money/blogs/outside-voices-
    careers/2014/02/24/

the-most-common-job-interview-questions-
    and-how-to-answer-them
Levinson, M. (2007, December 11). How to network:
    12 tips for shy people. *CIO.* Retrieved from
    www.cio.com/article/164300/How_to_
    Network_12_Tips_for_Shy_People?page=
    2&taxonomyId=3127
Male, B. (2010, April 29). How to network like a pro.
    Business Insider. Retrieved from www.busines
    sinsider.com/how-to-network-like-a-pro-
    2010-4?op=1
MUSC. (n.d.). Behavioral-based interview ques-
    tions. Retrieved from http://academic
    departments.musc.edu/hr/university/emp_
    corner/leaders/interviewtools/behavioral
    based.pdf
Riley Guide. (n.d.). Networking advice. Retrieved
    from www.rileyguide.com/nettips.html
Ryerson University Career Centre. (2014). Net-
    working. Retrieved from http://www.ryerson
    .ca/career/
Swanson, D. (2013, April 9). 7 tips to nail a Skype
    interview. *Forbes.* Retrieved from www.forbes.
    com/sites/learnvest/2013/04/09/7-tips-to-
    nail-a-skype-interview/

Videos

Ohio State University Fisher College of Business
    Office of Career Management. (2012, February
    14). How to answer "behavior based interview
    questions." Retrieved from www.youtube.com/
    watch?v=qKBubKO-798
Virginia Western Community College. (2009,
    September 25). Mock job interview questions
    and tips for a successful interview. Retrieved
    from https://youtu.be/BkL98JHAO_w

CHAPTER THREE

Routine and Informational Messages

Hero Images/Getty Images

Learning Objectives

A. **Determine** the purpose of a message.
B. **Assess** the audience's needs.
C. **Select** the best channel for the information.
D. **Communicate** information clearly and precisely.
E. **Craft** effective email communications.
F. **Develop** a strategic approach for writing sentences and paragraphs.
G. **Create** a short informational memo report.
H. **Create** a progress report.

The Story So Far

In Chapter 2, we looked at how job candidates can successfully network and prepare for interviews. We followed the cases of James Patel and Carrie du Plessis as they used two different approaches to networking in attending an organized networking event and using personal and professional networks. We also looked at how interviewers choose and select questions depending on the positions they have to hire for, and we followed how James Patel prepared for and participated in a job interview. Both candidates used the STAR (Situation, Task, Action and Results) approach to explain how their individual experiences allow them to demonstrate fit with the job that the organization is seeking to fill.

In Chapter 3, now that three of our student candidates have secured positions at APPFORMS, we look at some of their day-to-day activities, where they have to use their skills and knowledge to complete assigned tasks. We follow Sean McNeill, Lara Leveaux, and Maya Chen as they compose and send workplace emails, memos, and reports.

Introduction

Most of the messages created at work convey or request information. These messages might confirm a meeting date, ask for details about a project, or provide instructions.

In constructing these messages, the sender must

1. determine the purpose of the message
2. consider the audience that will receive the message and any factors that might affect the communication
3. select the most appropriate channel for the communication.

First, the sender determines what information must be communicated and why. If, for example, the sender needs to obtain information regarding the progress of the construction of a new app, she needs to clarify exactly what information she needs. Perhaps she needs the names of people involved in the development, perhaps she needs to know if the app is ready to move from the idea stage to the construction stage, or perhaps she needs a **timeline** to allow her to coordinate human resources. She must also determine what she wants the recipient to do in response to the request. Should the recipient arrange a meeting to discuss the app? Email a progress report? Respond immediately? Clarifying exactly what the sender wants and what she wants her recipient to do focuses the message, facilitates the flow of work, and minimizes time spent on sending and resending emails. Research has shown (Mark, 2006) that interruptions in the workplace are quite common and come from both internal sources (people interrupting themselves and switching to other tasks) and external sources (phone calls, emails, or co-workers). Senders of messages must be mindful that their email or memo will most likely create an interruption for the receiver. Clarity will minimize the time the receiver has to spend reading, interpreting, and responding to the message in the manner that the sender requires.

The sender also assesses the audience and considers any element that might interfere with the delivery of content. If, for example, a message is delivered to a new co-worker requesting him to report on sales, the message might need to contain particularly specific instructions on how to proceed. The sender might need to clarify particular elements that are typically addressed in this type of report and the standard form of delivery. The sender might need to adjust sentence lengths and word choices for an audience unfamiliar with the process. Since the message is delivered to a new employee, the message cannot contain acronyms or jargon with which this audience is unfamiliar. In considering audience, senders consider the degree of formality expected by the audience, the background knowledge of the audience, and the cultural expectations of the audience.

Given the purpose and the audience, the sender then selects the best channel. Would the message best be delivered in person because of its sensitivity, its complexity, or the need to address questions quickly? Is a text message sufficient given an audience familiar with the type of request? Or is an email more appropriate? If an email, what form should it take? What should the subject line of the email be to inform the receiver of the need to respond immediately or at leisure? And what channel should the audience use to respond? Is a quick conversation to report progress sufficient or is a more formal report necessary?

This chapter addresses purpose, audience, and channel in delivering effective workplace communications. Because these messages facilitate the quick and easy exchange of information, they are generally direct, stating clearly and precisely the purpose of the message. In each of the following scenarios, the sender makes a series of decisions about what to include, why, and how.

Emails

The Case of Sean McNeill: Informational Email

On his first day on the job, Sean is asked by his supervising coach, Manderson Renault, to compose a message to the marketing team introducing himself. Manderson asks Sean to show him the message before sending it. Sean considers this task to be a fairly simple one and composes the following message:

To:	Marketing@Appforms.ca
From:	Sean.McNeill@myuni.ca
Date:	January 11, 2016
Subject:	I'm here!

Hello! Sean here. I'm the new co-op student on the second floor, Marketing. I just started so I have no idea what I will be doing here, but as soon as you find out, let me know! Looking forward to the term!

Sean's supervisor reads the draft email and asks him to reconsider his approach. First, he points out, Sean should consider the purpose of the message. He was asked to introduce himself. How would he like the marketing team to see him? The email message is his first impression and should consider the professional relationship Sean would like to establish with the team. What message does the email convey? And what does Sean want the audience to do or to feel as a result of the message?

Sean considers his supervising coach's comments and thinks about what he wants the message to do. The email as is does not project a professional image. Sean used his university email address rather than his new work address, which presents him as a student rather than a young professional. The use of exclamation points and the casual approach further undermine his professional appearance. The humour intended in stating that he doesn't know what he is doing affects his credibility. The lack of an appropriate closing and the lack of a signature block also show a lack of professionalism. Manderson recommends that Sean use either the serif font Georgia in 11 point or the sans serif Verdana in 10 or 12 point. The internal standard for email at APPFORMS is Verdana because of its onscreen readability.

Manderson also points out that Sean has not considered his audience. The form of the message Sean has written is more appropriate for a text message to a friend than an email to co-workers. The message will be received by everyone on the marketing team, from recent hires to senior management. APPFORMS's relaxed and casual workplace environment does not mean an informal, chatty response is appropriate. Manderson asks Sean what his audience would like to know about him—perhaps his full name and where he is from—and to use the message as a way to establish a working relationship.

Sean reconsiders the purpose of his message. He wants to use it to establish a professional relationship with his co-workers. Although he would like to appear friendly and competent, he wants to be regarded as a professional, not as a student. He would also like to build his professional network. He decides that it is best to err on the side of formality in his message, rather than informality.

To:	Marketing@Appforms.ca
From:	Sean.McNeill@Appforms.ca
Date:	January 11, 2016
Subject:	Greetings from co-op student Sean McNeill

To the Marketing Team:

Hi, my name is Sean McNeill, and I will be working with you for the next three months as a co-op student from Nova Scotia University.

APPFORMS' innovative spirit and team atmosphere drew me to the company. My supervising coach, Manderson Renault, has already shared with me some of the marketing team's current projects, and I am excited to contribute whatever I can to them.

I look forward to meeting all of you over the next few days. If you need to get in touch with me, I can be found at my desk near 2nd floor reception or through the contact information in the signature block below.

Best regards,

Sean

Sean McNeill, Marketing Assistant
APPFORMS Canada ■ 1600 White Horse Way, Halifax, NS A1B 2C3
phone: (902) 555 1424   email: Sean.McNeill@Appforms.ca

Sean's revised message clearly identifies his purpose for sending the message. He announces his purpose in the subject line and states what he is doing with the company in the first paragraph. He indicates that he will meet his co-workers soon and offers his contact information. He also communicates his interest in APPFORMS and the position.

His revised message also considers his audience. Because his audience consists of busy professionals, he uses a direct yet friendly approach. He imagines that his audience might wonder how to contact him, so he anticipates this need by including where he can be found and how he can be reached. The format of the message also addresses his audience's needs. He includes a clear subject line so that the audience knows what the message is about. He uses white space to make the message more readable in an online email format. He includes a signature block in a standard form familiar to his audience.

Manderson then assigns Sean his first task. He asks him to look at the various apps currently available in Halifax for identifying and tracking bus routes. He would like Sean to write a report for him on the basic content, cost, and customer feedback of these existing apps. Some information has already been compiled by another member of the marketing team, Misha Hancock. Manderson asks Sean to request the information from Misha and to begin work as soon as possible since Manderson will need the information at next week's strategy meeting. Misha, he says, is away at a conference in Toronto for the rest of the week, but she took her computer with her.

To:	Misha.Hancock@Appforms.ca
From:	Sean.McNeill@Appforms.ca
Date:	January 11, 2016
Subject:	Request for transit app information

The subject line explains the purpose of the message.

Hello Misha,

I am the new co-op Marketing Assistant at APPFORMS. Manderson Renault has asked me to gather information for a report to be presented next week on currently available apps that identify and track metro buses.

Sean explains the reason for the request

Manderson has indicated that you have already compiled a list of available apps and some information. I am writing a report on the content, costs, and customer feedback on transit apps and would find this information useful.

He clearly asks for what he needs.

Can you send me the information you have gathered? If you could send the information through email by tomorrow, I can begin work in preparation for next week's strategy meeting.

Sean clearly states the method of delivery and the urgent need for information without being rude or abrupt.
By stating that he needs the information for next week's strategy meeting, Sean explains the urgency without going into too much detail.

Thank you.

Best regards,

Sean

He uses three short paragraphs to enhance readability. He understands that because Misha is away at a conference, she may only have time for a quick read of the email. The placement of the request after the white space at the start of the paragraph highlights the question.

Sean McNeill, Marketing Assistant
APPFORMS Canada ■ 1600 White Horse Way, Halifax, NS A1B 2C3
phone: (902) 555 1424   email: Sean.McNeill@Appforms.ca

Sean's message clearly and directly **states the purpose** of the message. He refers to Manderson and the strategy meeting to **explain the background** of his request and indicate the importance and timeliness of the information. He makes a **specific request** for information. He also indicates that the information can be delivered by email and ends by thanking Misha.

Sean realizes that she may be quite busy at the conference and might not have much time for reading emails. He uses white space to effectively divide the message into sections and to highlight the question that starts the third paragraph. He hopes that this use of white space will make the message more readable. He also omits any irrelevant statements out of respect for Misha's time and to maintain professional formality.

Misha responds.

To:	Sean.McNeill@Appforms.ca
From:	Misha.Hancock@Appforms.ca
Date:	January 11, 2016
Subject:	RE: Request for transit app information

Hi Sean,

Welcome to APPFORMS!

Please see the attached document. Some information that may be of use to you has already been gathered. The following information is included in the attached document:

- copies of descriptions of 3 apps, HaliGO (Apple), MyMetro (Google Play), and Where's My Ride (Google Play)

- customer prices for Halifax, Toronto, and Ottawa transit apps

- available customer feedback for Tom's Toronto Google Play Android app

- list of customization features for HaliGO and MyMetro

I look forward to meeting you next week.

Sincerely,

Misha

Misha Hancock, Digital Strategist
APPFORMS Canada ■ 1600 White Horse Way, Halifax, NS A1B 2C3
phone: (902) 555 2828   email: Misha.Hancock@Appforms.ca

Like Sean, Misha selects an appropriate font and point size. She chooses 10-point Verdana, which is the standard font and point size for internal APPFORMS online communications. She also presents the summary of information included in the attachment in a bulleted list to highlight the information, eliminate extra words, and enhance readability.

The Case of Lara Leveaux: Emailed Information Report

Lara has been working in accounting at APPFORMS for a few weeks. Her supervisor, Yue Goldberg, has requested that she calculate and report on the sales of the company's Maple Green app. This app helps users identify retail stores, restaurants, and growers that sell organic products.

Yue asks Lara to look at Maple Green's monthly earnings for the past year. She would like Lara to determine if the Best New App Award in March and the addition of interactive features in June coincided with increased sales. Lara is to report her findings to Yue and to the app development team.

Lara begins by gathering the monthly sales of the app, a $0.99 Android application. She finds the following sales totals for each month in 2015:

January	$1000	April	$1200	July	$1700	October	$2100
February	$500	May	$900	August	$2000	November	$2050
March	$250	June	$1300	September	$2250	December	$1995

To help her visualize the trends and determine what this information means, Lara creates a simple line graph to display the data:

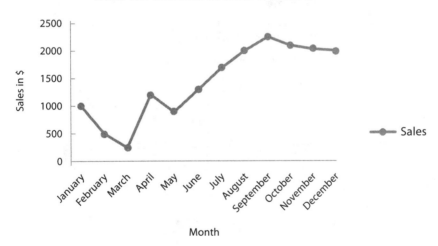

MAPLE GREEN SALES IN 2015

Being knowledgeable in creating charts from data, Lara ensures that the line graph encompasses as much information as possible to inform the reader about all aspects of the data. She ensures that the axes (*x* and *y*) are labelled appropriately. Since there are only 12 data points, she feels that the chart would be more useful if she included data labels indicating the sales figure for each month. She also has a clearly labelled chart title, but is aware that when she submits her report she will need to add a figure number and caption.

Lara analyzes the data to determine what the data mean. Sales were decreasing after the start of the year and then increased dramatically after the app won the Best New

App Award. Sales slumped again, but shot up with the introduction of new interactive features. Since then, sales have dipped slightly but remain high.

She plans her email to Yue and her team. She knows that the sales data is one of many pieces of information that they will use in their decision-making. She decides that a direct approach in presenting the information is best for an audience that needs to access the information quickly and easily. Lara chooses not to begin with social comments or questions, but to move directly to the information requested.

To:	Yue.Goldberg@Appforms.ca; Olya.Ortega@Appforms.ca; Angus.Nonu@Appforms.ca; Sergio.Chowdury@Appforms.ca
From:	Lara.Leveaux@Appforms.ca
Date:	January 11, 2016
Subject:	2015 Maple Green Sales Trends

Dear Yue, Olya, Angus, and Sergio:

Yue has asked me to look at the 2015 sales trends for the Maple Green app.

Sales rose with the Best New App Award but increased more dramatically and then stabilized with the introduction of new interactive features. The sales figures indicate that

- Maple Green sales jumped with the Best New App Award and then fell to previous levels;

- after the introduction of new interactive features, sales increased significantly and remained at about $2000 throughout 2015; and

- sales dipped by 10% in the last quarter.

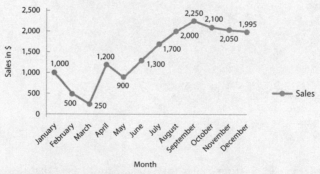

MAPLE GREEN SALES IN 2015

Please let me know if you have any questions or require any further information.

Regards,

Lara

Lara Leveaux, Accounting Assistant
APPFORMS Canada ■ 1600 White Horse Way, Halifax, NS A1B 2C3
phone: (902) 555 4242   email: Lara.Leveaux@Appforms.ca

Lara's email begins with a response to Yue's request for information: The award and interactive features resulted in increased sales. This decision to place the conclusion first allows her readers to easily access the information they need. She follows the conclusion with evidence. Lara includes a line graph to display the evidence for this conclusion, and places her evidence in a bullet list and a chart. These techniques facilitate comprehension; the list presents the information in brief, readable units, while the graph provides a visual representation of the data.

Memos

The Case of Sean McNeill: Memo Informational Report

Sean has gathered information from Misha and investigated the top three transit apps in Halifax. Manderson has asked Sean to bring copies of the report for distribution at the strategy meeting. He reminds Sean that the report should address content, cost, and customer feedback. Manderson shows him where to access APPFORMS's standard memo form and reminds him that the Georgia font is the preferred font for internal print communications within the company.

Sean does not know what exactly falls under the heading of content, and he doesn't want to appear incompetent. He is also unsure of what his audience will do with the information, so he doesn't know whether he should organize the report by app or by category (content, cost, and feedback). He fears that he will appear lacking in knowledge or initiative, but he decides that asking what is included under content and how his audience can best use the information is in his best interest and the interest of the marketing team.

Manderson is pleased that Sean has asked for clarification. He tells Sean that the company is seeking a niche in the marketplace and that typically the team looks at existing, related apps to determine their strengths and weaknesses and to identify opportunities and threats that APPFORMS would face if they launched a new application. They are particularly interested in the interactive features of each app. Customer feedback, though often misleading, can reveal issues of usability and customer satisfaction.

Sean immediately recognizes that Manderson wants him to do a SWOT analysis, which he learned how to do in his Introduction to Marketing course. With a better idea of what his audience needs, he drafts his report.

APPFORMSCanada

MEMORANDUM

TO: Marketing Team
FROM: Sean McNeill
DATE: January 18, 2016
SUBJECT: Comparison of metro bus apps

This memo report provides a comparison of the interactive features, customer feedback on usability, and cost of the top three metro transit apps in Halifax: HaliGO (Apple), MyMetro (Google Play), and Where's My Ride (Google Play). The research indicates that HaliGO has the most interactive features and the highest customer ratings, but is the only fee-charging app of the top three.

INTERACTIVE FEATURES

All three metro transit apps, HaliGO, MyMetro, and Where's My Ride, include interactive maps to enable users to find bus routes and locate stops. All three apps also identify the user's current position through a GPS. All three apps identify major landmarks along routes.

HaliGO offers the most interactive features. The following lists identify unique interactive features of each app for maps, personalization, and sharing:

Interactive Map Features

HaliGo
- information bubbles for landmarks along routes
- walking directions to stops
- in-transit recalculation of trips affected by road construction, accidents, or events

MyMetro
- special service buses identified

Personalization

HaliGO
- arrival alerts for users' final destinations
- ability to save routes for trips and destinations
- ability to add other transit services including taxi, tour bus, and rental bike locations
- real-time departure/arrival information

Marginal annotations:

In keeping with memo style, Sean omits both a greeting and complimentary close. Because the document will be distributed within APPFORMS, no return or recipient address is included.

Sean provides a summary of his conclusions at the start of the memo. The information that follows provides evidence for these conclusions.

Manderson has indicated that the team is especially interested in the interactive features, so these features are addressed first. Sean uses headings for readability.

Sean uses bullets in this section to enhance readability.

The first paragraph is brief, yet includes all the necessary information. He tells what the report is about and indicates how the report is organized. The list of elements to be compared reflects the order in which they are discussed in the report.

MyMetro
- ☐ arrival alerts for users' final destinations
- ☐ option to save trips to calendar from app

Where's My Ride
- ☐ text-to-speech functionality
- ☐ round-trip fee calculation

Share features

HaliGO
- ☐ ability to share routes through email from app

CUSTOMER FEEDBACK

The three apps are relatively new and limited customer feedback is currently available.

HaliGO's rating is 5/5. Of the seven comments, four say the app is "great." One reviewer especially appreciates the arrival alert function. Negative comments include site crashing and inaccessibility on certain routes where 3G connection is weak.

MyMetro has a 3/5 rating with four reviewer comments, all negative. The reviewers say the app is hard to use. In areas where multiple buses travel the same route, buses are not distinguished on the app's map. One reviewer complained that the app is poorly designed, in particular noting the difficulty in reading white text on a black background on the home screen.

Where's My Ride has no customer comments but an average rating of 4/5 stars with three reviewers.

COST

HaliGO: $0.99, with additional $0.99 charge for taxi location feature

MyMetro: free

Where's My Ride: free

Please let me know if you require any additional information.

The Case of Maya Chen: Memo Progress Report

In addition to her work as a financial analyst, Maya participates in APPFORMS's corporate social responsibility (CSR) initiatives. She leads a program called Link that introduces senior high school girls to careers in business and computer science. Girls are partnered with APPFORMS's employees in these fields for one month. During this time, the girls meet their mentors, "shadow" them at work, and participate in seminars. The month concludes with a lunch and presentation of certificates.

It is February, and Maya has already started preparing for the event, which takes place in April. A meeting of area managers is scheduled for next week, and Maya has been asked to submit a **progress report** to the group. She has already outlined the calendar of events, sent information flyers to local high schools and a regional homeschoolers' association, and selected, with a committee, a list of potential candidates. She has yet to match the girls with employees or to select the seminar topics and presenters.

The audience for Maya's progress report are managers who are familiar with the program. Link attracts the best and brightest students in the area and has a good reputation in the community and among APPFORMS's employees. Although the program is familiar to the managers, they are less familiar with the selection criteria, the logistical concerns, and the budget. Although she is writing an internal document, because the progress report is aimed at managers, Maya will need to maintain a level of formality appropriate for communication to people in high-level positions.

Maya considers the arrangement of her report. Because the program is one of many that involve students, she decides to begin with a description of the program's purpose and a brief overview. In the body of the report, she will address work that has been completed and work that has yet to be done. The organization of the report follows its function; since the report reviews work in the past and addresses work for the future, a chronological pattern of organization is most logical. Maya also knows that the area managers will expect her to address any changes in expenses to date.

APPFORMSCanada

MEMORANDUM

TO: Pierce Sanchez; Ziva Yaron; Vic Tremblett; Larissa Zhao; Chester Sanipass
FROM: Maya Chen
DATE: February 25, 2016
SUBJECT: Progress Report: 2016 Link Program for High School Girls

This report summarizes the work completed to date on the Link program for high school girls, identifies work still to be completed, and addresses potential obstacles.

BACKGROUND

The APPFORMS' Link program pairs employees with high school girls interested in careers in business or computer science. Since the program started in 2012, 62 girls and 37 employees have participated. During the month-long program, students meet with mentors and follow them through work activities. The month concludes with a lunch for participants. At the lunch, each student participant receives a certificate of participation and a $500 university scholarship.

WORK COMPLETED

Since January 4, the following activities have been completed:

- ☐ Creation of a schedule of Link events for the month of April
- ☐ Creation and distribution of promotional materials to all high schools in the Halifax area as well as the Homeschoolers' Association
- ☐ Confirmation of the participation of Dr. James Baker, Dalhousie University, as one of the three seminar speakers
- ☐ Committee selection of 24 suitable candidates for the program
- ☐ Commitment of seven employees to the program after all employees were sent initial request by email on February 24

NEXT STEPS

1. Select 10 of the 24 candidates.
2. Match students with employee volunteers.
3. Identify topics and speakers for the remaining two seminars.
4. Arrange location and caterers for the closing lunch event.

CURRENT AND ANTICIPATED PROBLEMS

1. Of the 24 suitable candidates for participation, 10 are interested in human resources and 8 are interested in accounting; however, none of the employee volunteers are from human resources, and only two volunteers are from accounting. To address this problem, I will recruit more employees specifically from the HR and accounting areas. Selection of the final 10 student participants will be determined by available employees. We can only place 1 student with each employee.

2. The cost for printing the brochures for school distribution increased significantly from last year. To address this issue, we can lower costs by either cutting the number of participants to nine or changing the venue and meal selection for the closing lunch event, or we can reallocate funds.

3. One of the managing partners typically attends the closing lunch event and presents the certificates and scholarships; however, all three managing partners are unable, due to prior commitments, to attend the event to be held on May 2 this year. To address this problem, I will seek recommendations for an appropriate substitute.

Preparation for this year's Link program is well underway and will be completed by the start of the program on April 1.

⊙ SCOPE

As we look at the experiences of Sean, Lara, and Maya, we can identify the elements of SCOPE: strategy, content, outcome, presentation, and ethics.

Strategy provides the basis for every choice one makes in the workplace. When Sean writes his introductory email, Manderson guides him through the process, highlighting to Sean the need to keep the audience in mind when crafting workplace messages. Manderson tells Sean to think carefully about the purpose of his message as well as its style and form. Each element conveys to the reader a certain impression of Sean, including what he expects the receivers to do after reading the message.

If style and form do not distract the reader, *content* can take centre stage. Sean, Misha, Lara, and Maya use bulleted and numbered lists to make structure explicit and the content stand out. Lara uses visuals to support the conclusion of her analysis of the sales of a particular app. All of them use clear and concise sentences with direct statements supported by evidence (attachments and graphs), and also make direct requests of their audiences. Much thought is required when creating workplace messages because of the scarcity of time that receivers often have.

The *outcome* of well-thought-out workplace messages is to reduce multiple exchanges on the same topic. Sean's clear sentences allowed Misha to respond quickly, despite her travel and time constraints, and presented Sean in good light to Misha—positive outcomes on both accounts. Lara used concise sentences, presented her information in a bulleted list, and used the rhetorical tools of compare and contrast to support her argument. It is likely that her message will also have a positive and desired outcome. Maya presented a structured progress report by using separate headings to identify progress, challenges faced, and a request for support. This structure will orient her audience to the state and status of the Link program and allow decision-makers to step in and provide assistance where needed.

Presentation includes the form and format of the message as well as the channel or vehicle used for the message, email, or memo. Most workplace messages are intended to be either informational or persuasive in nature, but even informational messages need to be persuasive to get the audience to read the message. For example, Sean used an effective subject line to encourage Misha to read his message. He needed to present his request to Misha (who has time constraints) in a manner that would encourage her to respond to his request. Sean, Lara, and Maya all had to present their findings or progress reports so that managers can make business decisions and assist where needed.

If strategy is the basis of all the choices made in the workplace, then *ethics* is the foundation of these choices. It is easy to become lazy when so many details need attention in the modern workplace. The easiest way would be to present someone else's reports or analysis as one's own. However, this approach is not sustainable and is bad for an individual's credibility. Sean could easily have found some online report on the transit apps and presented it to the marketing team as his own. Instead, he did his work honestly and benefited from the process. Similarly, Lara found the raw sales data of the Maple Green app but went further to provide a visual representation of the data. Her original work supported the decision-making process. Maya clearly outlines the status of the project and the challenges faced and makes direct requests for assistance.

Clear and concise writing includes using the active voice. While using the passive voice is not incorrect, it tends to make sentences longer and can confuse the reader. Being ethical communicators requires you to be as forthright as possible, keeping the needs, sensitivities, and nature of the target audience in mind. Finally, Sean and Lara collected information for their reports from external primary sources. They need to keep track of these sources and ensure that the information is accurate. This will help Sean and Lara build good working relationships with their co-workers.

Chapter Summary

Effective and ethical workplace communication requires much thought and deliberation. While we may tend to send or respond quickly (sometimes impulsively) to workplace emails and messages, we should always pause before doing so. We should think about the need to send the message in the first place, the content and form of the message, and the channel or vehicle for conveying the message. Except for instant messaging or phone conversations where employees can pose quick queries to one another or check on the availability of co-workers, most workplace communication is asynchronous, meaning it does not and need not occur at the same time. Despite time constraints that everyone faces in the workplace with multiple tasks that all need attention, it is always good strategy to think through each message before sending it to any audience. While it takes time to construct progress reports and analytical reports, thought must be given to the length of these communication channels or vehicles. Writing concisely, making clear requests, performing good quality analysis, presenting evidence-based arguments (which we will discuss in detail in Chapter 4), and making structure explicit by the use of indentation, bulleted lists, and informative headings all help to shorten messages, make them more effective, and achieve the desired outcomes.

Discussion Questions

1. Discuss the various components that make up an email or memo used to convey information to senior management. Make reference to sorting information into categories, choosing the order of the information, style, and format.

2. As the co-op intern in an app development company doing work-related research, you discover an app that monitors what people write in private text messages. The purpose of the monitoring is to alert authorities in case of malicious or law-breaking activities. Would you bring this information to your team to create a similar competing app or would you inform your team manager so that the company can alert the public about possible ethical issues with such an app? What are the implications and ethical issues of your actions?

3. If you found that the app from question 2 was created by the company you are working for, what would be your action be? If you decide to write to senior management informing them that the app is unethical, what channel would you choose? Discuss the key components you would use to convey your message.

4. You need to collect some urgent information from a co-worker. Is it a good idea to mark "URGENT" in the subject line and mention the urgency a few times in the body of the email?

5. How can you make structure explicit in a business message? What is the benefit of doing this? Does form make content more readable or can great content alone make a business message effective?

6. What is the purpose of citing sources when you collect information for analysis and reporting?

Exercises

1. Universities, like all large organizations, have standards that govern communications. Dalhousie University's guidelines, for example, describe the appropriate colours and language usage for banners, webpages, stationary, and other documents. Look at the editorial style

guide for your university or college or look at Dalhousie's guide, located at www.dal.ca/web team/web_style_guide/editorial_style_guide .html, then answer the following questions.

a) What is the purpose of editorial style guides and other communication standards? What image do these standards convey?

b) Standards change over time. Note, for example, Dalhousie's section on Honorifics and Professional Titles. The guide suggests using Mr. or Ms. for persons without a degree or special title. Identify other places where standards might change as the culture and language preferences change.

2. You have just been hired at your ideal company. Write a memo of introduction to your new co-workers.

3. In your role as marketing assistant, you have been asked both to participate in a recruitment event at your university and to promote the event through your personal network. The company would like to attract the very best students to the organization. You have three main audiences. Your first audience is international students; your company seeks to recruit more of these students. Your second audience is the Career Services Centre; you would like it to direct high-quality students to apply to the company. Your third audience includes your friends and fellow Commerce Society members, who may find a position with your company challenging and fulfilling. How will you promote the event in an email to each of these groups? How you will adapt the message for each group? How will the content vary for each group?

4. As part of your volunteer work at a local school, you have received the following items for an auction at the annual school fundraiser:

spa treatment
cottage rental
hockey tickets
food basket
set of bone china for eight
hand-carved wooden bench
canoe trip
ski lessons
children's dance classes
birthday party clown
apple pie
tutoring
sleepover at the school
oil change
unlimited coffee refills
gourmet dinner for six
handcrafted quilt
a year of lawn service
outdoor grill
guided tour of Montreal architecture
a dozen Tim Hortons donuts
two weeks of doggie daycare
cricket bat
student artwork
babysitting
pony rides

Organize these items into categories for the auction booklet.

5. Using the context provided in discussion questions 2 and 3, write an email or memo to senior management about the issues raised in those questions.

Good Advice or Bad?

1. In his blog post "How to Email a Professor" (http://mleddy.blogspot.ca/2005/01/how-to-e-mail-professor.html?m=1), Michael Leddy offers several recommendations:

a) Use your university email address.

b) Include the purpose for writing and the course number in the subject line.

c) Select an appropriate greeting like "Hi" or "Hello," but not "Dear" since an email message is not a letter.

d) Make requests politely.

e) Proofread the email.

f) Close with your full name, course, and class time.

Good advice or bad? Why?

2. In university, Greg typically uses the greeting "Dear Professor" followed by the last name in his emails, even though the professors generally respond with their first names. When he began his summer internship at a bank in Edmonton, he was introduced to all his co-workers, even his supervisors, by their first names. He does not know how to address his first work email to his immediate supervisor, Mr. Jia Liang. His friend Peng Peng suggests he begin the email with "Dear Jia Liang." Good advice or bad? Why?

3. Randy has to send an email to 75 members of the school's Management Society. He has recently read a document from I Will Follow Services (www.iwillfollow.com/email.htm) that states, "As you can imagine, use of the 'bcc' is somewhat unethical and therefore its use is discouraged." Good advice or bad? Why?

4. In "The New Rules of Business Etiquette" (www.forbes.com/sites/susanadams/2013/10/04/the-new-rules-of-business-etiquette-3/), Susan Adams cites Vicky Oliver as saying, "It's bad boss etiquette to harass your employees with notes after hours or on the weekend. If you receive one from the boss on a Saturday, she says, you can safely ignore it for 24 hours. 'You are being more than polite by doing that,' she says. 'You're also carving out a little boundary for yourself.'" Good advice or bad? Why?

Strategic Language: Sentence Structure

Using a variety of sentence structure adds interest to your writing. If every sentence uses the same structural pattern and is nearly the same length, the writing becomes hypnotic or soporific. Your audiences will be entranced by the rhythm or put to sleep by the repetition. The more structural patterns you have at your command, the more strategic you can be in your communications. To develop more controlled and strategic approaches to your messages, use a variety of sentence types. A variety of types will enable you to work with the placement of ideas and convey points in ways that enhance your message.

Sentences follow a few basic patterns:

- Pattern 1 (simple)—The first pattern is the simplest. It consists of a single complete thought. If I were to write *Arty*, you might ask, "Arty what?" The complete thought might be *Arty chokes*. This sentence tells what Arty did. The simple sentence follows a subject/verb pattern; *Arty* is the subject and *chokes* is the verb. Because the sentence is complete by itself, it is an independent clause.

- Pattern 2 (compound)—The second pattern combines two complete thoughts. It consists of two independent clauses combined with a conjunction—a connecting word like *and*, *or*, or *but*—or with a semicolon. An example is *Arty chokes, and Elly faints*. The compound sentence follows the subject/verb/conjunction/subject/verb pattern.

- Pattern 3 (complex)—The third pattern combines a dependent clause with an independent clause. A dependent clause makes no sense on its own. It has a subject and a verb, but it also has a subordinating conjunction such as *although, while, because,* or *since.* The dependent clause *While I read BuzzFeed* is an incomplete thought. *While I read BuzzFeed, the professor continued to lecture* is a complete thought. This sentence type follows the subordinating conjunction/subject/verb, subject/verb pattern.

- Pattern 4 (compound-complex)—The fourth pattern combines the second and third patterns. Its pattern is subordinating conjunction/subject/verb, subject/verb/ coordinating conjunction/subject/verb. *While I read BuzzFeed, the professor continued to lecture, and I missed the assignment directions* is an example.

In addition to the independent and dependent clauses used in these four patterns, sentences can have a variety of noun, adjective, and adverb phrases.

Write a new sentence that imitates the structural pattern of each of the following sentences. Example: Because customers want them, we will start selling peanuts. Answer: *Since I started work, I have earned $250.*

1. The cellphone died.
      subject/ verb

2. Business hours are 9 to 5.
      subject/   verb

3. The offensive text was deleted from the message board.
        subject/   verb

4. We should expand into overseas markets; however, we should first expand locally.
   subject/   verb/   coordinating conjunction/ subject/   verb

5. The sales representative offered several options, but none of the phones suited his needs.
        subject/   verb/   coordinating conjunction/subject/   verb

6. She gathered the information, and her co-worker wrote the report.
   Subject/ verb/ coordinating conjunction/ subject/   verb

7. The customer angrily approached the service counter and demanded a refund.
      subject/   verb/   verb

8. Although the website was informative, it was difficult to navigate.
   subordinating conjunction/subject/verb/   subject/verb

9. When the business reopened, the stock was larger, and the customers were pleased.
   subordinating conjunction/subject/verb/subject/verb/   coordinating conjunction/subject/verb

10. As a result of road construction, the business lost customers during the summer
    subordinating conjunction/   subject/ verb

    months, but sales recovered in the fall.
         subject/ verb

The way you arrange words in sentences can dramatically affect how your message is received by your audience. If you receive a message from your university stating, "While we are able to offer you a partial scholarship of $2000, we are unable to offer you a full scholarship," you might feel disappointed. The emphasis of the sentence is on what you did not get, rather than on what you did get. The placement of what you did not receive in the main or dependent clause emphasizes the bad news. If the sentence is worded as

"While we are unable to offer you a full scholarship, we are able to offer you a partial scholarship of $2000," you might still be disappointed, but the emphasis on what you will receive rather than what you will not receive could lessen the effect of the negative information and highlight your achievement.

Each sentence structure has a different effect on the meaning. A simple subject/verb pattern, Pattern 1, is especially useful for

a) delivering instructions
b) delivering complex information
c) adding impact to your assertion

Writing clear instructions requires simple steps with one action per step in logical order. For example,

1. Open your Word document.
2. Click on Insert at the top of the page.
3. Click on Chart.
4. Select the most appropriate type of chart for your information.

Delivering complex information also requires shorter sentences to ensure your audience follows the ideas. To explain the financial reasons for withdrawing support for a new convention centre would require simple sentences for an audience that does not understand economic terms.

If a series of longer complex sentences is followed by a short sentence, the simple sentence structure adds to the impact of the language. For example:

> Businesses should use social media to target young consumers. Although managing social media requires employee time and is therefore not "free," the cost of advertising through social media is less than advertising through traditional media such as newspapers and television. In addition, the majority of young people in urban areas now use smartphones, and young people carry these devices with them constantly throughout the day. Social media advertising is now essential.

This paragraph begins with a simple sentence to clearly and precisely state the point. Next are complex and compound sentences that explain and expand on the idea. The paragraph ends with a short, simple sentence. The simple structure and the shortness add emphasis, especially to the final word *essential*.

Compound sentences show the relationship between ideas in a sentence. They consist of two independent clauses of equal emphasis. They can also add detail to the sentence. The sentence "We market local products so consumers always have fresh fish" contains two clauses joined by *so*. The sentence shows the relationship between local goods and consumer benefits. The sentence "Banks now stay open for longer hours, but employees have resisted this change" shows the relationship between longer hours and employee attitude.

Complex sentences have a dependent and an independent clause. If the dependent clause is first, the independent clause or main idea receives the strongest emphasis. For this reason, complex sentences are useful in showing the relationship between ideas but adding more force to the main idea. In the sentence, "Although sales dropped sharply after the hurricane, sales in March exceeded expectations," the emphasis is on the exceeded expectations. In the sentence, "Although we cannot offer you a greater discount on the bike, we can offer you a free helmet valued at $79," the emphasis is on the free helmet.

If the independent clause comes before the dependent clause, its strength is lessened because the strongest part of the sentence is at the end. The pause created by the period adds emphasis to the last words. In the sentence, "Parking is limited because of road construction," the emphasis falls on the road construction.

Strategic use of sentence structure can add flow, emphasis, and power to your writing. The arrangement of words, in addition to the choice of words, affects how the reader receives the information.

Additional Resources

Twitter

Ivey Business School @iveybusiness
"Our mission is to develop business leaders who think globally, act strategically, and contribute to the societies within which they operate."

Additional Internet Source

Changing Minds (2014). Retrieved from http://changingminds.org/

CHAPTER FOUR

Analysis and Argumentation

© iStock/Yuri_Arcurs

Learning Objectives

A. **Develop** skills in critical listening, critical reading, and critical thinking.
B. **Understand** the concepts of analysis and synthesis.
C. **Recognize** that each situation requires a different set of analytical tools.
D. **Use** analytical tools to assess and solve business problems.
E. **Incorporate** techniques of argumentation effectively.
F. **Present** the findings of analysis in an effective manner.

The Story So Far

In Chapter 3, we saw how the various students have begun their work at APPFORMS. Sean McNeill learned how to create effective workplace emails. Lara Leveaux used her analytical skills to create an **informational report**, and submitted it by email as a short report. Maya Chen and Sean also created short reports they submitted to APPFORMS's managers as memos and progress reports. While short reports are the focus of a later chapter, Chapter 3 demonstrated the use of memos and emails to provide information to business decision-makers.

In Chapter 4, we look at a human resources task assigned to Carrie du Plessis, and see how she arrives at her recommendations. The task concerns the employee retreat, and was an agenda item of the daily morning partners' meeting presented in the introduction. Another agenda item at the same meeting was new products and business, which James Patel has been tasked to research, analyze, and make recommendations. Maya faces a different type of workplace situation, one caused by her, which also requires thought and analysis. It will eventually lead to cultural sensitivity training, which was also an agenda item at the partners' meeting.

Introduction

Companies hire people who will advance the company's goals in its various business aspects. When managers write job descriptions for vacancies in the various organizational departments, they consult with hiring managers and human resources personnel to determine the required qualifications for these roles. Managers search for and recruit people who have demonstrated that they meet or exceed these requirements. A few requirements are common to all roles, whether they are in marketing, accounting, engineering, sales, or finance. These include time management, personal integrity, critical thinking or analytical skills, verbal and written communication skills, including **argumentation**, and interpersonal skills. In this chapter, we will focus on two of these skills—analytical and argumentation skills—and walk through a few scenarios that require those involved to think critically about a problem and then devise appropriate ways to present these findings using argumentation techniques.

Analysis, Synthesis, and Effective Communication

The *Oxford Dictionaries* define *analysis* as "the process of separating something into its constituent elements." It is derived from the Greek word *analusis*, which means to break up or to loosen. Several definitions exist for different contexts (mathematics, logic, philosophy, and science), but they all essentially mean the same thing. Analysis is a method of understanding relationships between ideas. It is the process of identifying characteristics, identifying the relationships between these characteristics, creating categories to understand these relationships, and evaluating the information. Analysis is also used when applying new information. If you look at a company website, identify the characteristics of the site, and apply theories on social media to the website, you are analyzing the website through application and understanding.

Root cause analysis is one type of analysis. Some of the other types used in business situations to achieve strategic goals include cost-benefit analysis, SWOT **analysis** (Strengths, Weaknesses, Opportunities, and Threats), **business process analysis**, PESTLE **analysis** (Political, Economic, Sociological, Technological, Legal, and Environmental), and MOST **analysis** (Mission, Objectives, Strategies, and Tactics).

When something works well, we wish to replicate and improve upon the successful outcome. When something does not work well, we wish to identify areas that prevented the success, so that we can address the problematic areas, find ways to repair them, and avoid repeating past errors. Breaking an event or situation into its component parts enables us to find areas that were either malfunctioning or need to be repaired (like a bad motor or a false assumption about a situation) or functioning well (like best practices, good forecasting, or good relationship maintenance).

While analysis allows people to break things up into their component parts, the process of putting things back together to improve upon the existing whole and to replicate success or find better alternatives to an existing situation is the process of synthesis. The *Oxford Dictionaries* define *synthesis* as "the combination of components or elements to form a connected whole." It is derived from the Greek word *sunthesis*, which comes from *suntithena*, meaning "to place together." Analysis and synthesis, taking apart and putting together, thus go together. At various stages in a business, analysis is performed to find out the health of the business, the market, the competition, and the environment, and each of these requires reports such as progress reports, interim reports, or **status reports**. These reports present the analysis of internal and external business events and synthesize the findings of the analysis that was conducted.

However, breaking things down to their component parts and putting them back together does not constitute the entire process of analysis and synthesis. Often people tend to take things apart and describe the various components and finish their analysis with just the description. Once problem or success areas have been identified, different solutions for the problem or ways to successfully replicate the success can be explored. Then begins the process of synthesis, where each option is carefully evaluated for maximum benefit to the organization and recommendations can be put forward.

The next step in the process of critical or analytical thinking is the accurate and effective presentation of the results of the analysis and synthesis. Most business correspondence requires writers or speakers to use persuasive communication techniques. While we will cover persuasive communication in a subsequent chapter, it is worth noting here that the best way to produce effective persuasive communication pieces is by the careful use of argumentation techniques. The *Oxford Dictionaries* define *argumentation* as "the action or process of reasoning systematically in support of an idea, action, or theory." Argumentation is important when writing reports about results; requesting information from co-workers, management, or external stakeholders; or even presenting ideas to an audience.

Just as there are several approaches to analytical problem-solving, there are several techniques for analysis, synthesis, and argumentation. The process of analysis comprises several crucial pre-analysis steps. Critical reading of events or documents and critical listening of accounts delivered by people involved in these events allows the business communicator to consider all angles when critically thinking about these events. The analysis then will be more complete and the analytical tools that the business communicator employs will be more effective. Such an approach to analysis will result in better synthesis of the results and lead to more effective communication.

We will look at some of these analytical techniques in the context of APPFORMS. Carrie, Maya, James, Sean, and the others have already been using analysis and synthesis when they put together their respective résumés and cover letters, and presented some of their findings in their organizational roles, and the emails and memos they wrote. They will continue to use analytical techniques as they encounter tasks and problems and perform their duties.

The Case of Carrie du Plessis: Human Resources Scenario

Juanita Olson, director of human resources at APPFORMS, calls Carrie and tells her that the entire company is going to attend a two-day retreat the following month at Falls Lake Campgrounds and Resort. The purpose is partly to restore company morale, which is low due to the upcoming restructuring among the app development teams, and partly to brainstorm new and innovative ways to boost performance and productivity, and to give team members opportunities to come up with new ideas and work on pet projects. Juanita wants to include some **icebreakers** and team-building activities during the retreat and says there will be about three hours set aside for these. She asks Carrie to do some research, come up with a list of icebreakers and team-building activities, and make appropriate recommendations. Carrie needs to keep in mind the diverse workforce at APPFORMS and the sensitivities required while the organization undergoes restructuring.

Carrie begins her research in earnest. She has participated in team-building activities before and found them to be really useful. She has also had several professors who used icebreakers at the beginning of the semester. Students, especially in the first year of college or university, are often unsure of their surroundings and their classmates, and find it difficult to make new friends at first. Icebreakers are a good way to get to know classmates and possible future teammates.

Using the keywords "icebreakers and team-building activities," Carrie starts looking for ideas. She finds several websites and starts compiling a list, including the sources. She quickly realizes she has found far too many activities and she needs to categorize them into two separate lists. She also discovers that the activities on their own are not enough. The facilitator must be skilled at running these types of activities and in debriefing participants afterwards. Debriefing is the most crucial part of these activities. It helps the participants identify how the activities will help them build great working relationships with their co-workers, and shows them how the relationships can help them in their daily work. Carrie also learns that, while icebreakers can help people get to know each another, team-building activities help reinforce many of the strengths that people already possess and highlight areas for improvement.

With all this in mind, Carrie begins compiling a list of icebreakers. She decides to use a compiled list from the Lions Club website. The Lions Club is a reputable international organization with members from all professions and backgrounds. It is a diverse, not-for-profit organization. Carrie feels that the activities will have been tested and will therefore be useful for the APPFORMS's retreat. She creates a table with column headings for the icebreaker name, a brief description, the purpose of the activity, and a score on a scale of 1 to 5 (with 1 being least useful and 5 most useful). Carrie decides that she will rate each activity by how many objectives it achieves. For example, getting people to know each other is one objective, but getting to know their values helps lay the foundation for team-building, which is another objective.

Carrie creates a rating table to help her objectively rate each activity. She bases the criteria on the objective of the activity, how easy or complex it would be to do, its relevance and usefulness, and whether it would be interesting and fun. The more the activity can achieve, the higher the score. She believes her criteria are fair and will help her arrive at the correct choice of activities for the company retreat. As Carrie categorizes and sorts the activities, she is able to assess their usefulness. Rather than relying only on her own knowledge and experience, she uses a scoring or rating system to reduce the list of icebreakers into a more manageable list. Also, her process will help her document her analysis and can be used by others for rating similar programs or activities.

Table 4.1 Rating Table for Icebreaker and Team-Building Activities

Score	Criteria
1	Has one objective, is simple to do, and is somewhat relevant
2	Has one objective, is a little more involved, and is relevant
3	Has at least two objectives, is more involved, is quite relevant, and is interesting to do
4	Has two or more objectives, is more involved, is very relevant, and is interesting to do
5	Has two or more objectives, is more involved, is very relevant and useful, is interesting and fun to do, and will be memorable

Carrie's table will serve as a basis for her **decision matrix** (see Table 4.4). Before she creates a decision matrix, Carrie decides to create a table for icebreakers only. She includes all of the icebreakers from the Lions Club website.

Table 4.2 List of Icebreaker Activities

No.	Icebreaker Name	Brief Description	Purpose of the Activity	Score (1–5)
1	Seating Plan	People are seated alphabetically or by birthdays.	Get to know people	2
2	Marooned	Each team chooses 5 items they would want with them if they were stranded on an island.	Learn about other's values and problem-solving styles; promotes teamwork	5
3	Who's Done That?	Each team creates a list of useful skills and experiences.	Learn about team members' skills	3
4	Alliteration Introductions	People introduce themselves using alliteration; for example: "I am Magnificent Michelle" or "I am Superb Salman." Subsequent participants repeat the previous participant's name and add their own.	Get to know people	2
5	Chaos	Using props such as a ball, a pen, or a toy, people introduce themselves by saying their name and tossing the prop to the next person, who catches the prop, thanks them, says their name, and tosses the prop to the next person.	Energizes people and allows them to get to know each	3
6	Geographic Location	People create a map based on where they are from (or based on where they are assigned to).	Get to know people and where they are from	3
7	Name and Number	People are given an index card with their name and number. They mingle, try to meet as many people, and get their names and numbers. Afterwards, everyone tries to match the names with the numbers.	Get to know people	2
8	Pat on the Back	People write positive things about others on a piece of paper taped on to their backs.	Get to know people	2
9	Meeting Warm-Ups	People answer questions and others have to remember what is said.	Get to know people	2
10	"I Have Never"	Each person gets to finish the sentence "I have never..."	Get to know people	3
11	Two Truths and a Lie	People state two truths and a lie about themselves. The first person to guess which is the lie goes next.	Get to know people and their values	3
12	Me Too	In small groups, each person starts with 10 pennies, and names something he or she has done. Others who have done the same thing add a penny to the pile.	Get to know people in small groups	4
13	Common Ground	In small groups, people find out what they have in common.	Get to know people in small groups	3

Source: Icebreakers, team-building activities, and Energizers. *Lions Club International.* Retrieved from www.lionsclubs.org/EN/common/pdfs/icebreakers.pdf

Carries then decides to eliminate the activities with a score of less than 3. She creates a new table.

Table 4.3 Short List of Icebreaker Activities

No.	Icebreaker Name	Brief Description	Purpose of the Activity	Score (1–5)
1	Marooned	Each team chooses 5 items they would want with them if they were stranded on an island.	Learn about other's values and problem-solving styles; promotes teamwork	5
2	Who's Done That?	Each team creates a list of useful skills and experiences.	Learn about team members' skills	3
3	Chaos	Using props such as a ball, a pen, or a toy, people introduce themselves by saying their name and tossing the prop to the next person, who catches the prop, thanks them, says their name, and tosses the prop to the next person.	Energizes people and allows them to get to know each	3
4	Geographic Location	People create a map based on where they are from (or based on where they are assigned to).	Get to know people and where they are from	3
5	"I Have Never"	Each person gets to finish the sentence "I have never. . ."	Get to know people	3
6	Two Truths and a Lie	People state two truths and a lie about themselves. The first person to guess which is the lie goes next.	Get to know people and their values	3
7	Me Too	In small groups, each person starts with 10 pennies, and names something he or she has done. Others who have done the same thing add a penny to the pile.	Get to know people in small groups	4
8	Common Ground	In small groups, people find out what they have in common.	Get to know people in small groups	3

As she looks at the short list of activities, Carrie notes that only two of the activities have scores of 5 and 4, while the remaining activities have scores of 3. The activities with scores of 5 and 4 also have some team-building aspects to them. Carrie decides that these two activities would provide a good transition to the team-building activities that will follow. She now feels ready to create a weighted decision matrix to help her arrive at her final choices. A decision matrix lists all the options available and the criteria for evaluating each option. It is an important tool in the process of analysis. By eliminating the activities with a low score, Carrie can then make her final recommendations to Juanita.

She places the scores from Table 4.3 in the first column. Carrie decides to give a score of 1 for each criteria present in the activity and a score between 0 and 1 if some aspect of the criteria was present in the activity. If no criteria were present in the activity, she gives a score of 0. The final weighted score is the product of the score from Table 4.3 and the sum of the criteria scores. Although her rough estimate helped her create a manageable short list of eight activities, she feels that assigning scores will be more objective.

Table 4.4 Decision Matrix for Icebreaker Activities

Icebreaker Activity	Score from Table 4.3	Objective	Usefulness	Relevance	Involvement	Interesting/ Fun	Total	Final Weighted Score
Marooned	5	1.0	1.0	1.0	1.0	1.0	5.0	25.0
Who's Done That?	3	0.5	0.5	0.5	0.5	0.5	2.5	7.5
Chaos	3	0.5	0.5	0.5	1.0	0.5	3.0	9.0
Geographic Location	3	0.5	0.5	0.5	0.5	0.5	2.5	7.5
"I Have Never"	3	0.5	1.0	0.5	0.5	0.5	3.0	9.0
Two Truths and a Lie	3	0.5	0.5	0.5	1.0	1.0	3.5	10.5
Me Too	4	1.0	1.0	1.0	0.5	1.0	4.5	18.0
Common Ground	3	0.5	0.5	0.5	0.5	1.0	3.0	9.0

Carrie looks over her decision matrix and is now confident of making her recommendations for the two icebreaker activities. She chooses Marooned and Me Too and places them in a new table.

Table 4.5 Icebreaker Activity Recommendations

No.	Icebreaker Name	Brief Description	Purpose of the Activity	Score
1	Marooned	Each team chooses 5 items they would want with them if they were stranded on an island.	Learn about other's values and problem-solving styles; promotes teamwork	25
2	Me Too	In small groups, each person starts with 10 pennies, and names something he or she has done. Others who have done the same thing add a penny to the pile.	Get to know people in small groups	18

Source: Adapted from Icebreakers, Team-building Activities, and Energizers. *Lions Club International*. Retrieved from http:// www.lionsclubs.org/resources/EN/pdfs/icebreakers.pdf

Carrie then repeats the entire process with the team-building activities. Her master list consists of 10 team-building activities. She uses the same rating criteria and scales to score each activity. Table 4.6 shows her decision matrix for the team-building activities. Two of the activities, Pipe Cleaners and Three-Way Communication, have the highest scores and are clear winners, but Carrie wishes she could include Consensus too, even though its score is only 18. She decides to include all three in her recommendation report to Juanita. The Pipe Cleaners activity was fun and cross-cultural, while the Three-Way Communication activity stressed the importance of open communication among team members. Carrie understands that while consensus cannot always be achieved in team or group activities, the team-building activity called Consensus would definitely be useful.

Table 4.6 Decision Matrix for Team-Building Activities

Icebreaker Activity	Score From Table 4.3	Objective	Usefulness	Relevance	Involvement	Interesting/ Fun	Total	Final Weighted Score
Pipe Cleaners	5	1.0	1.0	1.0	1.0	1.0	5.0	25.0
Blind Numerical Order	3	0.5	0.5	0.5	0.5	0.5	2.5	7.5
All Tied Up	3	0.5	0.5	0.5	1.0	0.5	3.0	9.0
Build a Car	3	0.5	0.5	0.5	0.5	0.5	2.5	7.5
Human Machines	3	0.5	1.0	0.5	0.5	0.5	3.0	9.0
Rain	3	0.5	0.5	0.5	1.0	1.0	3.5	10.5
Consensus	4	1.0	1.0	1.0	0.5	1.0	4.5	18.0
Phrase Ball	3	0.5	0.5	0.5	0.5	1.0	3.0	9.0
Thanks Giving	3	0.5	0.5	0.5	0.5	1.0	3.0	9.0
Three-Way Communication	5	1.0	1.0	1.0	0.5	1.0	4.5	22.5

Source: Adapted from Icebreakers, Team-building Activities, and Energizers. *Lions Club International.* Retrieved from http://www.lionsclubs.org/resources/EN/pdfs/icebreakers.pdf

Carrie now begins to write a report on her findings to send to Juanita. She decides to start with a statement that she has identified two icebreaker activities and two team-building activities for the company employees to participate in during the two-day retreat. She then includes the tables she has created: Table 4.5 with her recommended icebreaker activities and Table 4.7 with her recommended team-building activities.

Table 4.7 Team-Building Activity Recommendations

No.	Icebreaker Name	Brief Description	Purpose of the Activity	Score
1	Pipe Cleaners	People are assigned to groups. Everyone is given three pipe cleaners and instructed to use them to form the most creative structure. Groups that combine their pipe cleaners to make a more creative structure are given special recognition.	Creativity	25.0
2	Three-Way Communication	People are assigned to groups: one representing face-to-face communication, one representing phone/instant messaging, and one representing email. Each group physically mimics and discusses the pros and cons of their assigned communication method.	Discussion	22.5
3	Consensus	Groups perform a noise for other groups to mimic.	Team-building, discussion, compromise, and negotiation	18.0

Carrie knows there will be three hours set aside to do these activities. However, she wonders if people might get bored doing only icebreakers and team-building activities for three hours continuously. To keep up the participant's interest, she recommends icebreakers that can be completed in 10 to 15 minutes, followed by a debriefing period of 10 to 15 minutes. Similarly, Carrie has recommended team-building activities that can be completed in 20 to 30 minutes, followed by a debriefing period of 20 to 30 minutes. She also recommends to Juanita that there be two 90-minute time slots set aside for the activities: one slot in the morning of the first day of the two-day retreat and the second slot in the afternoon of the second day.

Carrie reasons that everyone will be enthusiastic on the first morning of the retreat, so it is a good time to have people participate in these types of activities. The first slot will be for everyone in the organization (including the managing partners) and team members will be picked randomly from all departments and teams. So, for example, one team could have members from Team Apple, Team Android, someone from HR, one of the managing partners, and one co-op student. This will allow people to get to know people from the entire company and help them to identify with the entire organization, making the activity a rewarding experience.

The second slot should be during or after lunch of the second day. By that time, people will be thinking about going back to work and getting back to their projects. Carrie reasons that this second time slot would be ideal for people to do the activities with their own team to build team spirit and to help them reorient themselves back into their projects.

Carrie outlines all of her recommendations and reasoning in her report to Juanita. Although she includes in her report only the two tables that list the recommended activities, she attaches an appendix outlining her analysis and how she arrived at her recommendations. This way, Juanita can read through Carrie's short report and only look at the appendix if she has any questions about how Carrie reached her conclusions. Juanita could also call and talk to her if she has further questions.

The Case of Maya Chen: Intercultural and Interpersonal Communication

Maya nervously walks into the APPFORMS's office with her coffee in one hand and the *Chronicle Herald* in the other. As she heads toward her cubicle, she passes a red-faced Mohammed Yasin, assistant to Ziva Yaron, manager of Team Apple. Mohammed immediately turns away from her and stares at his laptop screen. Maya quickly goes to her cubicle. Jose Tsotsobe, one of the two Team Apple developers, catches Maya's eye and points to the newspaper in her hand. Maya still prefers to read news in print and she particularly likes the *Herald*. She scans the headlines. There is a report about some bombings in the Gaza Strip. Maya remembered that her discussion with Mohammed about the Israel–Palestine issue during lunch the previous day inadvertently caused him some discomfort. Lunchtime is usually a team affair and all team members, including Ziva, the manager, are comfortable discussing a wide range of topics. Yesterday, however, the conversation took a more serious turn, resulting in a tense work atmosphere.

As manager, Ziva is responsible for the entire team. She takes care of the team's needs, manages their targets, ensures maximum possible positioning for their apps at the Apple store, pushes her team's agenda at every meeting, and really cares for them. However, yesterday really tested her managerial skills. Mohammed is of Palestinian origin and Ziva is of Israeli descent. For the most part, Ziva got along really well with Mohammed as he is a great guy and really good to work with. Even so, out here in Halifax, far away from their respective countries of origin, Mohammed and Ziva shared strong feelings about the issues plaguing Israel and Palestine and sometimes things got testy. It didn't help that Ziva, a woman, was Mohammed's manager.

In light of the latest news from the Middle East, Ziva was fighting to gain composure of both herself and her team. Yesterday was particularly rough because Mohammed had said some things to Ziva at lunchtime that were not too polite. Then Maya's uninformed comments made the interpersonal climate among the team members even worse. Mohammed then continued with his harsh comments in response to Maya's statement, and she then called both of them terrorists. Ziva was of two minds: Should she talk to Juanita about this or go even higher? Or should she confront Mohammed and Maya individually or together and deal with it internally? She also wondered if she should involve all the team members. After all, they could see what was going on and the entire team's morale was at stake here. Meanwhile, both Mohammed and Maya were struggling with their own emotions while trying to figure out a way out of this situation.

Variations of this situation or other types of personality clashes often arise when groups of people work together. This scenario is discussed in a chapter on analysis and argumentation because it too is a business problem. Team dynamics and team or employee morale is a key factor that every manager or business leader needs to carefully consider when operating a business or managing a team. Bad morale or poor team dynamics can cause productivity to plummet and create a bad or even hostile environment at the workplace. Such situations need to be carefully analyzed, and clean and clear arguments need to be presented to team members so that good team dynamics and high morale can be restored. We will analyze the above situation from the point of view of all three affected employees: Maya, Mohammed, and Ziva.

This situation has multiple levels of complexity including gender, cultural sensitivity, and workplace hierarchy or power structure. Maya and Ziva are women, while Mohammed is a man. While Jose and others are present as team members, they have not directly added to or aggravated the conflict by saying or doing anything. However, as team members they are still involved indirectly, as witnesses to the altercation between Maya and Mohammed, and affected directly by the tension that is a result of the exchange between Maya and Mohammed. All three have different cultural backgrounds. Although all teams at APPFORMS are quite decentralized and have autonomous decision-making abilities, and within each team there is a fairly flat structure, all team members do report to the team manager. Ziva is the manager of Team Apple. Mohammed is her assistant, and Maya is the recently graduated student who has joined APPFORMS as a full-time employee. We begin with Maya.

Analysis of Maya Chen's Role

Maya has been thinking about her exchange with Mohammed ever since it happened the previous day. She realizes that she should not have blurted out what she said, particularly because she is not well informed about the situation in the Middle East. Known as a methodical person who is careful in her work and speech, Maya was surprised at her insensitive responses to Mohammed's claims about the Palestinian situation. She decides to list the sequence of events so that she can identify and flag areas where she erred. Once she understands what happened, she can determine a course of action and begin to rectify the situation.

Sequence of events during lunch the previous day according to Maya:

1. The team went to a Turkish restaurant to eat lunch.
2. The team ordered a sampler plate with hummus, baba ghanouj, kebbe, phyllo cheese rolls, tabouleh and fatouche salads, kabobs, and other dishes. (Despite the situation, Maya smiles as she lists the dishes. The food was good at this restaurant, she thinks to herself.)
3. Discussion veered toward how this kind of food is common around the Mediterranean Sea, especially in Israel and Palestine.
4. Discussion then centred on the Palestinian–Israeli conflict, with mainly Ziva and Mohammed talking about their own perspectives. Others at the table ate and listened. Mohammed began to get angry and said a few impolite things. ▶
5. Maya blurted out, "But you are all terrorists." ▶
6. Silence at the table.
7. Mohammed got up, spoke harshly, and left. ▶
8. Everyone quickly finished their lunches and left.
9. Ziva avoided Maya's eyes as they all returned to the office.
10. The rest of the day passes in silence with few verbal exchanges between any of the team members.

Maya looks at her list and notes the flagged items.

1. Discussion then centred on the Palestinian–Israeli conflict, with mainly Ziva and Mohammed talking about their own perspectives. Others at the table ate and listened. ►
2. Maya blurted out, "But you are all terrorists." ►
3. Mohammed got up, spoke harshly, and left. ►

Maya now realizes that, first, she should not have intervened. But, having intervened, she should have said something that eased the conversation or something that was more informed, rather than what she blurted out. Although Maya is an intelligent woman and does not usually make uninformed statements, this time she did. She decides that she must make an effort to rectify the situation. She lists the steps she must take.

1. Immediately write to both Ziva and Mohammed, apologizing for her comments.
2. Follow up with a face-to-face conversation.
3. Read up on the Middle East conflict to become more informed about the situation.
4. Stop forming opinions and judgments based on stereotypes.
5. Stop making statements that cannot be supported by evidence.
6. Maintain professionalism by saying what is relevant, providing evidence for any claims, making clear arguments, being courteous to everyone at the workplace, forming opinions and judgments based on good models and examples (for example, prototypes) and being compassionate to everyone.

Maya then proceeds to write an email to both Ziva and Mohammed, apologizing for her out-of-place comments and asks to meet with them personally.

Analysis of Mohammed Yasin's Role

Mohammed, too, has been thinking about the events that occurred during lunch the previous day. He knows that, although Ziva and he may have historical and cultural differences, they both live and work in Canada, where respect for everyone forms the basis of all social and workplace relationships. He likes working with Ziva. She is a good person and a great manager and he has long ago overcome his inhibitions of working for a female manager. Mohammed also knows that Maya is young and probably not aware of many of the events that led to the Middle East conflict. He should not have spoken so harshly to her and supposes that he got carried away by his emotions. While he does not want to suppress his emotions, nor deny his pain about the current situation in the Middle East, he realizes that Maya's comments were ill-informed and not meant to be spiteful. Her comments were directed to both Ziva and him. He decides to first meet with Ziva and then he will talk to Maya. Just then Maya's email arrives in Mohammed's inbox. He reads her written apology and notes that Maya has written to both Ziva and him. Mohammed nods in appreciation after he reads the email and then heads to Ziva's office.

Analysis of Ziva Yaron's Role

As the manager of Team Apple, Ziva is faced with a complex, team-conflict situation that requires sensitive handling. She decides that the matter is best handled by herself and within the team. She has always worked well with Mohammed. They have had discussions about the Middle East before, but it had never gotten this bad. Ziva realizes too that it was Maya's sweeping generalization about all of them that hurt the most. She was surprised by Maya's sudden statement, but then, Ziva has heard similar statements before, although from much older people. She does not want to blame either Maya or Mohammed for the tension, but rather ease the tension within the team. As she is thinking about the situation, she receives Maya's email. She is glad that Maya has realized her error and is making the effort to learn from this situation. She looks up and sees Mohammed heading toward her office and she smiles at him. She then gets up to greet him and together they head toward Maya's cubicle. Ziva asks Maya and the other members of Team Apple to come to the conference room for an impromptu meeting. It was worth spending the time now to address this situation. Ziva also decides to ask Juanita Olson to organize some team-building activities for everyone at APPFORMS that includes training about inter-cultural and interpersonal communication.

Argumentation

The *Oxford Dictionaries* define *argumentation* as "the action or process of reasoning systematically in support of an idea, action, or theory." A simple way to understand this is to consider it as a process of supporting a claim statement or assertion, with evidence from analysis, or logical reasoning. Argumentation then becomes a key process by which findings from analyses are synthesized in a manner that can be received effectively by the targeted audience. One can begin an argumentative process by first stating the claim, providing the relevant context and background, and supporting the claim with the necessary evidence. When the intended receiver raises an objection to the stated claim (the counterclaim), the business communicator can then provide a rebuttal, supported with further evidence. This cyclical process continues until either agreement on the claim is reached, or the communicator and the intended receiver both agree to move ahead.

We now look at another business scenario where James Patel uses analysis and argumentation processes to complete a business task.

The Case of James Patel: New Business Opportunity

James, the co-op marketing assistant in Team Android at APPFORMS, is asked by his manager, Pierce Sanchez, to start thinking about a new set of business apps that would allow corporate clients to perform **cloud-based** web analytics on business data. Pierce wants the business to grow to a reasonable size over the next five years. Before Pierce asks the design and development team to begin coding the apps, he wants James to perform a brief market analysis to look at supply and demand and make recommendations accordingly.

James goes back to his cubicle to think about the task. He begins by writing down exactly what Pierce has asked him to do: perform a brief market analysis on the need for mobile business data analysis apps. Pierce wants to know who the suppliers of business **data analytics** applications are (supply side) and who the consumers of these software applications are (demand side). Pierce also wants James to make some recommendations.

James realizes that the initial audience for his recommendations will be Pierce, APPFORMS's managing partners, and the design and development teams. However, the final audience will be business and corporate consumers who may use such a mobile app. James is quite analytical and has done market analysis assignments in his courses, but he decides to begin by looking at some online sources for strategies to approach this task. He then lists some key approaches to use. He picks the ones most relevant to his task and studies them.

Analysis Strategies

James identifies the following strategies as relevant to his task and writes them down.

1. Understand the task.
    *   List questions that arise.
    *   Return to the audience to get answers to the questions and any other clarifications.
    *   Visualize the task to see if there is a process to be followed.
    *   Identify key elements of the task or process and create a block diagram.

2. Use the process diagram.
    *   Check if the process is sequential (i.e., one process has to follow another).
    *   Identify which parts can be done concurrently.
    *   See if there are feedback loops in the process.

3. Gather and evaluate information.
    *   For each part of the process, determine whether information is available from a primary, secondary, or tertiary sources.
    *   Determine the type of information or data required.
    *   Evaluate the quality and source of the information.

4. Perform analysis.
    *   If necessary, perform data analytics (using an analytics software application like MS Excel) to generate numbers and charts to illustrate trends, etc.
    *   Estimate the likely costs and benefits of possible recommendations.
    *   Choose one or more options to recommend.

James decides to first clarify the problem and returns to Pierce to ask the following questions:

1. Would companies that develop data analysis software applications already have mobile apps for their products?

2. Am I only supposed to look at existing apps that work on the Android phones or could I widen the search to look at cross-platform apps?
3. Should I only look at web-based data analytics applications or also **business intelligence** (BI) dashboards and scorecards?

Visualizing the Problem

Pierce is pleased that James has returned to him to clarify the task and that James's questions are relevant. He tells James to broaden his search to include cross-platform apps and also to find out about BI dashboards and scorecards. He explains that companies that produce data analysis and BI software applications may have their own mobile phone apps, but the market appears big enough for APPFORMS to also enter. It is James's task to determine whether there really is room in the market for APPFORMS.

James returns to his list. He decides that the best way for him to proceed would be to identify the key elements of the task, and that visualizing the task will help him identify those elements. He then draws a diagram. On the supply side, he uses a cloud shape to indicate companies that offer data analytics in the cloud, and a rectangle to indicate companies that offer these applications on their own websites. On the demand side, he has a picture of a generic smartphone with arrows pointing toward it. He adds the names of the various mobile phone operating systems. He then uses a rectangle to indicate potential customers for these apps.

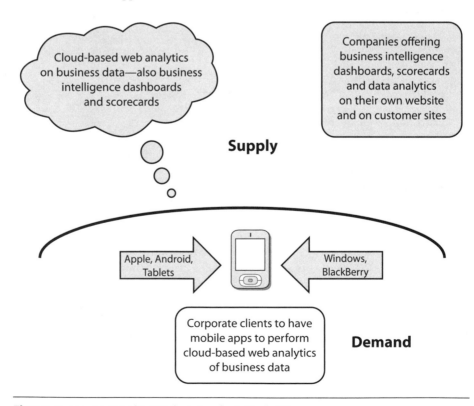

Figure 1 James Patel's Market Analysis Task Diagram

As he looks at his diagram, James realizes he is able to visualize the whole task into some of its component parts. He sees that there is a process involved and diagramming it will help him focus on specific areas.

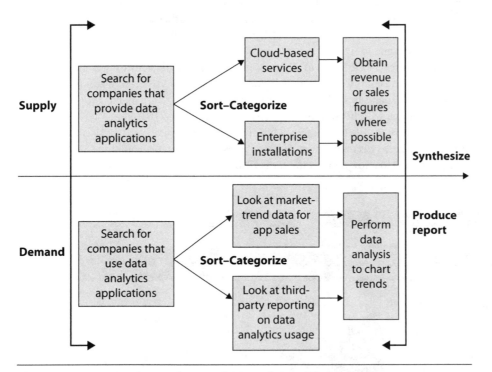

Figure 2 James Patel's Market Analysis Task Process Diagram

Instead of approaching everything at once, James sees that he could focus on one part of the task at a time by starting with either the supply side or the demand side. He knows from his marketing and sales courses that forecasting, based on customers' previous buying patterns, can be used to arrive at demand figures. These figures are sometimes easy to obtain, although not always.

Finding information on the supply side is easier. Companies often advertise their products, both on their websites and on third-party websites. James could visit both types of websites to find out

- how many BI dashboards and scorecards apps are currently available in the app stores;
- how many are cloud-based;
- how many are running from dedicated servers provided by the companies that made the apps; and
- how many are enterprise installations in the client's organizations.

He decides to start on the supply side with the data analytic services that are exclusively cloud-based. Then he moves on to companies that host their data analytic services on their own websites. In this manner, James progressively collects information about the supply side, creating a table to show his work in progress (see Table 4.8). He carefully places the source of his information alongside the table title. Notes to explain some of the terms go below the table. He includes a figure of a standard BI dashboard as a reference for himself.

James continues to document information about other apps he finds, sorting and categorizing them according to how the data analytics services are provided. He then moves to the demand side.

Since Pierce asked James to do a market analysis, he decides to present his data in both tabular and chart form. He also does a brief SWOT analysis on some of the top cloud-based and company-hosted BI apps. James then writes a short memo report outlining his information, with his sources in a separate document so that Pierce can access them when needed. Since the task required only research, not extensive analysis and interpretation, James keeps his report brief. He concludes with a recommendation that the market is large enough to allow apps from APPFORMS to enter and be profitable.

Figure 4.3 Sample BI Dashboard

Source: Customer relationship management and business intelligence (2010, May 30) [Blog post] Retrieved from http://20100157.blogspot.ca/2010/05/customer-relationship-management-and.html

Table 4.8 Top 16 Vendors of Business Data Analytics

No.	Name of Company	Cloud Only	Website and Cloud	Mobile Apps Y/N	Type and Notes
1	1010data	X	X	Roambi* Y	Works with multiple Hadoop** software providers
2	Actian			Y	Works with multiple Hadoop software providers
3	Amazon Web Services	X		Y	Works with multiple Hadoop software providers
4	Cloudera		X		Provides Apache Hadoop support for enterprises
5	HP		X		Works with multiple Hadoop software providers
6	Hortonworks		X		Provides Apache Hadoop support for enterprises
7	IBM		X		Uses its own Hadoop distribution
8	InfiniDB				Works with multiple Hadoop software providers
9	Infobright				Works with multiple Hadoop software providers
10	Kognito				Works with multiple Hadoop software providers
11	MapR				Provides Apache Hadoop support for enterprises
12	Microsoft		X		Offers complimentary software
13	Oracle		X		Resells and supports Cloudera
14	Pivotal				Uses its own Hadoop distribution
15	SAP		X		Works with multiple Hadoop software providers
16	Teradata				Offers complimentary software

Source: Henschen, D. (2014, January 30). 16 Top Big data analytics platforms, *Information Week*. Retrieved from http://www.informationweek.com/big-data/big-data-analytics/16-top-big-data-analytics-platforms/d/d-id/1113609?

*Roambi: Can get data analytics from most sources onto the mobile phone

**Apache Hadoop: Provides the open-source data processing platform on which vendors provide data analytics capabilities

Pierce is pleased with James's findings and asks him some follow-up questions. James outlines the process he used to complete his task, presents evidence for his claims/recommendations (initial statements stating a particular finding or conclusion), and responds to any rebuttals (counterclaims that question James's initial statements) that

Pierce has by providing additional evidence. James remembers from his business communication course that these are the elements of effective argumentation and he is glad that he is able to use them in such an effective manner at APPFORMS.

◎ SCOPE

Strategy plays a key role in analysis, and the analysis of events or situations informs the strategy of the organization. The three scenarios in this chapter all occur fairly frequently in most, if not all, organizations. They may take different forms, but every organization at some point or another embarks on a reflective and morale-building period with its employees, has to decide to expand its field of business and explore new ideas, and faces internal conflict among employees.

Although Carrie has a rather straightforward task, she does not jump to conclusions and uses a detailed weighted decision matrix to aid her analysis. The decision matrix is a key part of her strategy to tackle a straightforward task and helps her arrive at her conclusions in a methodical and replicable manner. This means that another person, following the same steps, can arrive at almost the same, if not the exact same, conclusions.

Maya faces an entirely different scenario because she spoke quickly without thinking and because of factors beyond her control. In order to build and maintain good working relationships with her co-workers, her strategy involved analyzing her actions and realizing her error. Her analysis helps her quickly resolve a potentially damaging situation in her workplace.

The strategy for expanding the business involved analysis of the strengths and weaknesses of the organization (internal factors) and exploration of the opportunities and threats (external factors). James performed his analysis mostly on the external factors, that is, opportunities (demand) and threats (competition) and arrives at his recommendation after analyzing the market for new apps.

Content is equally critical in both the analysis of an event and its presentation. It is also important that content is relevant to the context. That is, a thorough analysis of an event takes into account all the factors that led to the occurrence of that event. Analysis does not stop if some of the content is not available. But analysis should take into account any missing content, sources must always be documented and traceable, and, when and where possible, efforts need to be made to collect missing content. Care must be taken to arrive at informed conclusions despite missing content. This is done by documenting each step, which Carrie, Maya, and James have done. The steps must also be replicable. Being able to verify sources and processes and repeat the process becomes critical to any kind of analysis.

The *outcome* of analysis and synthesis of business events is to provide a strategic advantage to business decision-makers, regardless of their sphere of activity. Whether the outcome is to expand the field and scope of a business, negotiate a merger or acquisition, run a new ad campaign, solve financial problems, build up morale, buy new equipment, or negotiate insurance premiums, each and every business activity requires careful analysis of all of the factors that contribute to a successful outcome activity.

Presentation of analysis and synthesis of an event must carefully consider the audience. Carrie provides evidence and reasoning for her recommendations. Her reasoning is twofold: first, she creates a set of criteria to evaluate the activities and a scale to rate them according to her criteria. She then uses a decision matrix to help her select the best activities, and provides reasons for requesting two separate time slots for the activities, instead of one long session. Her reasoning shows that Carrie has a keen awareness of the needs of her audiences, which includes Juanita, her initial and primary audience, as well as her larger, secondary audience—the employees.

Maya, having committed an error of judgment, needs to present herself in a different light. Her approach is to be conciliatory by admitting to her error. Her careful choice of words will help her resolve the conflict within the team.

James's audience is both his manager, as well as others in the organization. He has to decide how to place his recommendations in his report. To expand or not expand into a new line of business applications will form his initial claim statement. He has to support these claims by clear evidence or logical reasoning. Although James provides evidence from sources he can verify, he needs to anticipate rebuttals or counterclaims to his claim statements. His analysis should anticipate these counterclaims and he should be prepared to submit further evidence or reasoning to back his assertions.

Ethics forms the core of analysis, and when analysis is done ethically, it is trustworthy. Laziness and bad time management lead people to do poor analysis. This can take the form of using information that can't be verified, making up data or information, skimping on the details, and rushing through the analysis. Good managers easily see through poorly performed analysis and recommendations based on improper or non-verifiable information. Most managers can also distinguish between description and analysis. When managers ask for analysis, they expect their employees to do due diligence to the task, make clear statements and arguments, and support their claims or assertions with verifiable evidence and/or sound reasoning. This will help them make better business decisions and show them that their employees are ethical and good communicators.

Chapter Summary

This chapter looked at the role of analysis and argumentation in the workplace. Almost every business situation, whether good or bad, requires employees to analyze their actions or internal or external events, identify the causes of the actions or events, explore alternatives to what was done, and make recommendations that solve business problems or issues. While analysis and synthesis forms one part of the process, clear articulation of the claims and assertions, backed by verifiable evidence and/or logical reasoning, form the basis of effective argumentation. We followed Carrie du Plessis, Maya Chen, and James Patel as they analyzed the tasks and events they were presented with. Each of them used a slightly different set of analytical tools, all with the same desired outcome of better business decision-making and better relationship building.

The analytical tools discussed in this chapter are not the only ones used in business. The steps to performing pre-analysis—critical listening, critical reading, and critical thinking—help employees understand the various components of the situation. It lets them see the big picture while looking closely into a situation to identify causes of success or failure. This kind of pre-analysis is applicable to any type or level of analysis. Likewise, the steps of argumentation discussed in the chapter are applicable to any situation or event. Even if you are only writing a one-line email, you need to put careful thought into the creation of that one line because it can contain an assertion and the evidence to back the assertion. The goal of this chapter is to help you develop your analytical thinking and argumentation abilities. These techniques will be used again in later chapters.

Discussion Questions

1. As the co-op intern in the accounting department of a company, you are asked to research insurance rates for medical, property, and liability insurance and make recommendations about the most feasible insurance company to use. How will you proceed? Discuss your steps. Would you use a decision matrix to aid your analysis? If so, why, how, and where?

2. "Option B is the most viable at present." How can one arrive at such a recommendation?

What steps or processes are involved when this claim or assertion is made?

3. Amanda Singh, sales manager of an electronics manufacturing firm, has been called to a meeting with senior management. As she enters the conference room, she sees her boss, the vice-president of sales, holding a phone to his ear. He asks Amanda to sit down. Seated around the table are the director of human resources, the vice-president of global marketing, the executive secretary, and the head of security. They all briefly nod at Amanda, but do not say or do anything else. What should Amanda make of this situation?

4. Keith Prasad is the director of marketing of a global clothing company based out of Ontario. His company outsources clothing from different parts of the world and markets them in North America. Most of the clothing is seasonal and trendy casual wear and occasionally some professional work clothing. He wishes to enter into the sports clothing market. He asks you, a marketing co-op intern at the company, to do a market analysis about the competition and demand and submit a report with appropriate recommendations. How would you go about this task? Discuss the steps involved in your analysis and synthesis.

Exercises

The exercises in this chapter involve the scenario presented below. Read the scenario and answer the questions based on the events described in the scenario.

The Case of Sean McNeill: Department Merger

Larissa Zhao, manager of Team Windows, calls Sean to her office. She states that, due to poor performance of both Windows Mobile apps and BlackBerry apps, there have been significant cost pressures throughout the company. She and Vic Tremblett, manager of Team BlackBerry, have had meetings with the managing partners and the director of human resources about merging the two teams. Larissa has been getting reports that morale has been a bit low in both the teams with rumours about a possible merger being discussed around the office. She tells Sean that the merger would not result in any job losses, but would mean that resources would be shared and development projects would be joined to improve the overall performance of both teams and increase sales for the company. She wants Sean to talk to members of both teams to get their opinions about the possible merger.

She and Vic already have a plan of action for merging the two teams, but she wants data to verify their plan. Larissa provides Sean with some of the questions that he could ask. She wants him to document the results of his interviews and email it to her within the next few days. Sean goes back to his cubicle and thinks about how to approach this task. He is a new co-op intern. He realizes that his report on the bus-route apps was well received by the marketing team, and that is why he has now been entrusted with this rather sensitive task.

1. What should Sean do first? Why? What does Sean need to know or do before he starts the interviews?

2. Does it matter if he talks to Team Windows or Team BlackBerry first?

3. If Sean decides to start the interviews with Team Windows, should he approach them by email or talk to them directly? Please explain the reasons for your answers.

4. In the early part of his interview with one of the developers in Team Windows, the developer asks Sean for some clarification. Sean is not in a position to provide the clarification. What should Sean's course of action be?

5. Why has Sean been entrusted with this task when Larissa and Vic could easily ask their own teams the questions?

Good Advice or Bad?

1. You are working on a market analysis task and have been looking at some trends to gauge the possible introduction of a new product line. Based on the analysis, you also need to forecast revenues for the foreseeable future. Your co-worker says that you should make revenue projections for up to five years into the future. Good advice or bad? Why?

2. You are helping a classmate with his analytical report and you come across several instances of bold claims but not much by way of evidence. Since he does not have time to collect more information before the report is due, you recommend that he add a few charts to make the report more believable. Good advice or bad? Why?

3. As you are working through your term assignment, you are searching for some information online and suddenly find a complete report that has analyzed the exact same problem you are dealing with in your assignment. You look at the date when the report was created and find that it is several years old. You tell yourself that this is perfect and quickly download it with the intention of updating the report and submitting it as your own work. Good advice or bad? Why?

4. You are working with your classmates on an industry analysis project. Your classmate tells you that the library has a subscription to a business resource database that provides in-depth analysis on many industries and organizations. All you need to do is to download the reports and submit them. Good advice or bad? Why?

Strategic Language: Using Rhetorical Tools in Argumentation

Common rhetorical tools used in business writing include process descriptions, mechanical descriptions, definitions, compare and contrast, cause and effect, assertion (which relies on backing and reasoning), and argument. We will briefly look at the definitions and examples of these tools.

1. Process description involves what, when, where, how, and the steps in the process. Example: A team of software developers is working on a project.

2. Mechanical description involves how something looks or works and what are its moving parts. Example: A kitchen blender has a base with a motor, a blade, a jar, and a lid.

3. Definitions state what a thing or process is and how or where it is used. Example: The definition of *velocity* is rate over time.

4. *Compare and contrast* describes two comparable events or things and recommends one over the other because of better features, performance, or price. It is used when something new is being compared to something known. While analogies are also used to describe similar processes or events, compare and contrast can be useful for performing **feasibility** or cost-benefit analysis. Example: Brand X photocopier is the recommended option because it has better features and longer warranty for an affordable price when compared to brands Y and Z.

5. Cause and effect is when a result can be linked to specific events. Example: Continuous heavy rain made the ground soggy and created a sink hole.

6. Assertions are based on evidence backed by data or sound reasoning. Example: The popular technology company CEO's resignation caused the company shares to drop by 10%, as reported by in the *New York Times*.

Rhetorical tools are based on the concepts of **logos** (logic or sound reasoning), **pathos** (emotional appeals), and **ethos** (ethics or credibility). Logos involves the use of argumentation by logical induction or reasoning from a specific event or situation to a generalization, which may be true but not necessarily a fact. Example: This winter, it snowed every Wednesday and the university declared a snow day each time. Every winter from now on, the university will likely declare a snow day every Wednesday.

A series of events caused the generalization, which could be true, but likely not.

Logos also involves argument by deduction from a generalization to a specific event or situation. In this case, the argument can be logical as long as the original premise is sound; otherwise, the logic can be faulty. Example: Most employed people have college degrees. You have a college degree. You will be employed.

The assertion that you will be employed is faulty. The person with a college degree may never get a job or may not want to be employed, proving the assertion false.

Arguments that use pathos use emotional appeals to convince the audience of a particular point of view. Arguments that use ethos use credibility, goodwill, or ethics to arrive at conclusions and attempt to convince the audience of a particular point of view.

Summary of Comparison and Contrast Words

	Comparison	Contrast
Coordinators	and	but, yet
Subordinators	although even though though while whereas	
Transition Words	however on the other hand	

Coordinators can join sentences and begin sentences. When they join sentences, place a comma before the coordinator.

Kim likes heavy metal, <u>but</u> Tom prefers classical music.

Kim likes heavy metal. <u>But</u> Tom prefers classical music.

Subordinators join dependent clauses to form sentences. When the dependent clause comes first, place a comma after it; if the dependent clause follows the independent clause, don't use a comma.

<u>While</u> Kim likes prime rib, Tom prefers rice and vegetables.

Kim likes prime rib <u>while</u> Tom prefers rice and vegetables.

Transition words do not join sentences; you have to use a semicolon (;) to join the sentences or begin a new sentence with the transition word.

Kim and Tom have different tastes in music and food; <u>however</u>, they both like to dance.

Kim and Tom have different tastes in music and food. <u>However</u>, they both like to dance.

In the following sentences, identify

* the pattern of reasoning (inductive or deductive),
* transition words, and
* elements of compare and contrast.

Once you have identified the above, rewrite the sentences in a more effective manner.

1. All noble gases are stable and helium is a noble gas, so helium is stable. However, gold is also stable, so gold must also be a gas.
2. Magnolias are dicots and dicots have two embryonic leaves; therefore, magnolias have two embryonic leaves.
3. Elephants have cells in their bodies and all cells have DNA, so elephants have DNA.
4. All cars have at least two doors and a Ford Focus is a car, so the Ford Focus has at least two doors.
5. All horses have manes and the Arabian is a horse; therefore, Arabians have manes.
6. Mary and Sue are friends. Mary enjoys fishing, running, and rock climbing. Sue likes fishing and rock climbing. Sue must also like running.
7. Whereas all baseball players can make it to first base in at least four seconds, so Barry can make it to first base in at least four seconds, because he is a football player.
8. All football players weigh more than 77 kilograms. However, Ray weighs less than 77 pounds, but he is still a football player.
9. All observed houses on the South Street are falling apart and because Sherry lives on South Street, her house is falling apart.
10. Jenny is a dancer. Dancers are thin and tall; therefore, Jenny is thin and tall.

Additional Resource

Additional Internet Source

Eliminating Wordiness in Business Writing. Retrieved from http://grammar.about.com/od/ words/a/Exercise-In-Eliminating-Wordiness-In-Business-Writing.htm

CHAPTER FIVE

Maintaining External Business Relationships in Letters

Junophoto/Getty Images

Learning Objectives

A. **Assess** the audience's needs.

B. **Master** the basic form of the business letter.

C. **Create** a style of delivery that focuses on developing, maintaining, and enhancing business relationships.

D. **Develop** techniques for focusing on the audience relationship rather than bad news in negative messages.

E. **Focus** on what *can* be done rather than what *can't* in bad news messages.

F. **Communicate** information in a way appropriate for a given audience and situation.

G. **Practise** developing strategies for formal communications to stakeholders.

The Story So Far

In Chapter 4, we followed Carrie du Plessis, Maya Chen, and James Patel as they each tackled complex workplace tasks. Carrie created a short report based on her use of a decision matrix to identify the best topics for icebreakers and team-building activities for the APPFORMS company retreat. Maya faced a situation where she made an unsupported, generalized statement that caused tension within her team. She then analyzed her actions, and decided on her response. James Patel faced a straightforward task of researching certain aspects of APPFORMS's business and looking for possible new opportunities. All three employees used analytical skills learned in their university courses, and developed clear, evidence-based arguments to support their assertions.

While Chapter 4 focused on different techniques for analysis, synthesis, and argumentation techniques, Chapter 5 will show how these approaches are used when the company's executives write business letters to convey information, good news, bad news, or apologies. The purpose of the letters is to maintain business relationships with different types of external stakeholders.

Introduction

Business is establishing and maintaining mutually beneficial relationships. In order to establish and maintain these relationships, it is essential to

- develop empathy;
- adjust the content of a message to ensure it is both clear and sensitive to the audience's values; and
- craft messages that sustain a lasting partnership even when the message contains bad news.

Occasionally it is necessary to abandon a relationship that is no longer mutually beneficial, such as when a customer abuses staff or a supplier engages in unethical practices. For as long as the relationship is mutually beneficial, however, it is essential to nurture the relationship through effective, professional, and empathic business communications.

While email is appropriate for internal communication and even most external communication, the business letter is still used when the situation or audience requires a high degree of formality or when the sender wishes to emphasize the importance of the communication. A job offer or letter of resignation, a formal complaint or letter of apology, an invitation to a special event or request for action all may require a formatted business letter. This chapter focuses on creating effective formal communications with audiences outside the organization.

The business letter format has changed over time. The standard format used to have indented paragraphs, but today's business letters most often align all elements on the left, a style called the block format. By using the block format, a writer demonstrates knowledge of current business standards.

Letters from organizations have the sender's address in a letterhead format at the top of the page and include

- the full name of the organization,
- the street address, including the suite or office number,
- the city, province, and postal code, and
- the telephone number.

Some letters also include

- a web address,
- a fax number,
- an email address, and
- the organization's logo.

A personal letter is often used for documents such as cover letters. Personal letterhead format includes the name, complete address, telephone number, and email address of the sender.

The margins of a business letter are typically 2.54 centimetres (one inch) wide, the default established in most word-processing programs. Line spacing is typically 1.15, with a line space between paragraphs and three line spaces between the closing and the signature. Most word-processing programs include templates that follow these business standards. These standards meet the readers' expectations of structure and allow the reader to focus on the content.

Although the form of the letter is standard, the writer has choices within this form, and these choices can dramatically affect the reader's impression of the sender. For example, the purpose of a letter from a university to an incoming first-year student is to offer congratulations on acceptance into university and to provide instructions for confirming enrolment. To meet both purposes, the letter might combine formal elements appropriate for the importance of the occasion with less formal elements appropriate for establishing a relationship with a new student. The formal elements would include a business letter format, a conservative serif font like Times New Roman, and a traditional closing such as *regards*. To appear more approachable and conversational, the letter might temper the formality with less formal elements; for example, the use of contractions, a comma rather than a colon after the greeting, and accessible language.

Knowing when to adhere to structure and formality and when to deviate from them requires knowledge of formal elements in writing and awareness of the audience's needs. The letters in this chapter demonstrate how to adapt to audience and situation.

Font style and size may seem like trivial concerns, but font choice can have a strong impact on the reader. The letters of a serif font have small lines, called *serifs*, on the ends of each letter. Sans serif fonts do not have these small tags.

Serif Font
Times New Roman

Sans Serif Font
Arial

Serif fonts increase the readability of printed text, while sans serif fonts are better for online text. Notice, for example, that books are usually designed with serif fonts while PowerPoint slides and websites generally use sans serif fonts. The extra lines on serif fonts make letters easier to distinguish than with a sans serif font, allowing readers to increase their speed while reading long passages of text.

Serif fonts have a more traditional and formal look than the more modern-looking sans serif fonts. A printed document in Georgia, Baskerville, or Times New Roman font looks more serious and important than a message in Calibri, Arial, or Comic Sans. Because business letters are normally now sent to formalize information or to convey a sense of importance, the more traditional serif fonts are more appropriate.

Business Letter Examples

The Case of Gary Chambers: Good News Messaging

Gary Chambers works in communications at APPFORMS. The company supports technology in schools through an annual O-Snapp competition in which students are challenged to create an original mobile application aimed at Maritime youth. Gary has been asked to write letters of congratulations to the finalists and invite them to spend a day at APPFORMS. On this day, students will attend seminars on m-commerce, share their experiences creating apps, and job shadow an APPFORMS employee.

The message is aimed at an external audience, so a letter or an email would be appropriate. Gary decides, however, that the message requires a more official format. A business letter adds formality to the document and importance to the students' accomplishment. Since the day students will be invited to spend at APPFORMS is two months away, the few days required for postal delivery is not an issue. The cost of postage is a worthwhile expense for the community-building that the program provides. Also, Gary knows from his own experience the impact a letter, so rarely received these days, can have on the sense of accomplishment and pride of a young person.

Gary is aware that the format, style, and language of the letter reflect the image and reputation of APPFORMS. The student might share the letter with family and friends and so it could have a broad public relations impact. In addition, the letter establishes a relationship with the student. Gary would like to convey respect for the student by delivering a clear and error-free document and by using language that is accessible to a youthful audience but appropriate for an accomplished and successful emerging professional. Although the letter is a formal channel of communication, he wants to establish a natural, working relationship with the student. He will use language that is not so formal as to establish a barrier between himself and his audience, but not so informal as to diminish the importance of the award or to compromise his professionalism. Gary would like the message to have a strong emotional impact for the student.

His message needs to contain the note of congratulations, an explanation of the day at APPFORMS, and a request to accept the invitation by telephone. He knows that the message is likely to be read all the way through if

- it is less than one page in length,
- he begins with the congratulations to reveal immediately the purpose of the message and to gain his reader's attention,
- he personalizes the message to each recipient, and
- he maintains his focus on the needs of his audience.

Gary constructs the following personalized message to the first award-winner on his list:

APPFORMSCanada

1600 White Horse Way, Halifax, NS A1B 2C3
(902) 555 1212 APPFORMS@app.ca

> The company letterhead includes the company name, the street address, the city and province, the postal code, the phone number, and email address.

June 12, 2016

Ms. Felicity Sarandon
2700 Sprytown Court
Halifax, NS A0T 1F9

> Gary follows Canada Post guidelines for the recipient address both here and on the envelope. The first line states the recipient's name. The second line contains the recipient's street address, and the third line includes the municipality, province, and postal code.

Dear Felicity,

> Gary opts for the comma rather than the colon here to set a slightly less formal tone.

Congratulations! I am pleased to inform you that your app "Fishcakes" is one of the finalists in the APPFORMS O-Snapp competition. Your app to identify free and cheap eats throughout the Maritimes impressed the team at APPFORMS with its unique and youthful design and its relevance to Maritime youth.

> He personalizes the letter by using the student's name and referring to specific details of the student's app in the first paragraph.

> He begins with the purpose of the message: to congratulate the student on becoming a finalist.

We invite you to attend a special event for our finalists on August 25. In the morning, you are invited to meet the APPFORMS team and your fellow finalists and to tour our facilities. You will then have the opportunity to attend sessions on the emerging and exciting field of m-commerce. After lunch with our management team, you will meet individually with a person in a field of your choice, observe the work environment, and perhaps even assist with one of our exciting new projects.

> Gary keeps the focus on the student by making "you" the subject of the sentence.

Please let us know by August 10 if you accept this invitation by phoning my administrative assistant at (902) 555-4033. He will confirm your email address and ask you for some additional information. After we receive your acceptance, we will send you a complete schedule for the day and a T-shirt to wear to the event.

> Gary indicates clearly with specific instructions what the student should do in response to the message.

Congratulations again, Felicity. I very much look forward to meeting you.

Regards,

Gary Chambers
Coordinator, O-Snapp Competition

The Case of Hamish Iosepho: Letter of Complaint

Hamish Iosepho works as an administrative assistant at APPFORMS. Last year, the city contracted out snow removal. In January, one of the contractors, Smurfy's Lawncare and Snow Removal Service, damaged one corner of the APPFORMS building with a small bulldozer. APPFORMS filed a complaint with the city, which forwarded the complaint to the contractor. It is now June, and no repairs have been done. On behalf of APPFORMS, Hamish phoned the contractor to complain about the lack of response concerning the damage and request that the situation be addressed immediately. The contractor's receptionist said she would check into the problem and respond as soon as possible.

A week later, Hamish receives a letter from the company in response to his request. He opens the letter:

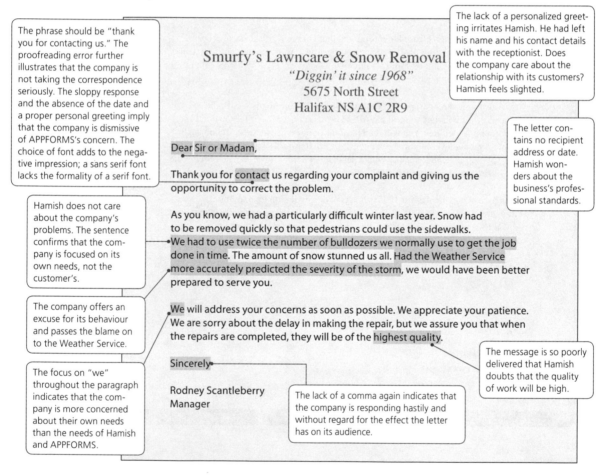

The phrase should be "thank you for contacting us." The proofreading error further illustrates that the company is not taking the correspondence seriously. The sloppy response and the absence of the date and a proper personal greeting imply that the company is dismissive of APPFORMS's concern. The choice of font adds to the negative impression; a sans serif font lacks the formality of a serif font.

The lack of a personalized greeting irritates Hamish. He had left his name and his contact details with the receptionist. Does the company care about the relationship with its customers? Hamish feels slighted.

The letter contains no recipient address or date. Hamish wonders about the business's professional standards.

Hamish does not care about the company's problems. The sentence confirms that the company is focused on its own needs, not the customer's.

The company offers an excuse for its behaviour and passes the blame on to the Weather Service.

The focus on "we" throughout the paragraph indicates that the company is more concerned about their own needs than the needs of Hamish and APPFORMS.

The message is so poorly delivered that Hamish doubts that the quality of work will be high.

The lack of a comma again indicates that the company is responding hastily and without regard for the effect the letter has on its audience.

Smurfy's Lawncare & Snow Removal
"Diggin' it since 1968"
5675 North Street
Halifax NS A1C 2R9

Dear Sir or Madam,

Thank you for contact us regarding your complaint and giving us the opportunity to correct the problem.

As you know, we had a particularly difficult winter last year. Snow had to be removed quickly so that pedestrians could use the sidewalks. We had to use twice the number of bulldozers we normally use to get the job done in time. The amount of snow stunned us all. Had the Weather Service more accurately predicted the severity of the storm, we would have been better prepared to serve you.

We will address your concerns as soon as possible. We appreciate your patience. We are sorry about the delay in making the repair, but we assure you that when the repairs are completed, they will be of the highest quality.

Sincerely

Rodney Scantleberry
Manager

The letter indicates to Hamish that Smurfy's does not care about the damage they caused. The letter seems to diminish his concern. Irritated by how the company has dismissed his complaint and the inappropriate response, Hamish is more determined than before to seek reparations. He writes to the district's councillor to voice his complaint:

APPFORMSCanada

1600 White Horse Way, Halifax, NS A1B 2C3
(902) 555 1212 APPFORMS@app.ca

June 23, 2016

Max Al Tawel
Central Peninsula District
24 Spring Garden Court
Halifax, NS A4C 3B2

Dear Mr. Al Tawel:

> The letter begins by clearly stating the purpose. The name and date provide essential identifying details.

I am writing to lodge a formal complaint about Smurfy's Lawncare and Snow Removal Service and its failure to repair damage done during snow removal on January 17.

On January 17, Smurfy's damaged the northwest corner of the APPFORMS building with a small bulldozer. On January 20, I filed a complaint on behalf of APPFORMS through the city's 311 call number. The representative said the contractor is responsible for the repairs, and the complaint would be forwarded to Smurfy's. No repairs were done, and on May 6, I phoned the company to request that the problem by addressed immediately. The receptionist thanked me for calling and promised to check into the problem. On June 23, I received an undated letter from Smurfy's assuring me that the problem would be addressed as soon as possible. I have attached a copy of the letter.

> This paragraph describes the problem in detail. Specific dates are provided, and Hamish refers to an attached copy of the letter from Smurfy's. The paragraph outlines the problem with short, clear sentences. Although Hamish is angry about the situation, he refrains from expressing this anger.

It has been several months since the damage was done to the building, and no repairs have been made. The damaged section of the building faces the company's visitor parking lot. APPFORMS attracts many people to the city from all over the country. The splintered wood, the hole in the façade, the scraped paint, and the orange cones reflect poorly on both APPFORMS and the city of Halifax.

> This paragraph describes the loss of reputation the company experiences as a result of the damage. Hamish also indicates that this loss of reputation reflects poorly on the city. This emotional appeal to the councillor's pride in the city strengthens his request to have the work completed.

According to the city's snow removal policy, damage to property should have been repaired by June 1. Smurfy's has not met this deadline. APPFORMS requests that you, as our district's councillor, address this problem with Smurfy's and ensure that the repairs are done within two weeks. Thank you for your time in assisting us.

Sincerely,

Hamish Iosepho

Hamish Iosepho
Administrative Assistant

> Hamish briefly summarizes the problem. He then states what action should be taken and includes a deadline. To show goodwill, he concludes by thanking the councillor for his time.

In writing his complaint, Hamish

- clearly states the purpose of his letter,
- describes the problem,
- explains the impact of the problem,
- states what action should be taken and by when, and
- ends on a positive note to express goodwill.

The Case of Abdul Hamza: Bad News Messaging

In addition to his work as a managing partner at APPFORMS, Abdul Hamza serves as a community councillor in the western part of Halifax. In a letter to the editor in this week's newspaper, a resident and business owner, Eddy Bateman, expressed anger over the city's request that he remove a sign he had placed along the highway advertising his family restaurant. The sign was professionally designed and painted. Local officials told Eddy that he could not place the sign on a limited-access highway, and it had to be removed immediately. In his letter, Eddy argued that the request to remove the sign goes against the community's goal to attract tourism; his sign could bring much-needed business to the area. In addition to writing to the newspaper, Eddy wrote a letter to the council that accused it of going too far with its regulations.

Abdul seeks to maintain the goodwill of the community member, but he also wants to uphold the community's standards for roadside signage, which other members of the community regard as visual pollution and as a distraction—and therefore a safety issue—on public highways. In the past, signs were permitted along the highways, but the large number of signs affected the beauty of the landscape, and they cluttered the roadside shoulder intended for emergency use. The community regulations, available online, clearly state that signs are no longer permitted.

The community council supports the removal of the sign, and Abdul is tasked with writing Eddy to inform him that, despite the sign's professional design and visual appeal, it cannot be placed along the highway. He composes his first draft, which focuses heavily on the legal justification of the bad news.

HALIFAX WEST COMMUNITY COUNCIL
1867 Confederation Drive
Halifax West, NS A2D 2I5
www.hwcc@ourgov.ca

June 14, 2016

Mr. Eddy Bateman
Farfetched Family Restaurant
500 Moosehead Place
Halifax West, NS A2D 3P9

Dear Mr. Bateman:

Thank you for your letter of June 7 to the community council.

As part of our area improvements, all signs along Highway 194 must be removed. Our research indicates that people in Halifax West do not like the excessive roadside signage that has appeared over the last two years. Although your sign has been professionally created, we cannot make an exception to the ban on signs. Our regulations (bylaw C-540) clearly state that "no mobile signage, meaning any sign intended for temporary use during business hours and erected and positioned without need of mechanical equipment, can be placed along a limited access public highway, which is defined as a thoroughfare over which no easement or right of access exists by property owners abutting said highway, thus enabling unimpeded traffic flow by vehicles."

Your sign cannot be placed along a limited access highway. Please refer to the Halifax West stipulations provided on our website.

In service to our community,

Abdul Hamza

Abdul Hamza
Halifax West Community Council

Abdul reviews his letter. He has opened the letter with a positive note of thanks. He then explains the reasons for the council's decision, and tells Eddy what actions he needs to take: Eddy should not place the sign along the highway and should review the bylaw.

The letter format is correct. The return address is followed by the date and the recipient address. The second paragraph looks a bit long, but Abdul thinks the letter has a sufficient amount of white space.

But he is not satisfied with the letter. It sounds cold and unsympathetic because of the legal language. Even the opening statement of thanks sounds harsh and impersonal. The message is strongly focused on the bad news.

Adbul considers the purpose of his letter. He wants Eddy to accept that he must obey the bylaw, but Abdul also wants to maintain a good relationship with a community member. The opening line is somewhat positive, but he has put a second positive statement (the reference to the professional quality of the sign) in a subordinate clause. This clause is followed by "we cannot." Abdul does not want to emphasize what cannot be done. He wants to state what Eddy can do, rather than focus on the negative.

He reviews the situation. Eddy is right that the community council wants to attract tourists to the area to improve the local economy. Abdul appreciates Eddy's efforts to establish a business consistent with this goal. Eddy's mobile sign is tasteful and professional. He also truly appreciates Eddy's letter since it reveals his interest in and dedication to the community.

Adbul decides to revise his letter to emphasize the mutual goals of both the community council and Eddy and to emphasize the positive aspects of Eddy's efforts. He wants to be clear that the sign cannot be placed on the highway, but rather than present the legal limitations, he would like to stress the possibilities. He wants to turn the focus away from the bad news of what cannot be done toward the positive of what can be done.

He drafts a new letter.

HALIFAX WEST COMMUNITY COUNCIL

1867 Confederation Drive
Halifax West, NS A2D 2I5
www.hwcc@ourgov.ca

June 14, 2016

Mr. Eddy Bateman
Farfetched Family Restaurant
500 Moosehead Place
Halifax West, NS A2D 3P9

Dear Mr. Bateman:

Thank you for your letter of June 7 to the council regarding the placing of signs on Highway 194. We appreciate your concerns and the opportunity to address them.

As you know, increased tourism can increase the prosperity of our community. The council applauds your effort to attract new business to the area through roadside signage, and we would like to support you in these efforts. In response to the community's growing concerns over the amount of signage on Highway 194 and the need to maintain the shoulder for emergency use, the council will erect two uniform signs to direct traffic to businesses in the area. These signs will eliminate the hazards of mobile signs along a limited access highway and preserve the beauty of our community. Although businesses appearing on the sign will incur a small fee to offset the costs, Halifax West will erect and maintain the signs. I have enclosed a drawing of the proposed uniform directional sign.

In addition to the uniform directional sign, you can place your current sign along adjacent roads. Whynot Road is a major thoroughfare leading to Highway 194. Your sign can be placed anywhere along the road as long as it does not block vehicle access or pedestrian walkways. I have enclosed a map of the area and highlighted areas where you can legally place your sign. If you would like additional details on the bylaws affecting signage, please refer to our website at Haliwest.ca/signage.

Thank you for your efforts toward a thriving Halifax West. Please let me know if we can include you on our new uniform directional signs or if I can answer any questions about sign placement.

Best regards,

[signature]

Abdul Hamza
Halifax West Community Council

Enclosures

The Case of Glenda Goodwin: Letter of Apology

Glenda Goodwin manages APPFORMS's social media platforms, including a company blog, Facebook, Pinterest, Twitter, and Google Plus. Along with her team, she manages APPFORMS's social identity, develops approaches for reaching stakeholders through social media, and interacts with customers to maintain an ongoing conversation.

This week has been particularly busy for Glenda. One member of her team had emergency surgery and is now absent, so her department is short-staffed. With the recent launch of a series of android apps, Glenda has felt pressure to increase the number and frequency of social media posts. One of her team members suggested the post "#whatIwant an app that does the thinking for me" as part of a conversation about an app that creates grocery lists from online recipes. Typically, content is proposed by team members, all members of the team review the proposed items, and the message is then posted. Rather than subject the proposed message for a quick review by the team, Glenda posted the item.

Within a couple of minutes, APPFORMS received 100 responses to the post. Two days previously, a radical group made global headlines when it overtook a girls' school serving a minority population, burned all of its books, and terrified the students, who were now too afraid to return to school. The hashtag "whatIwant" had been used by various groups to call attention to the need to support girls who want an education but who live in areas where the education of girls is forbidden or unavailable. The hashtag had been used in thousands of posts globally.

Glenda's team had seen the hashtag but had not verified its original meaning. Much of the team's energy was being spent on social media that focused on the release of the new apps, and they had not been monitoring current happenings and trends. Glenda was not aware of the hashtag's use to support girls' education, so the proposed post and comment did not raise alarms.

As soon as Glenda received the first responses from outraged stakeholders and members of the public, she investigated the issue. She was horrified to discover the implications of the post. These stakeholders were right; the use of the hashtag at this time was terribly inappropriate, and the reference to wanting an app that "does the thinking" at a time when girls are being denied the opportunity to learn was appalling.

Glenda immediately withdrew the offensive post. She knows she must issue an apology as soon as possible. Apologies from organizations are common now that organizations are held to high standards of corporate social responsibility. Because communication between consumer and business is more direct and more frequent through technology, Glenda realizes that her response must be quick, but, to avoid making the situation worse, carefully crafted. She will first send an apology using social media and then write an open letter of apology.

Models of these apologies are everywhere. Glenda starts by doing some online research. She finds an article by Josh Bloch of CBC News entitled "Age of the Public Apology: How Saying Sorry Has Gone Pro." Bloch cites Chris Lehane, author of *Masters of Disaster: The Ten Commandments of Damage Control.* According to Lehane, Bloch writes, the apology should be delivered soon after the offensive comment has been made. "I'm sorry" should appear early in the message, the message should indicate acceptance of responsibility rather than offer excuses, and the apology should state what actions will be taken and include assurances that the offence will not occur again.

She finds a similar structure outlined by Perfect Apology in "Sample Apology Letter: An Analysis of the JetBlue Apology" (www.perfectapology.com/sample-apology-letter.html). The article breaks down JetBlue's apology for poor customer service following a severe winter storm that caused travel delays. The airline's apology began with, "We are sorry and embarrassed. But most of all, we are deeply sorry." This beginning satisfies Lehane's suggestion to say "I'm sorry" early in the message. As the Perfect Apology article points out, the second paragraph of JetBlue's apology explains what happened in the incident without casting blame elsewhere, even on the weather. The letter goes on to acknowledge the harm the incident caused its customers. JetBlue then outlines the measures to be taken to ensure a similar problem does not occur again. The airline's desire to repair and maintain its relationship with its customers is evident in the offer of compensation and the statement, "Nothing is more important than regaining your trust, and all of us here hope you will give us the opportunity to welcome you onboard again soon and provide you the positive JetBlue Experience you have come to expect from us."

Glenda extracts from these sources her structure for the apology:

- a direct apology,
- an explanation of how and why the problem occurred,
- an acknowledgement of the hurt or dissatisfaction of stakeholders,
- the efforts to correct problem, and
- a desire to continue the relationship.

APPFORMS**Canada**

1600 White Horse Way, Halifax, NS A1B 2C3
(902) 555 1212 APPFORMS@app.ca

To our customers and our global community,

We are sincerely sorry.

> This sentence apologizes clearly and directly. Its placement at the start of the letter in a separate paragraph indicates the primary purpose in writing.

A few days ago, the world watched in horror as young women fled their school. Schoolbooks burned behind them. The fear and pain on the girls' faces, the flames consuming pages of history, math, and literature, and the disdainful glare of those who committed this violation are now etched in our collective memory.

> This paragraph explains what caused the problem. Glenda considers explaining the situation in more detail, but she does not want to appear to be making excuses. She opts for a simple, straightforward approach.

As the world watched in horror, our focus was internal. Without realizing the connection between #whatIwant and the terrible events at the school, we posted a message that seemingly dismissed the importance of women's education.

The inappropriate hashtag affected many of you in our community, and particularly girls and women. Our thoughtless use of the hashtag seemed to trivialize the value of girls' education. Many of you expressed justifiable anger at the use of the events at the school to promote a product.

> Glenda herself is mortified by the implications of the post. By using the hashtag to promote an app that "does the thinking," APPFORMS has diminished the importance of thinking for women. Here she seeks to acknowledge the harm caused by the post.

APPFORMS will restructure its process of reviewing and posting on social media. We realize, now more than ever, that the need to communicate with the public frequently and quickly should never supersede the need for careful monitoring of international events and public concerns. APPFORMS currently supports girls' educational programming in the local area. We will bolster these efforts as well as contribute to international efforts to raise money for the girls' school that has lost so much.

> In this paragraph, Glenda states what will be done to correct the problem and affirms the company's efforts to contribute to girls' education.

We look forward to working together to create a world in which all children receive what they want in an education.

Most sincerely,

APPFORMS Board of Directors and Management

> In this final sentence, Glenda seeks to establish a continuing relationship. She reinforces this goal with the words *working together*. She also echoes the word *want* from the hashtag to reaffirm the commitment of the company to this cause.

◉ SCOPE

The four scenarios in this chapter illustrate the elements of SCOPE: strategy, content, outcome, presentation, and ethics.

Strategy involves making choices to deliver a message while maintaining relationships. In developing a clear strategy, each writer assesses the audience and the purpose of the message. Whether the message is positive or negative, the ultimate goal is to maintain the relationship with the audience. The writer develops a strategy based on the content of the message and the recipient's needs and sensitivity to the issue. Gary Chambers develops a strategy based on his assessment of the needs of his young audience, and Glenda Goodwin develops a strategy based on the extreme sensitivity resulting from current events. The letter from Smurfy's Lawncare reflects a failure to develop a thoughtful strategy in dealing with consumers, and it irritates the recipient rather than repairs the relationship.

The *content* of a letter is dictated both by the information that needs to be expressed and the careful selection of detail. Rather than focus his message on what Eddy Bateman cannot do, Abdul Hamza focuses on what he *can* do by moving the sign and by using the new city-sponsored signage. By turning the focus from the delivery of bad news to how he can help Eddy, Abdul maintains positive relations. The deliberate selection of content is also evident in Glenda's choice of details. She wants to explain how the inappropriate hashtag came to be used, but does not do so because she runs the risk of appearing to make excuses for the mistake.

To achieve the desired *outcome*, the writer focuses on the audience's needs. The writer carefully analyzes the audience, selects the best approach for this audience, and addresses the audience's needs. The outcome Gary seeks is the student's participation at the event and the positive relationship that comes from community involvement. Abdul seeks to reinforce the policy for roadside signage, retain his constituent's commitment to the community, and come to a mutually satisfying resolution. Glenda seeks to repair the damage done by an offensive tweet and reinforce her company's values.

Each letter conforms to modern standards of *presentation*. Each writer uses a block format and standard elements of structure and design. Within this format, the writers make choices. Gary chooses a comma rather than a colon to establish a natural, relaxed relationship with the recipient. Glenda states her direct apology in a short, clear sentence to give it strength and to make the company's accountability clear. She uses short paragraphs to reinforce this message. The font and layout reflect the professionalism required in all of these scenarios.

Finally, the writers exhibit *ethics* in their approaches. They avoid ambiguous or misleading language. Their messages reinforce the values of the organizations they represent by considering the social consequences of their actions and words. Abdul considers carefully the social consequences of the legalese his first letter contains and the distance created by the language. He modifies his letter to focus on the needs of the people he serves and removes the inaccessible legal language. Each of the four letters exhibits professionalism that reflect ethical values.

Chapter Summary

This chapter presented methods for maintaining business relationships through formal channels of written communication with external audiences. To maintain these relationships, each writer considers the purpose of the message and the audience's needs. We presented four examples of letters that convey good news, a complaint, bad news, and an apology.

Discussion Questions

1. The modern business letter format is derived from standards of letter writing developed during the Middle Ages. *The Principles of Letter Writing* by Anonymous of Bologna and translated by James J. Murphy (http://medieval.ucdavis.edu/20B/Ars.Dictandi.html) instructs its medieval reader to craft a letter in five parts: the Salutation, the Securing of Good-will, the Narration, the Petition, and the Conclusion.

   The salutation offers a greeting appropriate for the rank or position of the intended audience or that identifies the relationship between sender and receiver, for example, "To Elizabeth, the closest of friends." The securing of good-will is intended to influence the reader through expressions of humility and favourable language. The narration explains the situation that prompts the message, while the petition calls for action. The conclusion closes the letter by affirming the benefits of the action or by simply bidding farewell.

   In what ways have modern business letters retained the standards from the Middle Ages? What aspects have been abandoned?

2. In New Zealand, the period is omitted after a title such as Mrs or Dr. When writing a business letter to a potential client in New Zealand, should you use the period as is customary in Canada or should you adopt the New Zealand standard? How do you determine when to adopt the standards of another country and when to use the business standards dominant in your own culture?

3. Writers are often instructed to begin messages with a "buffer," some positive or neutral information to soften and delay the bad news. Cushioning bad news is an effort to make the readers accept it. What characteristics of the audience would make this approach appropriate?

4. In 2013, Aaron Gilmore, a politician in Christchurch, New Zealand, was refused alcohol in a restaurant. He expressed his displeasure to the waiter. When his response became public, he tweeted the following: "I've apologised again for any offence that may have been taken from the behaviour of my group and I that a waiter may have received on Sat." What does he gain from his use of language? Is his use of language ethical?

5. Global standards are evolving with increased international communications. How can you maintain familiarity with business writing practices in other regions? What practices should you adopt in writing to an international business audience? How do you decide?

6. Various complimentary closes can be used in business letters. In what, if any, situations would you use each of the following closings? Under what conditions would you not use a particular closing?

Sincerely yours	Sincerely
Best wishes	Peace
Kind regards	Regards
Warm regards	Best regards
Fondly	Very best
Cordially	Affectionately
Love	I remain, as ever

Exercises

1. Your business makes eco-friendly packaging and annually awards a youth with a scholarship for an outdoor adventure camp. The awards are given to young people who demonstrate concern for the environment and actively engage in community projects such as recycling, tree planting, and collecting trash. The youth are nominated by their school or church.

Write a letter to this year's recipient, Kyler Tian, informing him that he has received the award. Invent the details of the message.

2. Broadband Internet service is subsidized in rural and northern areas. This subsidy is necessary to ensure these areas are economically viable in a modern, knowledge-driven world. An urban area group argues that subsidies are also needed for low-income city dwellers to ensure that they too are not economically disadvantaged. This group has asked a telecommunications provider to offer low-income families broadband Internet for $10 per month.

The company appreciates the need for inexpensive service in the community, but with recent updates and expansion, the company feels it cannot absorb the costs. Write a letter to the community group from the telecommunications provider that explains why it can't provide broadband Internet service for $10 per month but that maintains its relationship with the community. Invent the names of the organizations and other details as necessary.

3. Sarath Kearney of Show Us Your Crack Window Repair received the following letter from his security alarm company:

Dear Sir/Madam:

To accommodate the increasing demand for phone lines, the province will begin using 10-digit phone numbers. This decision by the phone providers means that we will have to update your alarm system and the system of every home and business we serve.

Your system must be updated for a 10-digit number by November 1 for your system to remain in working order. FAILURE TO UPDATE WILL RENDER THE ALARM SYSTEM INOPERABLE.

Your security system is set up for use with a seven-digit number. For uninterrupted security service, call our office at 902 555-9020 to arrange a time for our technician to visit your establishment. You will be charged our normal fee of $180 for this visit.

We are in no way responsible for the problems this update has caused.

The visit will require only a few minutes. Because we have so many businesses to attend to, please make yourself available for an entire morning (8–12) or afternoon (1–5) during which we can stop by.

Sincerely,
Security Blanket Alarm Company

Sarath is outraged by the cost of this service update. He believes that the company is taking advantage of the province's switch to 10-digit phone numbers to make money. The fee is high considering that all the update requires is punching three additional numbers into the system. His outrage is made worse by the company's focus on its own needs throughout the letter. He understands that the company must

make the change, but he is irritated by the security company's focus.

Revise the letter so that the relationship between Show Us Your Crack Window Repair and Security Blanket Alarm Company is maintained.

4. An automaker has been accused of violating advertising standards by producing a TV advertisement that shows a car and its young driver

travelling at high speed through an intersection just as the light turns green. It is clear that the car was travelling too fast to stop for a red light had it not turned green when it did. The ad is released during a period when a greater number of pedestrians than usual have been run over at intersections. The automaker had aimed to appeal to its customers' desire for excitement and the open road, but instead offended its audience with an apparent disregard for safety. Write an open letter of apology to the public for the company's insensitivity.

Good Advice or Bad?

1. In her 2014 article entitled "The Case for 'Living' Models" in *Business Communication Quarterly*, Valerie Creelman notes researchers' dismissal of the indirect approach to negative messages, in which the delivery of the bad news follows the writer's efforts to establish goodwill. Creelman writes, "Despite scholarly evidence supporting the use of indirect, buffered openings, researchers have nonetheless challenged the validity of this technique, concluding that it is dispensable, irrelevant, patronizing, and, in some instances, downright phoney" (p. 182). However, some textbooks and manuals state that when an audience is likely to be unreceptive to the news, the indirect message is the best approach. Good advice or bad? Why?

2. You have worked at a resort all summer and are preparing to return to university. Your employer is a family friend, and you have spent time with him all summer both on the job and at family events. His son is one of your best friends. He has asked you to submit a letter formally resigning from your position two weeks prior to your departure. It seems awkward to you to write a formal letter to a friend. The employer's son, your friend, says a casual approach is fine. He even suggests referring to the last boat trip you took together and your friendly competition for the best catch of the day. Good advice or bad? Why?

3. WikiHow suggests using "To Whom It May Concern" followed by a colon when writing a formal letter to an unnamed recipient. Another source suggests using "Respected Sir or Ma'am." Good advice or bad? Why?

Strategic Language: Adapting to Change

To maintain business relationships through written communication, writers must be able to adapt to the constantly shifting expectations of their audience. Expectations change because of generational differences, immigration, technology, and shifting social values. The debate on the use of *they* as a singular pronoun is one illustration of the way language reflects changing social values.

The use of *they* as a singular pronoun is a current example of the way changing social values affects grammar. William Strunk's *The Elements of Style* (1918) recommends the use of *he* unless the person referred to is clearly female. If the gender is unknown, *he* is an acceptable pronoun. Strunk points out that using *he or she* is awkward and affects the flow of the sentence.

The use of *he* to refer to anyone is no longer acceptable; however, the absence in the English language of a gender-neutral singular pronoun is problematic. One acceptable method is to alternate between *he* and *she* throughout the document. However, this still excludes people who do not identify themselves as either male or female. While new gender-neutral words have been proposed, such as the pronouns *xe*, *xem*, and *xyr*, which have been approved by the Vancouver School Boards, these words have not been uniformly adopted by users of Canadian English.

Another acceptable alternative to *he* is the use of the plural. Instead of "The researcher must check his sources," the writer could state, "Researchers must check their sources." Yet another alternative is to avoid the pronouns altogether. For example, the statement "Someone left his computer in the office," could be rewritten as, "A computer was left in the office."

Increasingly, *they* is accepted as a singular pronoun. When Facebook allowed its users in the United States to select from over 50 gender identities in February 2014, it also allowed users to select the pronoun others could use in reference to them. The choices included the use of the singular *they*. Shortly afterwards, *The Economist* published an article entitled "Johnson: Singular They," by R.L.G., celebrating Facebook's decision and pointing out that the singular *they* has been used for centuries. The sentence "Everyone should meet their sales goals in December" should be considered correct. The author tells readers to "think about your audience, gauge the effect you're going for, consider how formal the situation, and make the choice that works best" (www.economist.com/blogs/prospero/2014/02/pronouns#comments).

As the article in *The Economist* suggests, the decision of whether to use *he* or *she*, *his* or *hers*, *s/he*, *they*, or *their*, or another pronoun is based on the purpose, audience, and context. In formal business writing directed to an older or more conservative audience, the use of the plural to avoid using a singular *they* might be the best choice. Other audiences might see the use of singular *they* as progressive and therefore preferable. As with all decisions in writing, the word choice requires strategic decision-making and sensitivity to audience needs.

Additional Resources

Guidelines for Gender-Neutral Language. (2014). Government of Canada. Retrieved from www.noslangues-ourlanguages.gc.ca/bien-well/fra-eng/style/nonsexistguidelines-eng.html.

The Perfect Apology. Retrieved from www.perfect apology.com.

CHAPTER SIX

Persuasive Techniques for Writing Short Reports—Informative, Progress, and Status Reports

Learning Objectives

A. **Understand** the reasons for writing short reports.
B. **Understand** the purpose of short reports.
C. **Understand** form and content while writing short reports.
D. **Recognize** the importance of making structure explicit in a short report and the various design elements of such a report.
E. **Develop** skills and strategies to present complex information in a short report.
F. **Incorporate** techniques of argumentation, persuasion, and presentation effectively when writing short reports.
G. **Present** oneself and the organization favourably by using evidence, rhetorical tools, and ethics while writing short reports.

The Story So Far

Chapter 5 was about maintaining relationships with external stakeholders. You saw how letters from an organization are created with attention to both form and content. These letters are intended to keep the receiver (client, supplier, etc.) interested and engaged, and to nurture a long-term relationship. We followed the cases of Gary Chambers, Hamish Iosepho, Abdul Hamza, and Glenda Goodwin as they wrote letters of invitation, complaint, bad news, and apology. The four examples highlight the importance of various aspects of writing letters to maintain external relationships. Meanwhile, three APPFORMS interns were tasked with studying the market for possible new apps. Their managers asked them to do some research and analysis, and provide progress updates by submitting short, informal progress reports.

Introduction

Reports, whether written or spoken, are often the main channel for communicating about organizational events to audiences within or external to an organization. The *Oxford Dictionaries* define a *report* as "a spoken or written account of something that one has observed, heard, done, or investigated." Managers often ask their employees to submit progress reports about work in progress. They in turn submit reports to their superiors about the progress of their projects and details of any changes in project status. These reports may include information about project completion, analyses or research about feasibility, or even investigations when something unexpected occurs. There are formal reports (status, progress, investigative, etc.) when employees produce a report based on their positions in the organizations. There are also normal reports (feasibility, analytical, or research) that are not based on any official positions or formal organizational procedures. Where there are legal requirements, then statutory reports are prepared in accordance to the requirements of the law. Informational, research, and analytical reports can also be based on the functional aspects in an organization where information, analysis, or research is required on certain aspects of the organization's activities.

Each of these reports, regardless of type or form, is often the culmination of a set of activities within an organization. Progress, interim, and status reports are the exception. Managers may require short status updates or slightly longer project updates to allow them to make business decisions and adapt to changing requirements of the project, such as the need for more resources, modifying techniques, or speeding up the project to meet deadlines.

The ability to write professional reports is an extremely important and critical skill for the business communication student. However, before learning to write full-length reports, it would be good for business communication students to understand the mechanics and need for understanding, creating, developing, and writing shorter reports. This skill will allow students to keep track of projects, ensure the projects get completed on time, highlight the organizational resources required to complete the projects, and keep their managers informed about the process and possible outcomes. There are various forms of short, informal reports and they play an important role in conveying critical business information to organizational decision-makers. In this chapter, we will focus on both the form and content of the short business reports. We will follow APPFORMS's employees as they write reports for a couple of business situations and work through the mechanics of the reports.

Form, Content, and Everything in Between

Short reports can follow specific formats or not. The report writer can always choose the format based on the context, the amount of time the intended receiver has to process the information provided, the specific information the receiver is looking for, and what the writer needs to convey in order to move the project along. While formal reports tend to follow clear formats for ease of reading, shorter reports can take any form, such as a simple paragraph as part of an email memo, a slightly longer version containing more details, or some combination of the two. As always, the writer needs to provide clear evidence to support any assertions or claims made. These can take the form of graphs, charts, tables, timelines, and so on.

Whatever format the writer chooses, he or she needs to ensure that the message is delivered clearly to the receiver, who can then take relevant decisions. Word-processing applications like Microsoft Word or Google Docs have standard forms and templates for most types of business communication pieces, including memos, letters, and short and long reports. While these templates are a great place to start, the format or structure for your specific business need will be dictated by the audience and the context, and the modern business communicator needs to choose carefully

Form of a Report

In the context of a business report, *form* addresses all aspects of a report's appearance, including its design. This includes length, the appropriate use of relevant and informative headings, indentation, bulleted or numbered lists (**enumeration**), and the appropriate use of paragraph breaks with clear and effective transitions between paragraphs and sections of the report. Form also includes the use of grammatically correct sentences, consistent use of active voice, and choice of font type and size for readability. The writer needs to make sure that every sentence is there for a purpose, which is to present the information clearly and honestly so that the reader can make clear business decisions. A report that is attractive and readable but takes liberties with the facts is unethical and can lead to erroneous conclusions. It will be detrimental to both the writer and the business organization. However, a report that is true to the facts and gives clear recommendations, but does not have any structure or good form is also self-defeating because the reader will be unable to follow the writer's line of thought and may get frustrated in the process. This is why form and content are inseparable, and the writer must always present the content with the target audience in mind.

Content of a Report

Content refers to whatever the business situation requires. It can be a brief status update contained in an email to a manager or co-worker. It can be a short progress report discussing timelines and resource needs and submitted on a standard organizational template. It can be short reports documenting business events or incidents, such as first information reports, emergency medical technician (EMT) reports, accident reports on construction sites, financial stock market downturn reports, audit reports, or brief sales forecast reports. Content of longer research or analytical reports involves more detail and possibly more length. In addition to providing the background and context, such reports take time to develop a clear, evidence-based argument supporting any claims made at the beginning of the report. This does not mean that short reports can skip evidence-based arguments. These are always needed, regardless of the report's length, so that managers can follow the context and progress of any organizational task.

Most reports seek to answer the following questions:

- Who—who is creating the report, who it is meant for or who asked for it, and who, if any, are the internal or external stakeholders (people, groups, organizations) involved
- What—what the report is about, starting with a clear and informative report title, what the business gap is, and what possible options are available. What also refers to the recommendations or courses of action that need to be taken, what choices are available, and what strategies should be adopted and pursued
- When—any or all time-related references regarding the events being reported
- Where—the location of the events being reported on, as well as where the report is being created
- Why—why the report is called for and the reasons behind its creation, including context and background
- How—the methodologies involved in filling the business gap and in creating the report, how the events being reported evolved or came into existence, and how any recommendations or conclusions being made or drawn follow a certain line of thinking
  - Methodologies can be research, analysis, interpretation schemes, historical or archival information, and so on
  - Sources cited to add credibility can be internal and external
  - Recommendations and conclusions are arrived at after synthesizing the findings from research, considering multiple perspectives and options, and arriving at the best option for that point in time

Regardless of the type of report, the content for all business situations needs to start with some sort of claim statement. This statement (also called a topic sentence or topic statement or thesis statement) is aimed at answering the primary question or questions that may have been raised by the person or persons requesting the report. By providing a clear background or context for the business situation and identifying the reason for the questions, the writer is identifying the business gap. The answer to the questions will most likely be the solution for filling the business gap. Every time this is done successfully at the start of any report or business communication, the writer has created an effective introduction, which gains the readers' interest and encourages them to read further.

As discussed in Chapter 4, the business writer will begin to weave the narrative or content by using simple to complex rhetorical tools such as compare and contrast, cause and effect, and clear, evidence-based argumentation. The writer can frame knowledge to allow the reader to situate the topic under discussion, present new information based on known or accepted knowledge, and effectively use **clustering** and **roadmaps** to guide the reader.

We will now look at some scenarios where APPFORMS co-op students need to research or analyze certain business activities, and submit informational or progress reports to their managers.

The Case of Bahram Fonseca: Human Resources Hiring Project

Juanita Olson, director of human resources at APPFORMS, asks Bahram Fonseca, the HR co-op student, to come up with a hiring plan for when an organization faces a crisis. The purpose of this project is to provide HR managers with a customizable format to evaluate their hiring needs and make recommendations to organizational leaders. As Bahram begins work on the project, he looks at different organizational crises to see what steps the organizations took in order to respond to these crises, particularly from the HR perspective.

A couple of weeks later, Juanita asks Bahram to provide her with an update on his progress. Bahram decides to write a brief report for Juanita. After reviewing the different organizational crises he has examined, he decides to write about the Procter & Gamble Pampers Dry Max issue that the company faced in 2010 because it was a well-researched and well-documented scenario. He proceeds to make assumptions around possible HR hiring scenarios that the company may have taken in order to respond to the crisis. Bahram decides to use a standard short report form that introduces the topic, provides context, and walks through some analytical approaches he has taken to proceed with his assigned task. He chooses 12-point Garamond font, for ease of reading. He also decides to use appropriate labels, headings, and subheadings using the Microsoft Word styles menu. He adds a decision matrix on possible hiring scenarios and provides a timeline for the project completion. Finally, Bahram includes a short list of references for sourcing the information he has used for his assigned task.

Introduction

In 2010, Procter and Gamble (P&G) faced a serious issue of customers, particularly mothers of babies using the newly introduced Pampers Dry Max Diapers, complaining that the new diapers were giving their babies serious diaper rashes. Initially, P&G insisted that the diapers were not to be blamed for these reactions, but under growing pressure from concerned mothers, store owners and the media, P&G responded to the crisis. As I have been tasked to look at a human resources angle for such corporate scenarios, particularly with respect to hiring new staff to help mitigate the crisis, I looked at a few sources that could provide information to support the creation of a hiring plan for the organization. Since the Dry Max controversy has continued to unfold, new information has come to light. Specifically, I looked at the possibility of P&G working on the recovery of the Pampers brand equity through additional hiring of full-time employees as well as outside contractors.

Background

> As Bahram begins to edit his short report, he decides to bold face all the headings and leave only subheadings in normal type, without bold facing

As the Pampers Dry Max issue unfolded, parents were growing more concerned not only about the safety of the diapers currently on sale, but the apparent decrease in quality of the diapers, unaware that P&G was slipstreaming in a new and improved format onto shelves across North America (Gillin, 2012). Assuming that part of rebuilding the brand would require P&G to hire new staff in key areas like public relations (PR), I developed a decision matrix to look at the options of full-time and part-time hiring of new staff, their training, and deployment.

Analysis

Sub-Issue 1 – Full-Time Hiring

First, I looked at the possibility of P&G bringing on board additional PR and communications officers to interact with media and various other public entities. I have completed a preliminary analysis of three hiring scenarios. Using a simple weighting scheme of 1, 2 and 3, I created a decision matrix to summarize the results of the analysis and this is depicted in Figure 1.

At first glance, two to four new hires seems optimal, although additional analysis will need to be done to confirm this. The areas to be placed under scrutiny are total cost, ease of implementation, long-term value provided by the staff, and the speed at which we can implement the option. Two things seem to pop out as unusual when we look at the matrix: hiring an additional four to seven employees is rated as being easier to implement,

continued

As Bahram is reviewing and editing he feels that this sentence is rather complex. He feels he will need to rewrite this for improved readability

and faster to implement than two to four employees. The reasoning behind this is that hiring and training of four to seven new staff would be just as easy as hiring and training two to four new staff as they can simply select more applicants from the same total number of applicants and interviewees from a single round of interviews, allowing a greater marginal utility to be reaped from each additional new hire, leading to a higher rating for four to seven than two to four new hires.

Decision Matrix: Full-Time Hiring Scope			
Category/# of New Hires	2 to 4	4 to 7	7 to 10
Cost	3	2	1
Ease of implementation	2	3	1
Long-Term Value	1	3	2
Speed of implementation	2	3	1
Total	8	11	5

Bahram notes that he could put the table caption at the top of the table, as it will provide early information to the reader about the contents of the table, before the reader starts reading down the table

Table 1: Full-Time Hiring Plan Decision Matrix

He feels that this sentence too requires a rewrite

In terms of speed, P&G can conduct training sessions with more people attending, while delivering almost the same amount of value in terms of training to a larger group of new hires, again leading to greater marginal utility per new hire, leading to a higher score. This will allow P&G to best manage their resources and maximize the total long-term value of each individual additional staff member, assuming they do not leave the firm in the foreseeable future. They can add value by mitigating the damage to P&G's brand image and reputation as the crisis is being dealt with. Additional analysis will have to take place on the expected turnover associated with PR officers, as well as the cost of potentially using an outside headhunting agency to recruit them. A timeline outlining progress so far and additional steps with respect to this issue is provided in Figure 1.

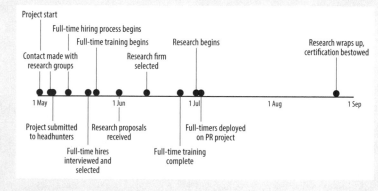

Figure 1: Preliminary Project Timeline

References

Reuters (2010, May 06). Parents Claim "Pampers" Diapers Caused Chemical Burns. *Fox News*. Retrieved from http://www.foxnews .com/story/2010/05/06/parents-claim-pampers-diapers-caused-chemical-burns.html

P. Gillan. (2012, August 29). Attack of the customers: The Pampers Dry Max crisis [Blog comment]. Retrieved from http://gillin.com/blog/2012/08/attack-of-the-customers-the-pampers-dry-max-crisis/

Bahram looks at the first draft of his short report to Juanita. He realizes that he will have to edit the report to ensure that it is free of errors. He looks at a few of the sentences he has written and realizes that he will need to rewrite them to improve readability. Bahram often struggles with his habit of writing long, complex sentences, which seem grammatically correct, but contain too much information. He realizes that this habit could frustrate the reader and decides to shorten the sentences, without losing the key information he wishes to convey. Bahram then proceeds to edit and proofread his report before sending it to Juanita.

The Case of Kirsten Hamed: Financial Markets Analysis

Niamh Trescothick, director of payroll and finance, asks Kirsten Hamed, the finance department's co-op student, to study a report by Goldman Sachs regarding the third wave of recessions. In the report, Goldman Sachs indicated that the fallout from the 2008 US housing mortgage collapse will result in a third wave of recession, specifically relating to emerging markets in the East Asia. Niamh wants Kirsten to read up about this situation and submit a report with her findings. The purpose of Kirsten's report is to see if APPFORMS can create an app that could help investors and investment analysts get current financial market information from all of the stock exchanges in the world so that they can respond to market fluctuations. But prior to embarking on creating such an app, it is important to understand what exactly was happening in these financial markets.

A few weeks after asking Kirsten to write the report, Niamh wants to know the status of her progress. Kirsten is completing her first co-op internship and is very thorough with her work. She decides to put her findings to date into a short report. After studying the original report from Goldman Sachs and looking at other sources and articles on the same subject to get a broad understanding of the situation, Kirsten feels ready. Her short report will review the financial crisis as outlined in the Goldman Sachs report, and list the outcomes and timeline she needs to produce her final report. Niamh can then take that information to decide whether to proceed with the creation of the app and use APPFORMS's resources to do so.

EMERGING MARKET INVESTMENT AND LENDING POLICY

PROGRESS REPORT

PREPARED BY:

Kirsten Hamed, Co-Op Student, Payroll and Finance Department, APPFORMS

PREPARED FOR:

Niamh Trescothick, Director of Payroll and Finance, APPFORMS

INTRODUCTION

As Kirsten reviews her report, she realizes that she can remove the underline in the headings. Since the heading is separated by good spacing, the underline does not enhance the heading

This report has been prepared to outline the progress made in creating a new investment and lending policy for emerging markets facing the third wave of the 2008 financial crisis. The Global Markets Institute, Goldman Sachs's division for public policy and regulations, oversees and facilitates advisory services for policymakers, investors, and regulators on a global scale (Goldman Sachs, 2015). The advice and recommendations given to clients directly impacts the economic climate the firm operates in, and contributes to determining future investment strategies for all departments of the firm.

The recent announcement of the third wave of the financial crisis specifically impacts many of the Global Markets Institute's clients. Emerging markets are predicted to suffer heavily and investors will require extensive guidance as the crisis approaches. In order to completely understand this situation, I will be creating a policy recommendation report. The report will outline policy strategies for investors in emerging markets during the crisis. The report is expected to be completed and ready for presentation by November 25.

ISSUE AND BACKGROUND

Kirsten's note to herself: remove underline.

The policy recommendation report will enable investment companies to provide a cohesive investment and lending policy recommendation to clients who will be most affected by the third wave of the financial crisis. In order to give the best possible recommendation to clients, many different factors must be considered. Personal preferences and biases, future market conditions, and the risks inherent to the situation must all be considered before coming to a final conclusion.

There is a real and immediate need for policy change in emerging markets. The third wave of the financial crisis is driven in large part by the economic downturn currently taking place in China, one of the largest and most influential emerging markets (Moshinsky, 2015). Chinese policymakers have been promoting excessive borrowing to encourage investment in their commodities industry since the initial financial crisis in 2008. These practices have resulted in wasteful investments and a 100 % increase in the nation's debt/GDP ratio since 2007 (Bird, 2015). Implementing a new investment and lending policy strategy in markets such as China will be necessary in order to slow this rapid downturn, secure current investments, and lay the foundation for emerging markets to return to a stable condition.

IMPLEMENTATION PLAN AND PROGRESS

There must be a strong policy plan in place for investors to ensure that they will be in a position to successfully face the coming crisis. In order to expedite the creation of this plan and focus efforts, I have broken down the work to be done into three stages, culminating with the final policy recommendation report. They are as follows:

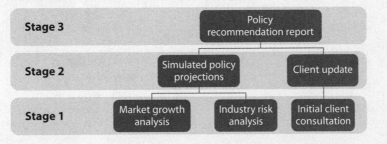

Figure 1: Proposed Stages for Final Report Delivery

Stage 1 provides the foundation on which the final report will be built. An initial consultation has already been held with each of the Global Markets Institute's major clients to outline our plan and gauge their willingness to comply with possible policy recommendations. The market growth analysis predicts the magnitude of negative growth expected for each of the emerging markets throughout the course of the financial crisis. The industry risk analysis will then calculate probabilities for expected investment returns in specific industries, given the expected market growth. Both of these analyses must be completed before Stage 2 as the simulated policy projections are contingent on their results.

The policy projections will predict the outcomes of several different policy strategies for clients regarding both their personal expected financial position, and the expected impact on the market as a whole. By taking into consideration future market and industry conditions as well as client preferences, these projections will enable investment analysts to identify the best policy for each client and clearly predict what the full

continued

impact of that policy will be. The client update will coincide with the completion of the simulated policy projections, at which time we will be able to answer questions regarding the nature of the policy we will be recommending, as well as give a definitive date for the completion of the full policy recommendation.

Stage 3 includes the completion and presentation of the policy recommendation report. This report will detail the expected results of the chosen policy and outline the most appropriate implementation strategy and timeline for each client. Specific progress, due dates, and notes for each task are listed in Table 1.

Table 1: Project Timeline

Project Overview			
Task	% Complete	Due	Notes
Market Growth Analysis — All Sectors	100	Nov 18	Projections completed for short term (1 year) and extrapolated for long term (5 years)
Industry Risk Analysis	75	Nov 18	Behind schedule on commodities analysis
Simulated Policy Projections	25	Nov 23	Includes expected outcome of conservative, moderate, and liberal investment policies
Policy Recommendation Report	15	Nov 25	Includes recommendations for Southeast Asia, China, India, and South and Central America

The positive impact of completing this project will give us a better understanding of the potential financial crisis and look at creating smartphone applications that can provide relevant information to financial analysts and investors on how to proceed in times of financial market turbulence.

References

Bird, M. (2015). $50 Trillion in Debt: This is what the '3rd wave' of the 2008 financial crisis looks like. *Business Insider*. Retrieved 18 November 2015, from http://uk.businessinsider.com/the-third-wave-emerging-market-debt-2015-10

Goldman Sachs. (2015). *Goldman Sachs | Research*. Retrieved 18 November 2015, from www.goldmansachs.com/what-we-do/research/index.html

Moshinsky, B. (2015). Goldman: Welcome to the "3rd wave" of the financial crisis. *Business Insider*. Retrieved 18 November 2015, from http://uk.businessinsider.com/goldman-sachs-were-in-the-the-third-wave-of-the-2008-financial-crisis-2015-10

The report that Kirsten produces is about four pages long. She could have produced an even shorter report of just a couple of pages, listing only her progress. However, being a co-op student and wishing to demonstrate her analytical and critical thinking skills and her attention to detail, she wrote the slightly longer report. She ensures that her short report provides all the information that Niamh would need to make a decision. The report highlights Kirsten's ability to perform analysis, and provides evidence of sources and methodologies used to arrive at certain conclusions and recommendations.

The Case of Dharini Gagnon: New Opportunity

Dharini Gagnon is another co-op student at APPFORMS. She is doing her second internship at APPFORMS, and is quite aware of the tasks typically given to co-op students. She has established relationships in the company, and made such a great impact during her first internship at APPFORMS that she was invited back. Dharini comes with a background in marketing, really enjoys doing market research, and plans to pursue a career in the technology industry with a focus on marketing. APPFORMS is just the type of organization in which Dharini thrives.

Larry Lamba, director of business development, with whom Dharini has worked before, calls her to his office to discuss a new task he has for her. Many companies have started to move their in-house information technology (IT) services to the cloud. Companies that provide cloud-based IT services provide dedicated servers for organizations to use to store their data, as well as email and other communication technology support. Using cloud-based IT services frees organizations from worrying about managing their IT requirements themselves, and allows them to focus on growing their businesses.

Larry had heard news that IBM, one of the largest technology companies in the world, was not doing so well in the cloud computing business because it was not able to compete with Amazon, Google, and other organizations that appeared to be more agile. In response to market changes and demands, IBM sold its server division to Lenovo (to whom it had already sold its laptop division). IBM also acquired a cloud services provider, SoftLayer, to help improve its cloud services. Larry felt that there was an opportunity here for APPFORMS to come up with a series of apps to help IT personnel and organizational decision-makers take advantage of the growing cloud computing market. Larry was aware that Pierce Sanchez, manager of APPFORMS's Android division, had tasked one of his co-op students to conduct a feasibility study on business intelligence (BI) apps for the cloud. Confident in Dharini's abilities, Larry asks her to look at the IBM case and report on the options IBM had to counter competition from Amazon and Google.

Larry now wants to know what progress Dharini has made in completing her task. She was very excited to do this task, and had begun her research on IBM's response to the market challenge, which was the need to position IBM as a provider of superior cloud computing services. Dharini decides to provide Larry with a short, informative report. Even though it is a short report, she still provides an informative title, clear headings, graphs and charts as necessary, references for her sources, and a project timeline. It is common for informative, progress, and similar short reports to contain a task or project timeline, so decision-makers will know when the task or project is likely to be completed. Dharini decides to use 12-point Calibri font for ease of reading. She likes Calibri because it is a sans serif font and is good for reports, particularly if they are published online. She includes an introduction, has a clear body, and ends with a brief conclusion. For her references, she uses APA (American Psychological Association) format, but decides to provide even more guidance to the reader by identifying the paragraphs where she cited sources. While this is not necessary, Dharini knows it will help readers quickly find the sources they may be interested in learning more about.

IBM Progress Report for Cloud Computing in Banking (Africa-Mauritius)

Introduction

Note from Dharini to self: proofread

IBM's global position has lately been at risk due to competition within the cloud computing industry. IBM has spent a lot of time underestimating its competitors, like Amazon, in the cloud computing division. Currently, many start-ups are choosing to be on the cloud of companies like Amazon or Google, instead of the IBM cloud. Figure 1 shows the performance of IBM in the cloud services space. We can see the steady decline, but proactive strategies could allow IBM to improve its cloud services business. In this report, I will indicate the possible strategies IBM could adopt to regain market share in the cloud computing business, focusing specifically on one such strategy.

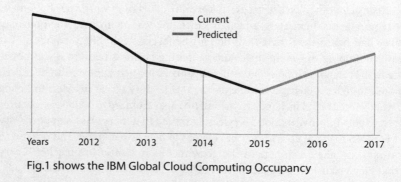

Fig.1 shows the IBM Global Cloud Computing Occupancy

It would be good for IBM to look at emerging markets to establish itself in the cloud business. Emerging markets like Africa, China, India, Brazil, etc. offer IBM opportunities to grow its business in the cloud. I will explore one such opportunity where IBM could focus on just one country, Mauritius, and begin the process of gaining market share. The reason for doing this, as opposed to a broader analysis, is to allow us to step through the possible strategies IBM could take and where in this process APPFORMS could have an opportunity to provide apps to IT persons, bank employees, lay customers, etc., that leverages IBM's cloud services and our app technologies to draw data from such cloud services to provide relevant business information to users.

Here Dharini provides a clear rationale for why she is following this approach. This rationale will then help Larry Lamba decide if this is the right approach for Dharini or whether she needs to focus on something else. Thus, a progress report serves two purposes: (1) it updates business managers on the status of a task/project; and (2) it suggests changes or modifications to the task.

Cloud Computing in Banking

IBM's cloud technology can help banks in Mauritius by offering secure deployment options to develop new customer experiences, by enabling effective collaboration internally and externally, and by improving market speed, responding to economic uncertainties, interconnected global financial systems and demanding customers (IBM Sales and Distribution, 2013).

Dharini looks at this sentence, feels maybe it is too long and thinks about shortening it. She will do this when she begins editing and proofreading the report, before sending it to Larry Lamba

This sentence also serves as the initial claim statement or topic sentence for Dharini's report

The Finance and Banking Industry in Mauritius has been flourishing, and Mauritius is being referred to as Africa's next banking hub. Mauritius, which happens to be among the wealthiest African countries on a per capita basis with GDP that surpasses almost every other African country by about 70 %, has a financial system that is known for being among the most sophisticated on the continent (Wallace, 2013, para. 1). One strategy for IBM would to get the major banks in Mauritius to put their trust in IBM's cloud services to improve their banking services and expand their reach to all their banking customers. This would increase IBM's presence in Africa, and would boost IBM's position in the global cloud computing race.

IBM has invited one of the leading banks in Mauritius, the Mauritius Commercial Bank (MCB), to collaborate with IBM, and get acquainted with cloud computing (Global Private Banking Awards, 2015). Apparently, IBM is also planning to approach the State Bank of Mauritius and the Bank of Mauritius, which are also among the leading financial institutions in Mauritius, to adopt cloud computing so as to increase their market growth and banking efficiency. If IBM is successful at conquering those banks, it will get the attention of other African financial institutions that are competing against each other. This will lead to an increased demand for IBM cloud services on the African continent, and that would really help improve IBM's reputation on the international podium.

continued

Prospective Partnerships and Mergers & Acquisition in Mauritius

Another strategy that IBM could adopt in order to grow its occupancy in cloud computing within Africa, starting with Mauritius, is to work together with the established companies there that already have expertise in cloud computing. This could help improve IBM's reputation and competitiveness.

Orange Mauritius is the dominant Internet and telecommunications establishment in Mauritius, and offers a comprehensive range of cloud solutions to assist companies in their strategic business transformation (Orange Cloud Solutions, 2014). GoCloud Ltd, another Mauritian company, incorporated in 2014, offers end-to-end cloud computing and strategic IT consulting services to small and medium enterprises (GoCloud, 2014). Since the company is doing well for itself, it would be in IBM's good interest to strike an M&A deal with the company or to opt for a partnership agreement with them. These are at least two growth opportunities for IBM in Mauritius.

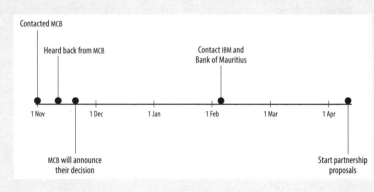

Fig. 2 shows the Work Progress Timeline

Dharini has to decide whether to go with this timeline, which presents the options IBM has, or her own task completion timeline

Conclusion

The timeline in Figure 2 indicates possible strategies for IBM's effort to reclaim its market share in the cloud computing business. In the final report, I will investigate and provide recommendations on how APPFORMS can possibly partner with IBM and financial institutions to create a suite of apps that can help users get more out of IBM's cloud computing services.

REFERENCE LIST

> Dharini's note to herself: do I need this underline here?

Paragraph 3

IBM Sales and Distribution (2013). *Cloud computing for banking.* Retrieved from http://www-935.ibm.com/services/multimedia/Cloud_Computing_for_Banking__Janvier_2013.pdf

Paragraph 4

Wallace, Paul. (2013). *Mauritius: Africa's next banking hub?* Retrieved from http://www.thebanker.com/World/Africa/Mauritius/Mauritius-Africa-s-next-banking-hub?ct=true

Paragraph 5

Global Private Banking Awards (2015). *Winner 2014* Retrieved from http://www.privatebankingawards.com/winners/2014-winners/

Paragraph 8

Orange Cloud Solutions (2014). *Orange Cloud Solutions.* Retrieved from http://www.orange.mu/pdf/cloud.pdf

GoCloud (2014). *Providing Complete Suites of Cloud Solutions* Retrieved from http://www.gocloud.mu/#!about/cgvz

At four pages, Dharini's report is short. It is a little more complex than Kirsten's and Bahram's reports presented earlier, and requires more analysis; however, like the other short reports of Hamed and Fonseca, relies on information collected from external sources.

Note that all three reports in this chapter's case studies have similar structural elements. They provide informative headings in bold, and use normal type headings to distinguish the second level headings from the first level headings. They all use APA format for in-text and endnote citations.

⊙ SCOPE

Strategy is important in every aspect of business decision-making. It is strategy that drives business decision-makers to task their direct reports to conduct market research, issue identification and analysis, and write reports. However, managers like to know how their staff is doing with their various projects in case the managers need to change strategies. Employees need to effectively use writing and communication strategies to convey complex information to their managers. Bahram and Kirsten use standard report formats to create their progress reports, while Dharini is a little more informal in her approach. Regardless, all three have a clear structure consisting of introduction, body, and conclusion. They provide a context for their task, outline what they have done and will be doing, and present a plan or a timeline to inform their respective managers about the task and the potential completion date.

Content presented in an unstructured form can cause a lot of confusion and make it hard for readers to find the real message. Bahram, Kirsten, and Dharini use clear structure, headings, guideposts, and timelines to highlight their findings and make their content easy to access. Their visuals have captions and they refer to these visuals in the text to provide evidence for any claims that they made. The timelines indicate the progress of the task, except in Dharini's case where she provides a timeline for IBM's strategies, instead of one for the completion of her assigned task. These are content choices that she made.

The *outcome* for any communication is to further the relationship between the sender and the receiver. Managers ask for reports so they can position themselves to take the right decisions that their businesses demand, and so that organizational objectives are met in a timely manner. They need to know the status or progress of every task or project they are responsible for so that they can be agile and change course if the situation demands it. Being agile allows the business decision-maker to adapt to changing environmental conditions and ensures that their businesses can respond quickly to changes.

Presentation brings us back to form and design. Using standard forms with headings, subheadings, and numbered and captioned figures and visuals allows business managers to quickly see the relevant parts of the reports. Short reports need to get to the point, and provide clear and concise information to managers about is the status of the task. Presenting information in short reports requires as much skill as any other type of communication, particularly because managers need to know if they have to intervene, take quick decisions, change or modify the task, seek additional resources, and be alert to changing needs.

Ethics is always central to any communication. Faulty decision-making can result when writers are not ethical and provide misinformation. Care must be taken so that visuals do not convey false or wrong information. Tables summarizing findings should be supported by clear methodologies around data collection, data integrity, and honest effort. Finally, using visuals or direct quotations without citing the source or without paraphrasing will be detrimental to the business effort, and will only be self-defeating. Paraphrasing is a good way to explain an event or message in your own words while retaining the main points surrounding the event or message. This technique is useful when the writer or speaker does not wish to use full quotes to reproduce the exact version of the original message. While paraphrasing, the writer will still cite the source, but convey the message in a manner that is often simpler, yet retains the key information contained in the original quote. For example, the original sentence "Goldman Sachs, in its recent report on the financial crisis, has indicated that the third wave of recession is about to occur" can be paraphrased as follows: According to the recent report from Goldman Sachs, they expect a recurrence of the financial crisis very shortly.

Chapter Summary

In this chapter we presented the various aspects of writing short business reports. The first part of the chapter described how and why form and content were equally important, particularly in reports. Since reports typically have a lot of text, using explicit structure such as headings, bulleted lists, captioned visuals, relevant tables, and even choice of font and point size are key features that improve readability. The writer can then focus on creating meaningful and relevant content, cite sources, and provide status updates to decision-makers who have requested these short, informative reports. We saw examples of three reports as each co-op student reported on the progress of tasks assigned to them by their managers. Ethical approaches are always front and centre, and are especially critical when writing reports of any length. These were highlighted in the choices that the three students made as they performed their business tasks and wrote their reports. Each cited the sources of their work and presented timelines.

Here we note that the reports produced by Bahram Fonseca, Kirsten Hamed, and Dharini Gagnon are based on actual progress reports produced by students for a class assignment. The grammar has been completely edited, and the contexts changed. The reason for this inclusion is that the quality of reports produced by these students was quite high, and it is good to showcase them. The names of the students have been changed to protect their identities, and permission has been received from them to use them in this book.

Discussion Questions

The exercises in this chapter involve the following scenario. Answer the questions based on the events described in the scenario.

The Case of Mithra Charleston: Short Report Assignment on a Legal App

Percy Toufiq, director of the legal department at APPFORMS, asks Mithra Charleston, the department's co-op student, to analyze the legal issues surrounding the use of APPFORMS's apps by end users, and provide a detailed report of her findings. APPFORMS already has clear legal documentation about the use of apps created by the company, but since the app market is so dynamic, it is good practice to keep updated about changes to protect the company in case of litigation, copyright infringement by other app developers, and intentional or unintentional misuse of the apps by users. A few weeks after assigning the task to Mithra, Percy asks her to provide an update on her progress. Answer the following questions to choose the format Mithra should use to write her report.

1. What type of report is Mithra writing?
2. How long should it be?
3. How much detail should Mithra provide?
4. How can Mithra demonstrate her writing abilities and her analytical or critical thinking skills?

Exercises

1. How do informative and progress reports differ from analytical or research reports?

2. Are timelines necessary in progress reports? Why or why not?

3. What is the purpose of paraphrasing and why should you do it?

4. What is the difference between a recommendation and a conclusion?

5. What argumentation devices can a writer use to provide credibility for the claims made in a report?

Good Advice or Bad?

1. You have been asked to write a report about auto financing and lending practices. After looking at one source, you feel you have found everything you need. Your friends read your report and agree that you have done due diligence. Good advice or bad? Why?

2. You are running late in submitting a progress report. To make the deadline, you make up some imaginary milestones to create a timeline. Good advice or bad? Why?

3. Your supervisor asks you to submit a report to show how you are progressing at a task she asked you to perform. You decide to send an email to say that everything is fine and you are on track. Good advice or bad? Why?

4. You feel uncomfortable writing in first person, and active voice. So, for a short report you are writing, you decide to use a mix of third person and passive voice. Good advice or bad? Why?

Strategic Language: Formal and Informal English

The Columbia Guide to Standard American English (1993) provides a definition of formal English that may be applied to the language standards in any country: "Standard American English usage is linguistic good manners, sensitively and accurately matched to context—to listeners or readers, to situation, and to purpose. But because our language is constantly changing, mastering its appropriate usage is not a one-time task like learning the multiplication tables. Instead, we are constantly obliged to adjust, adapt, and revise what we have learned" (p. ix).

Standards of English may be seen as on a continuum from most formal to least formal.

Official or legal ▸ Professional and academic ▸ Casual or conversational ▸ Colloquial or slang ▸ Coarse or vulgar

Written and spoken language in professional contexts is more formal than in friendly or casual contexts. The ability to move adeptly along the continuum lets you establish appropriate relationships among different audiences. But sometimes it is difficult to determine the appropriate standard. For example, when working with a group of peers, casual/conversational and colloquial/slang language may initially be considered appropriate; however, if the group consists of individuals who have learned English as a second language or are native English speakers from outside Canada, the group's language may need to be more formal to ensure mutual understanding.

The standards of formal English can be manipulated to achieve desired ends. For example, when CBC News revealed that Royal Bank of Canada (RBC) had hired temporary foreign workers to replace Canadian citizen employees, RBC's CEO Gord Nixon responded with an open letter to the public (www.cbc.ca/news/canada/rbc-ceo-gord-nixon-s-open-letter-1.1385030). His letter used informal English, which diminished Nixon's power and aligned himself with the people the bank serves. In assuring his audience that the bank cares about public opinion, the letter referred to the public's expectation of the bank and stated, "And that's something we take very much to heart." In this sentence, Nixon uses several elements of informal English—the use of a conjunction (*and*) to begin the sentence, a contraction (*that's*), and an idiom (*take to heart*). This use of informal English may have been intended to confirm Nixon's position as an average Canadian, just like his audience.

Standards of formal English and English used in professional or academic contexts change over time. Current practices include the following:

- Formality in language choice
  - Complete words, without acronyms (*University of Toronto* rather than *U of T*) or contractions (*is not* rather than *isn't*)
  - Use of titles and surnames (*Dear Mr. Lemire* rather than *Dear Angus*)
  - Slang-free language (*I could not stop laughing* rather than *I literally died laughing*)
  - Idioms (*make use of* rather than *draw on*) and culturally rooted expressions (*Canadian government* rather than *Ottawa* when referring to the federal government) that are difficult for non-native English speakers
- Formality in format
  - Normal margin widths of 2.54 centimetres
  - Traditional block format for letters
  - Standard font and point size (Times New Roman, Ariel, or Calibri in 10, 11, or 12 point)
  - Left justification
- Formality in style
  - Standard punctuation marks with no exclamation points (!)
  - No more than four variations in style in the entire document (plain text, capital letters, italics, bold, and underline), no more than three within the space of a few lines, and underlining used rarely, if ever, for readability
  - APA style unless other internal guidelines established by the business or the academic environment are expected

Note that because degrees of formality, audience expectations, and channels of communication shift over time, these guidelines are not fixed. The passive voice, in which the subject of the sentence receives the action rather than does the action (*The mail was delivered by me* rather than *I delivered the mail*) is often considered an element of formality in writing. However, passive voice is more often a sign of weak writing or is used to deliberately obscure the cause of the action.

Identify the elements of informal (casual, conversational, colloquial, or slang) language and convert them to formal (official, legal, professional, or academic) language:

1. I'd rather not have a position in which I have to deal with a bunch of randoms.
2. The company delivers products or whatever to the Northern Territories.
3. But she can't complete the task if the team members behave like a bunch of imbeciles.
4. The product took off like a cat on fire.
5. The White House responded to Ottawa through a French interpreter.

Additional Resources

Additional Internet Resources

Purdue OWL (2016). Handbook on report formats. Retrieved from https://owl.english.purdue.edu/owl/owlprint/726/

University of Bradford. (n.d.). Introduction to report writing. Retrieved from www.bradford.ac.uk/academicskills/media/academic skillsadvice/documents/academicskills resources/writing-reports/Teach-Yourself-Introduction-to-Report-Writing.pdf

Grammar and Language Links

CPA. (2014). CPA Canada writing style guide. Retrieved from http://cpa.yellowpencil.selfip.com/style-guide/docs/CPA_Writing_Style_Guide_06_2014.pdf

Humber College. (n.d.). Business reports. Retrieved from https://www.humber.ca/liberalarts/sites/default/files/BUSINESS%20REPORTS.pdf

Kaplan University Writing Center. (2013). Formal vs. informal writing. Retrieved from https://kucampus.kaplan.edu/DocumentStore/Docs10/pdf/style/formal_vs_informal.pdf

Lund University. (2011). Academic writing in English: Formal vs. informal. Retrieved from http://awelu.srv.lu.se/grammar-and-words/register-and-style/formal-vs-informal/

RBC's Gord Nixon's Open Letter to the Public. Retrieved from http://www.cbc.ca/news/canada/rbc-ceo-gord-nixon-s-open-letter-1.1385030

CHAPTER SEVEN

Persuasive Techniques for Writing Long Reports

© iStock/David_Ahn

Learning Objectives

A. **Understand** the reasons for writing reports
B. **Understand** the purpose of reports
C. **Understand** form and content while writing reports
D. **Recognize** the importance of making structure explicit in a report and the various design elements of a report
E. **Develop** skills and strategies to present complex information in a report
F. **Incorporate** techniques of argumentation, persuasion, and presentation effectively when writing reports
G. **Present** oneself and the organization favourably by using evidence, rhetorical tools and ethics while writing reports

The Story So Far

Chapter 6 was about writing short reports, and the various aspects of form and content that go into the creation and production of these reports. We saw how co-op students Bahram Fonseca, Kirsten Hamed, and Dharini Gagnon worked through their assigned tasks and produced short reports with visuals and timelines. Each report was designed to provide the most relevant information to their managers, so that the managers could decide whether the students were progressing in the right direction.

Chapter 7 is about writing long reports and again discusses the various aspects of form and content that go into the creation and production of these reports. Here we pick up the storylines of Carrie du Plessis and James Patel from Chapter 4. Carrie had been tasked to create analytical reports on identifying and recommending the best icebreakers and team-building activities for the company retreat. She submitted a short report to the HR director. In this chapter, Carrie creates the complete long report, and we see the choices and decisions she makes as she does so. Similarly, we follow James Patel as he prepares his long report on the market potential for a business data analytics app. Our students are becoming proficient in their roles, and becoming known to their managers as reliable, hardworking people, capable of critical thinking and producing high-quality written work.

Introduction

Short reports give managers a sense of where a particular task is at, and how well or not it is progressing. Managers are particularly interested in receiving completed reports, so that they can inform their own superiors and use these reports in business decision-making.

For the business communication student, learning to write professional reports, regardless of type, is an extremely important and critical skill. Mastery of this skill involves

- understanding the need for the report;
- having an awareness of the audience for the report;
- understanding the context in which a report is requested;
- understanding the objectives of the report;
- having the ability to choose the appropriate form and structure to present the content;
- ensuring thorough credibility of the sources used to create the content; and
- using appropriate and relevant business language, free of errors, to convey the findings.

As students learn about the different forms of business communication, such as persuasive letters or memos, and structured communication pieces, such as newsletters or résumés, they begin the process of choosing the right form for conveying a certain piece of information regarding a business activity. Students understand and synthesize this knowledge and learn about increasingly sophisticated forms of conveying information about business activities—namely, reports and oral presentations.

Oral presentations will be addressed in Chapter 8. In this chapter, we focus on the form and content of business reports. After a discussion of some basic foundational concepts, we will follow the co-op students as they write their reports.

Form, Content, and Everything in Between

In formal reports, form guides content, but the two are inseparable and it is important to pay careful attention to both. There may be instances where content is so important that one tends to ignore form and focus on the content, which ends up being delivered in a less-than-organized manner. Even in such instances, it is important to follow the basic requirements of form, language, and structure so that the receiver of the information can easily locate the key points contained in the message.

So what exactly is form in a report? As with other types of business communication like memos, letters, and newsletters, reports take on certain forms or structures depending on the reason for the report, the type of audience that will read the report, and the nature of the content that needs to be delivered. As you read in Chapters 4 and 6, business writers weave the narrative or content by using simple to complex rhetorical tools such as compare and contrast, cause and effect, and clear, evidence-based argumentation. They can frame knowledge to allow their readers to situate the topic under discussion and present new information based on known or accepted knowledge. They also effectively use clustering and roadmaps to guide their readers.

We will now return to two of the scenarios from Chapter 4, and follow along as Carrie du Plessis and James Patel research or analyze certain business activities and submit reports to their managers.

The Case of Carrie du Plessis: Human Resources Scenario— Report with Recommendations

Carrie was tasked by Juanita Olson, director of human resources, to recommend some icebreakers and team-building activities that could be useful and appropriate at the upcoming APPFORMS's company retreat. Carrie has now completed her research and collected the information she needs to write her report. She will be writing a research and analysis report that requires her to make some recommendations.

However, the report needs to be short so that Juanita can take decisions. Carrie's reasoning is as follows. She must identify and recommend activities for the company retreat. The purpose is to boost employee morale ahead of a possible reorganization among the various APPFORMS teams. Carrie feels this is an important task for both her and the company; however, she knows the implications are not as critical as those involving an organizational incident. Such an occurrence needs more time and probably many people working together to investigate and gather information, as well as detailed analysis and longer reports. Carrie considers her task to be an important enough to do some level of analysis as she sorts through the various options and uses a weighted matrix approach to identify the best activities and make her recommendations. Carrie begins writing her report. She decides to give it a simple and informative title and to provide a short report summary at the start.

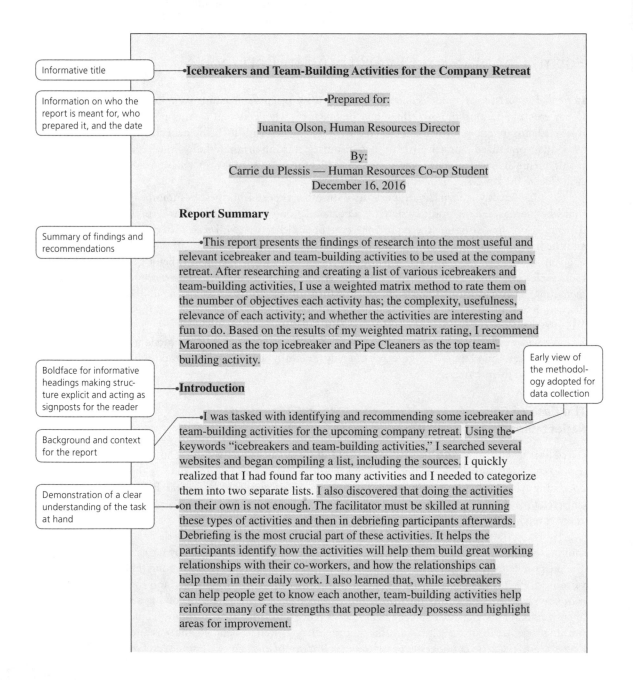

Informative title

Icebreakers and Team-Building Activities for the Company Retreat

Information on who the report is meant for, who prepared it, and the date

Prepared for:

Juanita Olson, Human Resources Director

By:
Carrie du Plessis — Human Resources Co-op Student
December 16, 2016

Report Summary

Summary of findings and recommendations

This report presents the findings of research into the most useful and relevant icebreaker and team-building activities to be used at the company retreat. After researching and creating a list of various icebreakers and team-building activities, I use a weighted matrix method to rate them on the number of objectives each activity has; the complexity, usefulness, relevance of each activity; and whether the activities are interesting and fun to do. Based on the results of my weighted matrix rating, I recommend Marooned as the top icebreaker and Pipe Cleaners as the top team-building activity.

Early view of the methodology adopted for data collection

Boldface for informative headings making structure explicit and acting as signposts for the reader

Introduction

Background and context for the report

Demonstration of a clear understanding of the task at hand

I was tasked with identifying and recommending some icebreaker and team-building activities for the upcoming company retreat. Using the keywords "icebreakers and team-building activities," I searched several websites and began compiling a list, including the sources. I quickly realized that I had found far too many activities and I needed to categorize them into two separate lists. I also discovered that doing the activities on their own is not enough. The facilitator must be skilled at running these types of activities and then in debriefing participants afterwards. Debriefing is the most crucial part of these activities. It helps the participants identify how the activities will help them build great working relationships with their co-workers, and how the relationships can help them in their daily work. I also learned that, while icebreakers can help people get to know each another, team-building activities help reinforce many of the strengths that people already possess and highlight areas for improvement.

With all this in mind, I resumed my search with more focus. I decided to use a compiled list from the Lions Club website. The Lions Club is a reputable international organization with members from all professions and backgrounds. It is a diverse, not-for-profit organization. These activities will have been tested and will therefore be useful for the APPFORMS's retreat.

Indentation of the first line of each paragraph and making structure explicit

Explanation of the reason for using only one source for the information

Methodology

Line spacing between headings and the start of the paragraph to make structure explicit and provide white space

To select from this list, I created a table with column headings for the icebreaker name, a brief description, the purpose of the activity, and a score on a scale of 1 to 5 (with 1 being least useful and 5 most useful). I rated each activity by how many objectives it achieves. For example, getting people to know each other is one objective, but getting to know their values helps lay the foundation for team-building, which is another objective. I then created a rating table to objectively rate each activity. I based the criteria on the objective of the activity, how easy or complex it would be to do, its relevance and usefulness, and whether it would be interesting and fun. The more the activity can achieve, the higher the score. Table 1 shows my ratings. I believe my criteria are fair and helped me arrive at the correct choice of activities for the company retreat. Also, this process helped me document my analysis and can be replicated by others for rating similar programs or activities.

Reference to the table in the text

Detailed explanation of the methodology adopted for rating the activities

Table 1: Rating Table for Icebreaker and Team-Building Activities

By convention, table number and table caption appear at the top of the table

Score	Criteria
1	Has one objective, is simple to do, and is somewhat relevant
2	Has one objective, is a little more involved, and is relevant
3	Has at least two objectives, is more involved, is quite relevant, and is interesting to do
4	Has two or more objectives, is more involved, is very relevant, and is interesting to do
5	Has two or more objectives, is more involved, is very relevant and useful, is interesting and fun to do, and will be memorable

The purpose of my approach is to create a basis for a decision matrix. A decision matrix lists all the options available and allows for a score for each option. It is an important tool in the process of analysis. As I categorized and sorted these activities, I was able to look at and assess the usefulness of each activity. However, rather than rely just on my own knowledge and experience, I used a scoring mechanism to reduce the list of icebreaker activities into a more manageable list of options. From this reduced list of options, I could then make my final recommendations.

continued

Starting with the icebreaker activity, I reproduced all the activities from the Lions Club site into one table. Based on the scores I gave to each activity, I selected those activities with a score greater than 3, giving me a new table with a reduced list of activities, shown in Table 2.

Table 2: Reduced List of Icebreaker Activities

No.	Icebreaker Name	Brief Description	Purpose of the Activity	Score (1-5)
1	Marooned	Each team chooses 5 items they would want with them if they were stranded on an island.	Learn about other's values and problem-solving styles; promotes teamwork	5
2	Who's Done That?	Each team creates a list of useful skills and experiences.	Learn about team members' skills	3
3	Chaos	Using props such as a ball, pen, or toy, people introduce themselves by saying their name and tossing the prop to the next person, who catches the prop, thanks them, says their name, and tosses the prop to the next person.	Energizes people and allows them to get to know each	3
4	Geographic Location	People create a map based on where they are from (or based on where they are assigned to).	Get to know people and where they are from	3
5	"I Have Never"	Each person gets to finish the sentence "I have never..."	Get to know people	3
6	Two Truths and a Lie	People state two truths and a lie about themselves. The first person to guess which is the lie goes next.	Get to know people and their values	3
7	Me Too	In small groups, each person starts with 10 pennies, and names something he or she has done. Others who have done the same thing add a penny to the pile.	Get to know people in small groups	4
8	Common Ground	In small groups, people find out what they have in common.	Get to know people in small groups	3

Source: Icebreakers, team-building activities, and Energizers. *Lions Club International.* Retrieved from www.lionsclubs.org/EN/common/pdfs/icebreakers.pdf

Two of the activities in the reduced list shown in Table 2 have scores of 5 and 4, while the remaining activities have scores of 3. The activities with scores of 5 and 4 also have some team-building aspects to them and will provide a good transition to the actual team-building activities that will follow. I then created the weighted decision matrix to help me arrive at my final choices. I placed the scores for each activity from Table 2 in one column, giving a score of 1 for each criteria present in the activity and a score between 0 and 1 if some aspect of the criteria was present in the activity. If no criteria were present in the activity, I gave a score of 0. The final weighted score is the product of the score from Table 2 and the sum of the criteria scores. The scores will be more accurate than my rough estimate. Table 3 shows the weighted decision matrix for the icebreaker activities.

> Explanation of the analysis

Table 3: Decision Matrix for Icebreaker Activities

Icebreaker Activity	Score From Table 3	Objective	Usefulness	Relevance	Involvement	Interesting/Fun	Total	Final Weighted Score
Marooned	5	1.0	1.0	1.0	1.0	1.0	5.0	25.0
Who's Done That?	3	0.5	0.5	0.5	0.5	0.5	2.5	7.5
Chaos	3	0.5	0.5	0.5	1.0	0.5	3.0	9.0
Geographic Location	3	0.5	0.5	0.5	0.5	0.5	2.5	7.5
"I Have Never"	3	0.5	1.0	0.5	0.5	0.5	3.0	9.0
Two Truths and a Lie	3	0.5	0.5	0.5	1.0	1.0	3.5	10.5
Me Too	4	1.0	1.0	1.0	0.5	1.0	4.5	18.0
Common Ground	3	0.5	0.5	0.5	0.5	1.0	3.0	9.0

Based on my decision matrix, I am confident of making my recommendations for the two icebreaker activities. The activities Marooned, with a score of 25, and Me Too, with a score of 18, are the top two activities. In a similar manner, I proceeded to compile a list of team-building activities. My master list consists of 10 team-building activities listed in Table 4.

continued

Table 4: Decision Matrix for Team-Building Activities

Icebreaker Activity	Score From Table 3	Objective	Usefulness	Relevance	Involvement	Interesting/Fun	Total	Final Weighted Score
Pipe Cleaners	5	1.0	1.0	1.0	1.0	1.0	5.0	25.0
Blind Numerical Order	3	0.5	0.5	0.5	0.5	0.5	2.5	7.5
All Tied Up	3	0.5	0.5	0.5	1.0	0.5	3.0	9.0
Build a Car	3	0.5	0.5	0.5	0.5	0.5	2.5	7.5
Human Machines	3	0.5	1.0	0.5	0.5	0.5	3.0	9.0
Rain	3	0.5	0.5	0.5	1.0	1.0	3.5	10.5
Consensus	4	1.0	1.0	1.0	0.5	1.0	4.5	18.0
Phrase Ball	3	0.5	0.5	0.5	0.5	1.0	3.0	9.0
Thanks Giving	3	0.5	0.5	0.5	0.5	1.0	3.0	9.0
Three-Way Communication	5	1.0	1.0	1.0	0.5	1.0	4.5	22.5

Source: Icebreakers, team-building activities, and Energizers. *Lions Club International*. Retrieved from http://www.lionsclubs.org/resources/EN/pdfs/icebreakers.pdf

Using the same rating criteria and scales to score each activity, I was able to identify the top two team-building activities. Two of the team-building activities, Pipe Cleaners and Three-Way Communication, have the highest scores of 25 and 22.5 respectively and are clear winners, but I looked at the team-building activity called Consensus and felt that I should include it, even though it has a score of 18. The Pipe Cleaners activity is fun and cross-cultural, while the Three-Way Communication activity stresses the importance of open communication among team members. While consensus cannot always be achieved in team or group activities, the activity called Consensus would definitely be useful and that is the reason I have included it as an option in this list. Table 5 shows the list of recommended icebreaker activities and Table 6 shows the list of recommended team-building activities.

Table 5: Icebreaker Activity Recommendations●————

> Summary and the rec-
> ommendations in a table
> format (Tables 5 and 6)

No.	Icebreaker Name	Brief Description	Purpose of the Activity	Score
1	Marooned	Each team chooses 5 items they would want with them if they were stranded on an island.	Learn about other's values and problem-solving styles; promotes teamwork	25.0
2	Me Too	In small groups, each person starts with 10 pennies, and names something he or she has done. Others who have done the same thing add a penny to the pile.	Get to know people in small groups	18.0

Table 6: Team-Building Activity Recommendations

No.	Icebreaker Name	Brief Description	Purpose of the Activity	Score (1-5)
1	Pipe Cleaners	People are assigned to groups. Everyone is given three pipe cleaners and instructed to use them to form the most creative structure. Groups that combine their pipe cleaners to make a more creative structure are given special recognition.	Creativity	25.0
2	Three-Way Communi-cation	People are assigned to groups: one representing face-to-face communica-tion, one representing phone/instant messaging, and one representing email. Each group physically mimics and discusses the pros and cons of their assigned com-munication method.	Discussion	22.5
3	Consensus	Groups perform a noise for other groups to mimic.	Team-building, discussion, com-promise, and negotiation	18.0

continued

Implementing the Activities

Selecting the activities is one aspect of the task. However, understanding how they will be implemented will ensure that the activities are successful and people participating in these activities will get the maximum benefit from the participation. With this understanding and the awareness that there will be three hours set aside for these activities, I realized that people might get bored if they were to only do icebreakers and team-building activities for three hours continuously. So I have selected and recommended icebreakers that can be completed in 10 to 15 minutes followed by a debriefing period of 10 to 15 minutes during which participants can share their thoughts about the activity and the facilitator explains how the activity can help people in their daily work. Similarly, I selected and recommended team-building activities that can be completed in 20 to 30 minutes, followed by a debriefing period of 20 to 30 minutes. I further recommend that there be two 90-minute time slots set aside for these activities: one slot in the morning of the first day of the retreat and the second slot in the afternoon of the second day.

My reasoning is that everyone will be enthusiastic on the first morning of the retreat, so it is a good time to have people participate in these types of activities. The first slot will be for everyone in the organization (including the managing partners) and team members will be picked randomly from all departments and teams. So, for example, one team could have members from Team Apple, Team Android, someone from HR, one of the managing partners and one co-op student. This will allow people to get to know people from the entire company and help them to identify with the entire organization, making the activity a rewarding experience.

The second slot should be during or after lunch of the second day. By that time, people will be thinking of going back to work and getting back to their projects. This second time slot would be ideal for people to do the activities with their own teams to build team spirit and to help them reorient themselves back into their projects.

Conclusion and Recommendation

As presented in the report, I identified a list of icebreaker and team-building activities from the Lions Club website (www.lionsclub.org). Using a rating scale, I created a decision matrix to help select the top two icebreaker activities, Marooned and Me Too, and the top three team-building activities, Pipe Cleaners, Three-Way Communication, and Consensus. I have also briefly mentioned how and when these activities can be implemented.

The report that Carrie produces is six pages long. She could have produced an even shorter report of just a couple of pages, listing only her recommendations. However, being a co-op student and wishing to demonstrate her analytical and critical thinking skills and her attention to detail, she wrote the slightly longer report. However, she ensures that the report summary provides all the information that Juanita would need to make a decision. If Juanita skimmed the report, but carefully read the recommendations at the end, she would still find it short and informative to make a decision on choosing the activities. The report highlights Carrie's ability to perform analysis, and provides evidence of sources and methodologies used to arrive at certain conclusions and recommendations.

The Case of James Patel: New Business Opportunity— Report with Recommendations

In Chapter 4, we followed James Patel as he performed a market analysis on business apps that would allow corporate clients to perform cloud-based web analytics on business data. James's task was to look at demand and supply and make recommendations accordingly.

James thought through the task, obtained clarifications from his manager, and decided on an approach for collecting and categorizing the data. He then conducted his analysis and made his recommendations. Now he is ready to synthesize his findings in a report.

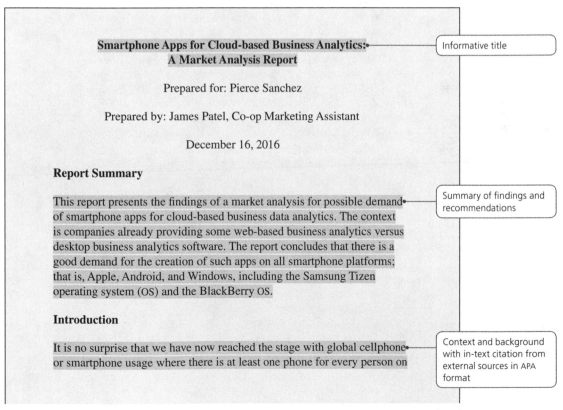

Smartphone Apps for Cloud-based Business Analytics: A Market Analysis Report

Prepared for: Pierce Sanchez

Prepared by: James Patel, Co-op Marketing Assistant

December 16, 2016

Report Summary

This report presents the findings of a market analysis for possible demand of smartphone apps for cloud-based business data analytics. The context is companies already providing some web-based business analytics versus desktop business analytics software. The report concludes that there is a good demand for the creation of such apps on all smartphone platforms; that is, Apple, Android, and Windows, including the Samsung Tizen operating system (OS) and the BlackBerry OS.

Introduction

It is no surprise that we have now reached the stage with global cellphone or smartphone usage where there is at least one phone for every person on

Informative title

Summary of findings and recommendations

Context and background with in-text citation from external sources in APA format

continued

the planet. Chaffey (2011) predicts that global mobile traffic data will increase 26 times between 2010 and 2015, that there will be one mobile device per capita by 2015, and that by 2015 two-thirds of the world's mobile traffic data will be video. Tennant (2016) writes that smartphones will be assisting users with everything from learning to cook or play music, and allow users to shop from anywhere, upload videos and pictures or listen to music, and even talk to people. Increasing numbers of business users of smartphones have found ways to get their work done on mobile devices. Beyond voice, text, and video communication, business users have begun using their mobile devices for business analytics as well, such as Slack™ for team communication. Verkooijen (2014) defines mobile business intelligence (BI) or mobile intelligence as "[t]he capability that enables the mobile workforce to gain business insights through information analysis using applications optimized for mobile devices." As this report will show, there are now an increasing number of companies providing web- or cloud-based business analytics applications in addition to desktop services. Moving business analytics to the web or the cloud allows business users to access business intelligence data as they go about meeting clients and allows them to take data-driven business decisions faster. There now appears to be a general momentum toward making business analytics accessible on mobile devices and, with these devices packing more features, power, and capabilities, industry analysts seem to agree that this will be an inevitable move.

To find out whether this is the growing trend and there truly is a market, I decided to clarify with Mr. Pierce Sanchez the exact nature of what I needed to research. These clarifications are listed below to guide the reader.

1. Perform a brief market analysis on the need for mobile business data analysis apps.
2. Identify the suppliers of business data analytics applications (supply side).
3. Identify the consumers of the software applications (demand side).
4. Make recommendations.

Methodology

I identified the following strategies as relevant to this task.

1. Understand the task.
   • List questions that arise.
   • Return to the audience to get answers to the questions and any other clarifications.

Margin annotations:

Academic article citation indicating the gap

Possible solution for filling the gap

Steps in trying to understand the problem or task

Combination of numbered and bulleted lists to make structure explicit. Also demonstrating to his manager James's methodical approach to the task

- Visualize the task to see if there is a process to be followed.
- Identify key elements of the task or process and create a process diagram.

2. Use the process diagram.
   - Check if the process is sequential (i.e., one process has to follow another).
   - Identify which parts can be done concurrently.
   - See if there are feedback loops in the process.

3. Gather and evaluate information.
   - For each part of the process, determine whether information is available from primary, secondary, or tertiary sources.
   - Determine the type of information or data required.
   - Evaluate the quality and source of the information.

4. Perform analysis.
   - If necessary, perform data analytics (using an analytics software application like MS Excel) to generate numbers and charts to illustrate trends, etc.
   - Estimate the likely costs and benefits of possible recommendations.
   - Choose one or more options to recommend.

Having listed the strategies, I approached Mr. Sanchez with some additional questions:

1. Would companies that develop data analysis software applications already have mobile apps for their products?

2. Am I only supposed to look at existing apps that work on the Android phones or can I widen the search to look at cross-platform apps?

3. Should I only look at web-based data analytics applications or also business intelligence (BI) dashboards and scorecards?

Mr. Sanchez suggested that I broaden my search to include cross-platform apps and also find out about BI dashboards and scorecards. Mr. Sanchez also indicated that companies that produce data analysis and BI software applications may have their own mobile phone apps, but the market appears big enough for APPFORMS to also enter. Visualizing the task will help me identify the elements of the task. My diagram is shown in Figure 1.

continued

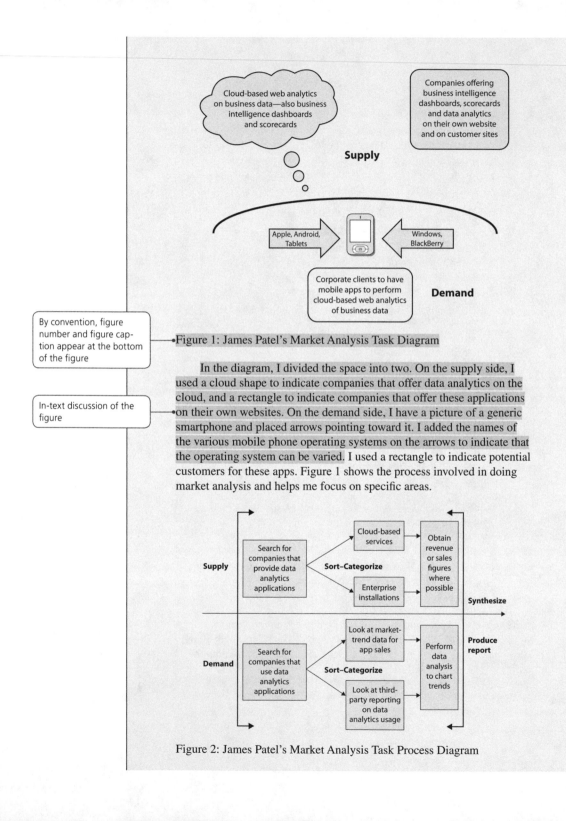

By convention, figure number and figure caption appear at the bottom of the figure

Figure 1: James Patel's Market Analysis Task Diagram

In-text discussion of the figure

In the diagram, I divided the space into two. On the supply side, I used a cloud shape to indicate companies that offer data analytics on the cloud, and a rectangle to indicate companies that offer these applications on their own websites. On the demand side, I have a picture of a generic smartphone and placed arrows pointing toward it. I added the names of the various mobile phone operating systems on the arrows to indicate that the operating system can be varied. I used a rectangle to indicate potential customers for these apps. Figure 1 shows the process involved in doing market analysis and helps me focus on specific areas.

Figure 2: James Patel's Market Analysis Task Process Diagram

Figure 2 provides a more detailed view of this market analysis process. As in Figure 1, the market analysis process is divided into the supply and demand sides. Instead of approaching everything at once and knowing that I can approach the task from either the supply side or the demand side, I decided to evaluate both to see which would be the best place for me to start collecting data. Forecasting, based on customers' previous buying patterns, can be used to arrive at demand figures. However, these figures are not always readily available. On the other hand, finding information on the supply side would be easier. Companies often advertise their products, both on their own websites and on third-party sites. I therefore decided to start with the supply side of this problem.

Supply Side

> Second-level heading or subheading – use of italics to indicate sub-heading. One can also use alpha-numeric or Roman numeral notations to provide a similar signpost

I decided to begin with the data analytic services that are exclusively cloud-based. Once I had collected information about those apps, I began collecting data on companies that host their data analytic services on their own websites. Table 1 shows the list of vendors who make or provide software services for corporations to conduct analytics on business data. The source for this information is cited alongside the table caption and there are some notes explaining the terms used in the table. Figure 3 depicts a typical BI dashboard.

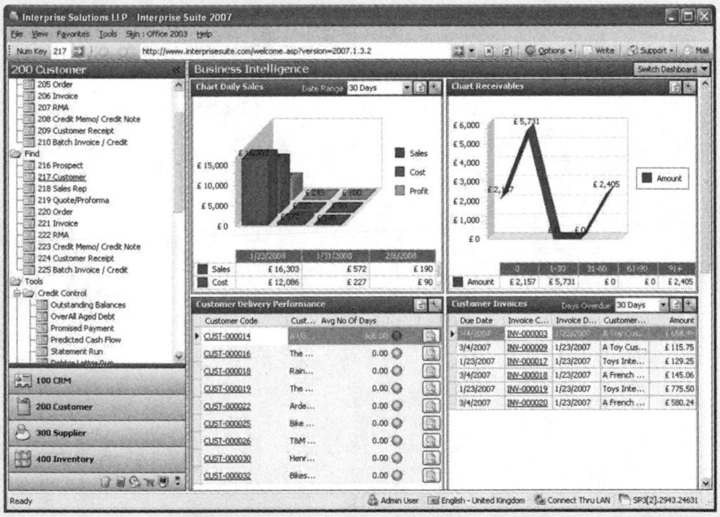

Figure 3: Sample BI Dashboard

continued

Table 8: Top 16 Vendors of Business Data Analytic

No.	Name of Company	Cloud-Only	Website and Cloud	Mobile Apps Y/N	Type and Notes
1	1010data	X	X	Roamb* Y	Works with multiple Hadoop** software providers
2	Actian			Y	Works with multiple Hadoop software providers
3	Amazon Web Services	X		Y	Works with multiple Hadoop software providers
4	cloudera		X		Provides Apache Hadoop support for enterprises
5	HP		X		Works with multiple Hadoop software providers
6	Horton-works		X		Provides Apache Hadoop support for enterprises
7	IBM		X		Uses its own Hadoop distribution
8	InfiniDB				Workd with multiple Hadoop software providers
9	Infobright				Works with multiple Hadoop software providers
10	Kognito				Works with multiple Hadoop software providers
11	MapR				Provides Apache Hadoop support for enterprises
12	Microsoft		X		Offers complimentary software
13	Oracle		X		Resells and supports Cloudera
14	Pivotal				Uses its own Hadoop distribution
15	SAP		X		Works with multiple Hadoop software providers
16	Teradata				Offers complimentary software

Source: Henschen, D. (2014, January 30). 16 Top big data analytics platforms, *InformationWeek*. Retrieved from http://www.informationweek.com/big-data/big-data-analytics/16-top-big-data-analytics-platforms/d/d-id/1113609?
*Roambi: Can get data analytics from most sources onto the mobile phone
**Apache Hadoop: Provides the open-source data processing platform on which vendors provide data analytics capabilities

Analysis of Findings

> A separate section on analysis of findings

Based on the data collected, we have a few options to consider. First, there is evidence of a growing number of companies that are providing web-based analytics for their clients. While most are desktop services, increasingly, companies are offering mobile BI options. Business users too are looking for data analytics on their mobile devices, both tablets or smartphones. With this in mind, I have listed some of the most relevant options we have and consider the pros and cons of each.

- Option A: Do nothing.
- Option B: Make a small test app for the most popular operating system and see how well the technology works, and whether it meets the needs of the business user.
- Option C: Get into full scale development of mobile BI apps for all the platforms.
- Option D: Select two or three most popular mobile platforms and partner with one or two data analytics companies to create targeted apps.

> List of available options

Option A: The "do nothing" option is tempting, but if we do nothing, we will miss out on entering the market when there are only a few players. Ramping up the development team will take time and we may not be competitive if we delay entry. However, the "do nothing" option allows us to focus on other consumer apps that we are already good at and grow the business.

> Discussions of pros and cons for each option

Option B: Making a small test app for one popular mobile platform like the Android (highest global market share) appears to be a good idea. However, focusing on just one platform will make us miss out on many users who use iPhones (second largest global market share).

Option C: Getting into full-scale development for all the mobile platforms will be a good option in the long run, but will exhaust our current resources and prevent us from supporting the apps we are currently selling.

Option D: Selecting two or three platforms, such as Android, Apple, Windows or even Tizen (Samsung's answer to Google's Android), will provide us with flexibility and the agility to get to market quickly. While there are millions of business users still using the BlackBerry phones, BlackBerry itself is currently undergoing changes, so it is best to hold development on this operating system. There is talk that BlackBerry may enter into a partnership with Android. There are very few companies that are developing mobile BI apps. Additionally, if we partner with one or two mid-range data analytics companies, then we will have an existing customer base that we can tap into and begin growing the business. As this business matures, we can consider adding other mobile platforms as well. While this will strain our resources a bit as we seek to redeploy our team resources, eventually the business can grow and new hiring can be done in each of the development teams to take on the extra workload.

continued

Recommendations and Conclusions

Having collected relevant data on the companies currently providing cloud-based data analytics and some mobile data analytics, and having also analyzed projections of the number of business users of smartphones, I presented four possible options for developing apps for mobile BI. Considering the pros and cons of each option, I recommend that APPFORMS begin the development of mobile BI applications for the Android, Apple, and Windows operating systems. Additionally, APPFORMS can partner with companies like Cloudera and Actian to develop specific apps for the data analytics applications provided by these companies. Later on, once the business matures, we can look at developing apps for other operating systems like Tizen and BlackBerry. Gartner, the world's leading information technology research and advisory company, predicted that business intelligence and analytics will remain the top focus for Chief Information Officers (CIOs) through 2017 (Gartner, 2013) and have even produced reports discussing return on investments (ROI) on customer-facing mobile apps (Marshall, 2014). Since mobile apps are a vital part of any business, digital or otherwise, business analytics on mobile devices will be all the more crucial in providing up-to-the-minute data analytics on how a business performs and help decision-makers take data-driven business decisions.

References

Chaffey, D. (2011). Mobile usage statistics 2010–2015, *Smart Insights*. Retrieved from http://www.smartinsights.com/mobile-marketing/mobile-marketing-analytics/mobile-usage-statistics-2010-2015/

Gartner (2013). *Gartner predicts business intelligence and analytics will remain top focus for CIOs through 2017*. [Press release]. Retrieved from http://www.gartner.com/newsroom/id/2637615

Marshall, R. (2014). *How to estimate ROI for customer-facing mobile apps*. Stamford, CT: Gartner. Retrieved from https://www.gartner.com/doc/2789317?ref=SiteSearch&sthkw=customer%20usage%20of%20data%20analytics&fnl=search&srcId=1-3478922254

Tennant, D. (2016). Smartphones reviews. *Top Ten Reviews*. Retrieved from http://cell-phones.toptenreviews.com/smartphones/

Verkooijen, K. (2014). Mobile business intelligence: Key considerations for implementation projects. *Journal of computer information systems 54* (1), 23–33.

Clear recommendations

Ending with citation of another credible and reputable source to support the recommendation

Separate references section following APA format

James's report is longer than Carrie's report. It is more complex and requires more analysis, even though it too relies on information collected from external sources. Whereas Carrie had only one external source, James sought additional sources to support his recommendations. He uses academic articles and well-known research companies like Gartner to provide information to support his claims. However, both reports have similar structural elements. They provide informative headings in bold, and James uses italics to distinguish his second-level headings from the first-level headings. Many word-processing applications provide styles that have standard heading styles for multiple levels. He uses the APA (American Psychological Association) format for in-text and endnote citations. Where he retrieves information from the Internet, he mentions the URL of the source site. In some cases, online sources have what is called a digital object identifier (DOI). Where available, this too can be presented in the references section beside the cited work.

◉ SCOPE

Strategy as always is key to identifying the solutions to any business task or issue, positive or negative. Carrie du Plessis found her task to be a positive exercise. Her approach in identifying sources for icebreaker and team-building activities and using the list from the Lions Club was a good strategy because it saved her time. Her source was credible and the reputation of the organization helped her reach her decisions faster. However, Carrie employed additional analytical strategies to help her select from the large list of activities and make her recommendations. In the case of James Patel, the problem was bigger, though it too was a positive one. There were aspects of the problem, particularly from the users' perspective, where complete information was not available. So he arrived at conclusions and made recommendations based on reasonable and testable assumptions. This will allow his manager to take the correct business decisions. Both Carrie and James then adopt a clear strategy in constructing their reports. They need to be easy to read and also demonstrate to their managers that Carrie and James, even though they are only co-op students, can think clearly, do analysis, and articulate their findings in a manner that is easy to follow.

Content in a report or any form of communication is intended to provide information to decision-makers and motivate their actions. Poorly structured content can make it difficult for readers to understand what they are required to do after reading the report or other communication. The greatest content can be buried in poorly constructed sentences and poorly designed forms of communication. Form and content go hand-in-hand and care needs to be taken to design reports or any form of communication in a manner that allows readers or audiences to follow the line of thought and motivate them to take the actions that the producers of the reports wish them to take.

The *outcome* for any communication is to further the relationship between the sender and the receiver. Managers ask for reports so they can position themselves to take the right decisions that their businesses demand, and so that organizational objectives are met in a timely manner. Reports are also key to help the businesses determine where there were failures and what needs to be addressed and possibly fixed. In the case of positive or desired outcomes, managers need to know how successful decisions can be replicated in different circumstances, with modifications to suit the new contexts, and how these successful decisions can be used to train employees and future leaders.

Presentation brings us back to the form and design. Both Carrie and James used standard forms. This allows their managers to quickly follow their line of thought and go directly to parts that were most relevant to their decision-making processes. Using clear structures, informative headings, numbered and captioned tables and figures, referring to the tables and figures in the main text, and providing **signposts** allow readers to absorb written presentations quickly. Managers and business leaders may not have the time to read full-length reports, so including summaries and clear takeaways in the conclusions are critical, but care still needs to be taken while presenting details in the report body.

Ethics again becomes central to the presentation of ideas and opinions in a report. While care must be taken to design a report and present information in a structured manner, extra care needs to be taken to ensure that the content itself is clean and clear, devoid of misleading interpretations, erroneous conclusions, and false data. Making up data only leads to problems. However, on occasion, made-up data can be used to demonstrate a point or a proof of concept. On such occasions, it must be clearly stated that the data is not real, but that it has been created only to demonstrate a point. It should further be stressed that such an exercise was conducted only to act as a simulation for a possible scenario to allow business decision-makers to prepare strategies to face hypothetical scenarios.

Chapter Summary

In this chapter we presented the various aspects of writing business reports. While there are multiple types of reports a business writer may need to produce, there are common factors to all types. Form, including structure, style, design elements, font type and point size, informative headings acting as signposts, grammatically correct sentences, transitions between sections, lists, figures, tables, and appendices, is a critical aspect of how well the content is received by the reader. Content that provides clear context and background, using analysis that follows accepted practices and leads to honest and logical claims and interpretations based on the evidence, clear evaluation of available options, and presentation of actionable recommendations and conclusions, can be used by managers to take relevant and timely business decisions. We looked at the examples of Carrie du Plessis and James Patel writing long reports and highlighted the various form and content approaches that the two co-op students adopted to showcase their findings. Ethical approaches are always front and centre and are especially critical when writing reports. These were highlighted in the choices that the two co-op students made as they performed their tasks and wrote their reports.

Discussion Questions

The exercises in this chapter involve the following scenario. Answer the questions based on the events described in the scenario.

The Case of Sean McNeill: Departmental Integration

Larissa Zhao, manager of Team Windows, and Vic Tremblett, manager of Team BlackBerry, have asked Sean to talk to members of both teams and ask them their opinions about the possible merger of the Windows and BlackBerry teams. They provided Sean with some of the questions that he could ask and want him to document the results of the interviews. They want the results in an email within the next few days. Sean conducts the interviews and makes notes on all of the interviews. He is now ready to write his report.

1. What type of report is Sean writing?
2. How long should it be?
3. Should Sean reproduce entire conversations in the report or just summarize the findings? Should he interpret the findings and offer his opinions?

4. Should Sean send the report only to Larissa Zhao and Vic Tremblett or to the team members as well?

5. How can Sean demonstrate his abilities at report writing and his analytical or critical thinking skills?

Exercises

1. Identify and list the best font types and point sizes suitable for report writing.
2. What is the meaning of making structure explicit?
3. When should you use numbered lists and when should you use bulleted lists?
4. Should every report have a report summary or executive summary?
5. Should reports have running headers?

Good Advice or Bad?

1. You have completed a report and realized that you did not collect all of the citations while writing it. You are now running out of time and need to submit the report. Your friend suggests that you grab some random website URL information and drop in some names as nobody actually checks the citations. Good advice or bad? Why?
2. You are using bold and italics for your headings and subheadings in your report. To emphasize certain aspects you think you should underline those areas. Good advice or bad? Why?
3. You source all your information from a Wikipedia page on your topic. Since you used only that one page, you feel you only need to cite the URL of that Wikipedia entry. Good advice or bad? Why?
4. You are rushing to complete a report and you are running out of time. Your friend suggests a contact who will do your report professionally for a fee. Good advice or bad? Why?

Strategic Language: Using Transitions in Writing

Transitions are words or phrases that help move the narrative along from one idea or sentence to the next and from one paragraph or section to the next. They guide readers or listeners to where the writer or speaker wishes them to go. When sentences, paragraphs, or sections start and end abruptly, readers are often confused and will lose interest in the topic and abandon the effort of following along.

There are several types of transitions. Transitions can be logical when they present a claim supported by step-by-step presentations of evidence (causal or otherwise). They can be structural, where a defined noun is followed by a verb. They can be phrasal by using words such as *however*, *but*, *therefore*, and *because*. And transitions can be verbal, where the writer moves from a known or widely accepted concept to the new concept.

How your letter or report is organized is crucial to the reader following your train of thought. Transitions can help the reader follow the narrative closely. Transitions between sentences in a paragraph help readers anticipate what is coming next. Here words or short phrases can be used effectively. Transitions between paragraphs connect two sets of relationships and can be done effectively by using phrases or even a sentence. One sentence at the end of the preceding paragraph and one sentence at the start of the next paragraph will help the reader keep the train of thought as they proceed through the narrative. Transitions between sections often require more than just words or phrases. They could even have an entire transition paragraph to orient the reader toward the writer's viewpoint. The Writing Center, University of North Carolina, Chapel Hill, North Carolina has a good list of expressions commonly used for transitions.

In summary, transitions help categorize relationships in a narrative, whether letters or reports. The various types of relationships between ideas in a narrative are listed alphabetically in the Table 7.1.

Table 7.1 List of Transitional Relationship Types and Examples

Relationships	Examples
Addition	also, again, as well as, besides, coupled with, furthermore, in addition, likewise, moreover, similarly
Consequence	accordingly, as a result, consequently, for this reason, for this purpose, hence, otherwise, so then, subsequently, therefore, thus, thereupon, wherefore
Contrast and Comparison	contrast, by the same token, conversely, instead, likewise, on one hand, on the other hand, on the contrary, rather, similarly, yet, but, however, still, nevertheless, in contrast
Direction	here, there, over there, beyond, nearly, opposite, under, above, to the left, to the right, in the distance
Diversion	by the way, incidentally
Emphasis	above all, chiefly, with attention to, especially, particularly, singularly
Exception	aside from, barring, beside, except, excepting, excluding, exclusive of, other than, outside of, save
Exemplifying	chiefly, especially, for instance, in particular, markedly, namely, particularly, including, specifically, such as
Generalizing	as a rule, as usual, for the most part, generally, generally speaking, ordinarily, usually
Illustration	for example, for instance, for one thing, as an illustration, illustrated with, as an example, in this case
Restatement	in essence, in other words, namely, that is, that is to say, in short, in brief, to put it differently
Sequence	at first, first of all, to begin with, in the first place, at the same time, for now, for the time being, the next step, in time, in turn, later on, meanwhile, next, then, soon, the meantime, later, while, earlier, simultaneously, afterwards, in conclusion, with this in mind
Similarity	comparatively, coupled with, correspondingly, identically, likewise, similar, moreover, together with
Summarizing	after all, all in all, all things considered, briefly, by and large, in any case, in any event, in brief, in conclusion, on the whole, in short, in summary, in the final analysis, in the long run, on balance, to sum up, to summarize, finally

Source: *Study guides and strategies* (n.d.). Retrieved from http://www.studygs.net/wrtstr6.htm

Identify the types of transitions in the following sentences and indicate the type of relationship as shown in Table 7.1. Also indicate whether the transition is logical, structural, verbal, or phrasal.

1. She didn't seem willing to sell the car this week, but in any case I don't get paid until the end of the month.
2. The music had a retro sound but at the same time incorporated a complex modern rhythm.
3. In their advertising business, saying things directly was not the rule. That is to say, they tried to convey the message subtly though with creativity.
4. The research was presented in a dry style, although it was coupled with examples that made the audience tear up.
5. The Quakers gathered each month with attention to deciding the business of their meeting.
6. Consensus was arrived at by all of the members exclusive of those who could not vote.
7. The children were happy. On the other hand, and perhaps more importantly, their parents were proactive in providing good care.
8. When there is a trusting relationship coupled with positive reinforcement, the partners will be able to overcome difficult situations.
9. Highway traffic came to a stop as a result of an accident that morning.
10. She scanned the horizon for any sign though in the distance she could not see the surprise coming her way.
11. He stumbled on the nesting pair incidentally found only on this hill.
12. Some friends and I drove up the beautiful coast chiefly to avoid the heat of the city.
13. There were a few talented artists in the class, but for the most part the students only wanted to avoid the alternative course.
14. The chapter provided complex sequences and examples illustrated with a simple schematic diagram.

Additional Resources

Additional Internet Resources

Purdue OWL (2016). Online Writing Lab. Retrieved from https://owl.english.purdue.edu/owl/resource/560/01/

APA Style. American Psychological Association. Retrieved from http://www.apastyle.org/

Grammar and Language Links

English Language Smartwords—Transitions and Phrases. Retrieved from http://www.smartwords.org/linking-words/transition-words.html

The Writing Centre at UNC–Chapel Hill. Retrieved from http://writingcenter.unc.edu/handouts/transitions/

CHAPTER EIGHT

Persuasive Techniques for Short and Long Presentations

Learning Objectives

A.   **Understand** the reasons for doing presentations.
B.   **Understand** form and content when preparing presentations.
C.   **Understand** the importance of making structure explicit in a presentation and the various design elements of a presentation.
D.   **Develop** skills and strategies to present complex information in a presentation.
E.   **Incorporate** techniques of argumentation, persuasion, and presentation effectively when delivering presentations.
F.   **Present** yourself and the organization favourably by using evidence, rhetorical tools, and ethics when preparing and delivering presentations.
G.   **Learn** the various aspects of public speaking—tone, pace, pauses, flow, eye contact with audience, use of space, letting go of crutches, dropping filler words and phrases—to deliver good to great presentations.

The Story So Far

Chapters 6 and 7 were about writing short and long reports, and discussed the various aspects of form and content that go into the creation and production of these reports. In Chapter 6 we saw how Bahram Fonseca, Kirsten Hamed, and Dharini Gagnon created short progress reports. In Chapter 7, we followed Carrie du Plessis and James Patel as they each created analysis and recommendation reports for the tasks they had been assigned to (first presented in Chapter 4).

So far in this book, we have followed the various stages of students' preparation as they attend university, prepare their career portfolios, use their written and oral communication skills effectively, and successfully start their work term placements. We are now at a stage when, toward the end of their co-op work terms, students are being asked to present their work to management. Carrie, having submitted her report in Chapter 7, has now been asked to present her recommendations to the APPFORMS senior management. Sean McNeill, who had been asked to conduct an interview with members of two APPFORMS's departments that could be integrated, is now going to present his findings. In Chapter 8, we will see how Carrie and Sean go about preparing their presentations.

Introduction

In today's globalized work environment, delivering presentations is a skill that everyone needs to develop. Whether one works in an exclusively client-facing role in marketing, sales, finance, or entrepreneurship, or in more back-end roles such as in accounting and auditing, human resources, payroll, or administration, everyone has to prepare and deliver presentations at one point or another. The audiences typically vary with the role and can consist of internal or external stakeholders or a combination of the two. Regardless of the audience, it is the ability of the presenter to effectively communicate simple to complex business information that determines whether the presentation is successful and the audience understands the key points.

The presenter's ability is revealed by how she or he sets the tone through delivery, pace, volume, and clear engagement with the audience by making eye contact and by talking about the benefits to the audience as it sits and watches and listens. It is always the presenter doing the presentation, with props and slides acting only as presentation aids. The presenter may also provide visual and oral cues for the audience. However, care must be taken to ensure that presentation aids such as slides do not distract the audience from the narrative. The presenter needs to work strategically in choosing what to present, how to organize the information, what to highlight, and, most importantly, what to omit. Appendices contain extra, but relevant, information, and appear at the end of a report or a presentation.

Chapter 8 addresses issues of style, design, and organization, as well as delivery that make effective presentations. We will follow Carrie du Plessis and Sean McNeill as they create their presentations and prepare to deliver them.

Form, Content of Presentations, and Everything in Between

In formal presentations and reports form guides content, but they are inseparable and it is important to pay careful attention to both. There may be instances where content is so important that one ignores form and focuses on the content, which ends up being delivered in a less-than-organized manner. Even in such instances, it is important to follow the basic requirements of form, language, and structure so that the receiver of the information can easily locate the key points contained in the message.

So what exactly is form in a presentation? As with other types of business communication like memos, letters, newsletters, and reports, presentations take on certain forms or structures depending on the reason for the presentation, the type of audience, and the nature of the content that needs to be delivered. The form or structure allows the audience to easily follow the narrative and find what they need in order to take business decisions. A quick look at any commercially available presentation application such as Microsoft PowerPoint, Prezi, Apple Keynote, or Google Slides will give you certain standard forms and templates for most types of business presentations. While templates are a great place to start, the form or structure for your specific business need will be dictated by the audience and the context. The modern business communicator needs to choose a template carefully.

Form of a Presentation

In the context of a presentation, form addresses all aspects of appearance, including its design. It involves length (i.e., number of slides, where slides are used), appropriate use of relevant and informative slide titles, indentation, bulleted or numbered lists (enumeration) with short sentences in each bulleted or numbered point to convey important and relevant information, and the overall look and feel of the presentation. Form also includes the use of grammatically correct sentences, consistent use of active voice, choice of font type and size for ease of readability, and making sure that every sentence, figure, table, or graphic is there for a purpose. This allows the presenter to present the information clearly and without deceit so that the audience can take clear business decisions. A presentation that is beautiful to watch but takes liberties with facts or data is unethical and can lead the audience to erroneous conclusions and will be detrimental to both the presenter and the business organization. However, a presentation that is true to the facts and gives clear recommendations, but does not have any structure or good form, is also self-defeating as the audience will be unable to follow the presenter's line of thought. They may get frustrated in the process and eventually tune out. This is why form and content are inseparable, and the presenter must always present the content with the target audience in mind and with a view to engaging the audience.

Design Elements in a Presentation

The organization and design of presentation slides are critical elements in a presentation because they determine the narrative. Although it is the presenter's delivery and style that guides the audience, the slides that aid the presentation must not distract the audience. To do this, the presenter needs to follow certain simple steps.

1.   Create an easy-to-read yet informative presentation title that will catch the audience's attention.
2.   Inform the audience about the presenter.
3.   Create an agenda slide to serve as the starting point.
4.   Add visual signposts to the slides such as arrows that are highlighted to indicate where in the presentation the presenter is at.
5.   Ensure that slide titles are all the same font and point size throughout.
6.   Ensure that all slide text uses the same font and point size throughout.
7.   Ensure that all figures, tables, and graphics are appropriately captioned.
8.   Ensure there is enough contrast between slide background and foreground and font colour (e.g., black background, light-coloured fonts, or vice versa).
9.   Strategically choose design and colour schemes provided by the presentation application.
10. Ensure the length of the presentation (i.e., number of slides) is appropriate for the time allotted for the presentation. A good guideline is to allow one to two minutes of speaking time per slide.
11. Avoid text-heavy slides. Use short sentences or sentence fragments for each bullet point instead of long paragraphs.
12. Where text is used, try to keep the line length to between five and seven words.
13. Where line length exceeds one or two lines, insert extra line spaces between bullet points.
14. As far as possible, avoid animation. If using, use it sparsely and strategically.
15. Cite sources of all externally or internally obtained information, tables, graphics, quotations, etc.
16. End with a thank-you slide that invites questions.

Content of a Presentation

Content of the presentation depends on the need of the business situation. It can be a short progress presentation discussing timelines and resource needs. It can also be short presentations documenting business events, such as brief sales forecast presentations, lab results, company policy changes, and updates. Content of longer research or analytical presentations involves more detail. In addition to providing the background and context, such presentations take time to develop a clear evidence-based argument supporting any claims made at the beginning of the presentation.

Like business reports, most presentations seek to answer the following questions:

- Who—who is creating the presentation, who it is meant for or who asked for it, and who, if any, are the internal or external stakeholders (people, groups, organizations) involved
- What—what the presentation is about, starting with a clear and informative presentation title, what the business gap is and what possible options are available. It also includes recommendations or courses of action to be taken, choices available, and strategies to adopt and pursue
- When—any or all time-related references regarding the events being presented
- Where—the location of the events being presented, as well as where the presentation is being created
- Why—why the presentation is called for and the reasons behind its creation including context and background
- How—the methodologies involved in filling the business gap and in creating the presentations, how the events being presented evolved or came into existence, and how any recommendations or conclusions being made or drawn follow a certain line of thinking
  - Methodologies can be research, analysis, interpretation schemes, historical or archival information, and so on.
  - Sources cited to add credibility can be internal and external.
  - Recommendations and conclusions are arrived at after synthesizing the findings from research, considering multiple perspectives and options, and arriving at the best option for that point in time.

Regardless of the type of presentation, the content for all business situations needs to start with some sort of claim statement. At the start of any presentation, the presenter needs to answer any potential questions from the audience with the claim statement, also known as a topic statement. When the business communicator provides a clear background or context for the situation and identifies the reason for questions, they are identifying the business gap. The answers to questions will most likely be the solution for filling the gap. Every time a presenter does this successfully at the start of a presentation or business communication, he or she has created an effective introduction, which gains the audience's interest and motivates the audience to stay engaged in the presentation.

Style and Delivery in a Presentation

Once a presenter has prepared the presentation slides, he or she can then begin to work on the delivery. Different people have different presentation styles and techniques as they deliver their presentations. Many feel nervous when they have to go out in front of an audience and have many pairs of eyes watching them. Eventually, however, most people are able to overcome these fears and go on to become good to great presenters or public speakers. New online applications such as Presenters Podium allow students to practise their presentations in front of cameras and record their final presentations. Peers then evaluate the presentations with constructive critiques and help the speaker improve delivery style and technique.

There is no great mystery to public speaking. While a few are able to do it naturally, most have to practise to get better. Oratorical skills can only be improved with practice and public speaking is no different than a stage performance. Actors have to practise their lines, alone at first, and then with the other actors with whom they will share the stage. Presenting in public requires the same level of practice and comfort with the material being presented. However, it is good to be aware of and pay attention to the following aspects of presenting in public.

1. Style and delivery are crucial to engage the audience, but the content must also be strong, relevant, and strategically arranged to keep the audience involved and engaged. Pace is most crucial. If you speed through, you will lose your audience and they will understand nothing of your content, so your presentation time is wasted. If you are too slow, you will also lose the audience. Adapt the content to suit the time limit provided. Too many vocal tics (e.g., *um* and *uh*) interrupt the flow to such an extent that there is no coherence. The key to style and delivery is practise, practise, practise.

2. The next thing to keep in mind is voice modulation, tonal variations, and inflections. Most people have very good public speaking voices, but you must put it to good use by raising the volume a bit. Avoid a monotone as nothing will put an audience to sleep faster. A steady pace helps a speaker develop and use tonal variations effectively.

3. Confidence and enthusiasm are not in most grading rubrics, but are definite factors that elevate a presentation from good to very good, or from very good to excellent or masterful.

4. Finally, learn to "embrace the pause." The pause is one of the most effective techniques in public speaking. It allows you to hold your audience's attention and create a certain aura of drama and sense of anticipation. However, a pause is best employed when using a good steady pace. Listen to yourself as you practise your speeches and watch how often vocal tics like *um* and *uh* enter the speech. Once you master the art of pausing, you can become a great public speaker and engage your audience with vocal inflections, tonal variations, and emphases.

Combining Good Organization, Useful Content, Good Delivery Style, and Effective Use of Visuals in a Presentation

The elements discussed above can all be combined to generate a great presentation. These are listed below in a manner to help you design and deliver effective presentations. Often these elements form the basis of any rubric used to rate and evaluate presentations.

Organization

- Use an effective introduction that develops context appropriately, identifies a clear main idea, and provides a specific overview
  - Apply appropriate organizational strategy; structure is explicit throughout

- Include a meaningful conclusion with effective summary and strong take-away statement
  - Effectively use time provided, adhering to time limit

Content

- Clearly identify why this issue/situation/business problem was chosen
  - Identify criteria for or features of a possible solution
  - Consider alternative solutions and evaluate the pros and cons of each alternative
  - Explain how the recommended solution meets criteria
    - Provide detailed analysis of the problem and solution
    - Make a clear claim; provide evidence from research and proper warranting to back up the claim
- Cite all sources

Delivery Style

- Speak clearly, at an audible volume and adequate pace
- Use an engaging vocal delivery with a natural speaking rhythm and control over vocal tics
- Maintain eye contact with audience throughout
- Use controlled and purposeful gestures, without distracting physical tics

Use of Visuals

- Effectively integrate slides into presentation through gestures and by making explicit references in speech
- Use slides with a clear and specific purpose and an appropriate level of detail to support content and act as good signposts to guide the audience
- Use a design with clearly legible font and good contrast between the background and the fonts and images
- Effectively frame slides with titles and figure headings

As discussed in Chapter 4, the business communicator (writer or presenter) weaves the narrative or content by using simple to complex rhetorical tools such as compare and contrast, cause and effect, and clear evidence-based argumentation. Presenters can frame knowledge to allow the audience to be situated in the topic under discussion, present new information based on known or accepted knowledge, and effectively use clustering and roadmaps to guide the audience. We will now return to the scenarios from Chapter 4, where Carrie du Plessis and Sean McNeill researched or analyzed certain business activities and submitted reports to their managers. Both have been asked to make presentations to their managers and the senior executives at APPFORMS.

Short Presentations

The Case of Carrie du Plessis: Presentation on Icebreaker and Team-Building Activities

Carrie was tasked by Juanita Olson, director of human resources, to identify and recommend some icebreaker and team-building activities for the upcoming APPFORMS's company retreat. Carrie did the research and submitted a report to Juanita, in which she makes some recommendations. Juanita really likes the report and asks Carrie to do a five-minute presentation at the next board meeting. Carrie's audience will be the three managing partners, Goran Duro, Alvira Cairns, and Abdul Hamza, as well as the directors of payroll and finance, business development, communications, and legal.

Carrie is both happy that Juanita liked her report, and nervous that her audience is going to be the senior management of the company. The next board meeting is two days away, and Carrie realizes that she needs to start work on her presentation right away. She has made presentations for class assignments before, but the audience were her classmates and her instructors. She has never presented to other audiences before. However, she is confident of her abilities to present.

Carrie decides to use Prezi. Although she is a Mac user and has used Keynote to prepare her class presentations, she feels that Prezi is more effective for short presentations. It is also easy to use and, like most presentation applications, it has design templates and lets her use animation where needed. She has a free account on Prezi and has not yet had the need to get a paid desktop version.

She opens up the Word document containing her report and reads through it to refresh her memory about the material. She then logs in to her Prezi account and opens up a new Prezi. The blank Prezi comes with a default set of circle frames (other frame shapes are also available), numbered sequentially. She enters the title for her presentation and her name in the title block. Moving to circle frame 1, she enters some information about the task and the methodology she employed. She then adds the design criteria table and the decision matrix for the icebreaker. In circle frame 4, she adds the design matrix for the team-building activity. She then adds the table recommending the top two icebreaker activities, and in circle frame 6, she adds the table recommending the top three team building activities. She realizes that she will need two more circle frames and adds them to the Prezi canvas. In circle frame 7, she adds some bullet points about the implementation and finally, in circle frame 8, she summarizes her recommendations. She checks the sequence of her frames and can see them lined up in the circle-frame box on the left side.

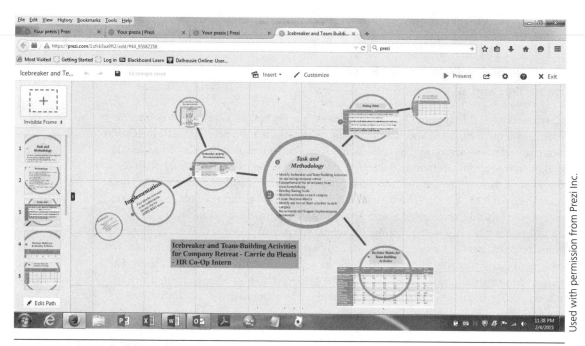

Figure 8.1 Carrie du Plessis's completed Prezi

She zooms out and takes a look at the Prezi, and then switches to presentation mode to see how it appears.

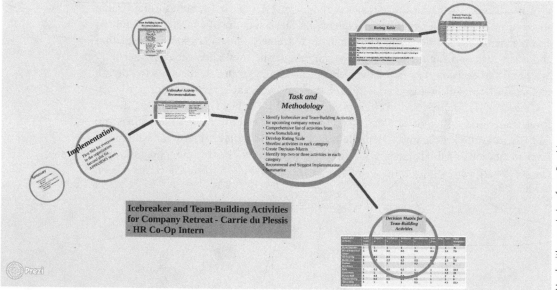

Figure 8.2 Completed Prezi in Presentation Mode

Carrie zooms into some of the frames to see if the information is presented correctly and there are no spelling or typographical errors.

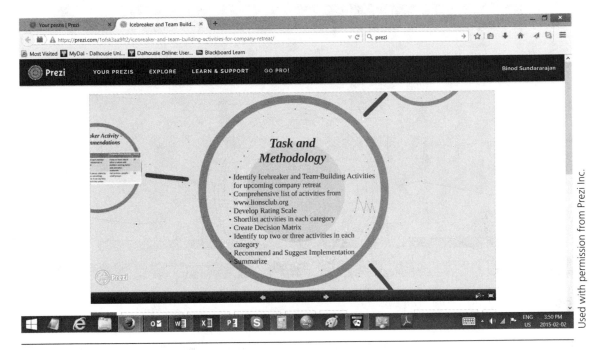

Figure 8.3 Carrie's First Frame Describing Task and Methodology

She then clicks through a few of the other frames checking for proper fit of the table inside the frames. In the case of the decision-matrix tables for both activities, she feels that the tables were too large. She decides since she had included these tables in her report, she need not present them here. If any audience member asks her questions about the decision matrix, she will briefly explain it to them, and refer them to the report that she submitted to Juanita. In the end, she decides to keep only the rating table and the tables recommending the activities. She then moves to the implementation and summary frames.

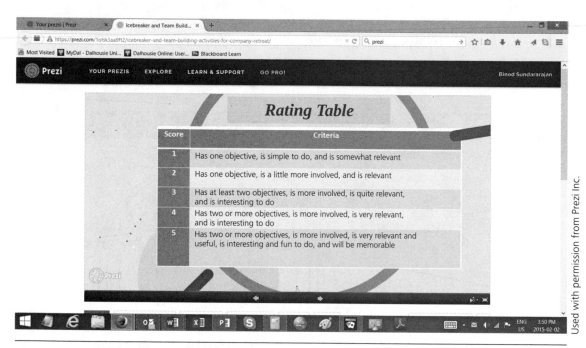

Figure 8.4 Rating Table Frame

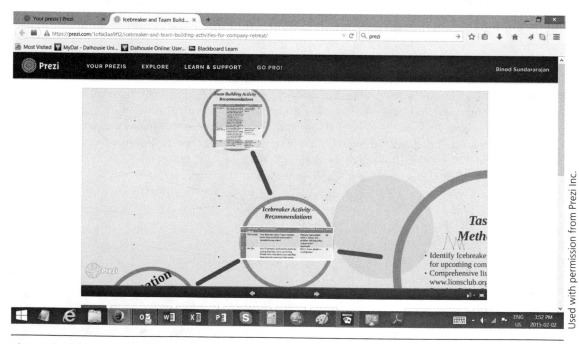

Figure 8.5 Tables with Recommendations

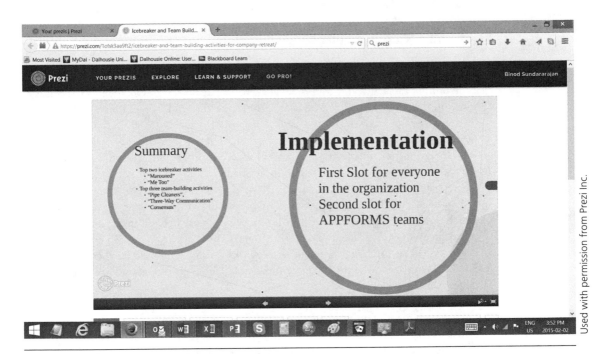

Figure 8.6 Implementation and Summary Frames

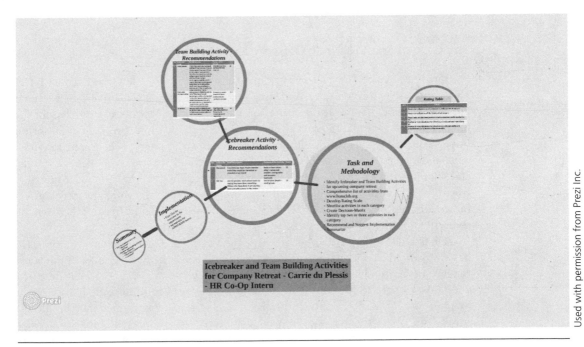

Figure 8.7 Carrie's Final Prezi

After making her final adjustments by ensuring she has used consistent fonts and point size and title sizes for the frames, and resizing the circle frames as much as possible, Carrie is happy with her Prezi. She now begins to prepare her presentation. She practises by first reading the material in each frame and clicking through the Prezi. She spends time talking to each frame and times herself. She decides she will spend 45 seconds at most on the title frame to introduce the topic, background, context, and methodology. She will then spend at least 60 seconds discussing the rating table in circle frame 2 and 60 seconds on each of the frames with recommendations. Finally, she will spend about 45 seconds on the implementation frame and the last 30 seconds she will use to summarize the recommendations. Carrie has always had an even pace for her presentations, but the repeated feedback from instructors and peers was that she needs to raise the volume of her voice a bit. Even though she will be presenting in the company conference room, which is not very big, she knows that she will need to raise her volume a bit more than her usual speaking voice. She always works to make good eye contact with everyone in the audience. Carrie is feeling confident as she works through and practises her presentation. She knows that she should get some more practice before the actual presentation and begins timing herself.

On the day of the presentation, Carrie presents her report with confidence, and is appreciated by everyone present. They all unanimously decide to adopt her recommendations, and select the highest-ranked activity in each category. Juanita then asks Carrie to assist her with implementing the activities during the retreat.

Long Presentations

The Case of Sean McNeill: Departmental Merger

Sean had been tasked by Larissa Zhao, manager of Team Windows, to conduct interviews and surveys among the Windows and BlackBerry team members regarding a possible merger of the two teams. Larissa provides Sean with the questions to use for the interviews and surveys. The survey questions were divided into two major categories, Importance and Agreement, with eight questions in each category. There were also four open-ended questions. Sean conducts the interviews and surveys, compiles the results, and submits a report. Larissa asks him to present the findings at the next board meeting, where the audience will include the senior management of the company. Since it is a rather complex topic, Sean will have 20 minutes to present his findings and there will be about 10 minutes afterwards for a question-and-answer session.

He is really happy at the opportunity and begins preparing his presentation. He has always worked with Microsoft PowerPoint and loves the new features in the latest version. He is also aware that the default presentation screen ratio is 16:9 widescreen and makes a note to himself to switch it to a 4:3 screen ratio once he has designed his presentation and is ready to present. Sean is a good presenter, but he always speaks too fast. Knowing that he has 20 minutes for his presentation, he decides to only include the most important aspects of his findings so that he can address them at a slower pace. That way he will not sound rushed or finish too fast and be out of breath.

Sean then lists what he will include in his presentation:

1. Title slide with a simple and clear title and his name
2. An agenda slide with chevron arrows to act as signposts
3. One slide with background information and context
4. Two slides with the survey questions
5. One slide for the open-ended questions
6. Slides of the survey analysis results, including
   a) his descriptive analysis of the survey responses
   b) bar graphs, giving information on the mean and standard deviation for each chart
7. One slide summarizing the findings from the survey and the open-ended questions
8. A thank-you slide that invites questions

Once Sean is ready, he opens his report and PowerPoint. He looks at the various design styles and chooses Organic. It is a neat and professional design, with a light background and a default black font. He decides not to use any animation as it could distract from the serious nature of the content. Sean curbs his natural tendency to crack jokes and add humour, as the business situation does not require it. The audience will already be engaged and they will want to know more about the findings and not Sean's funny side. He then begins adding the content according to his plan.

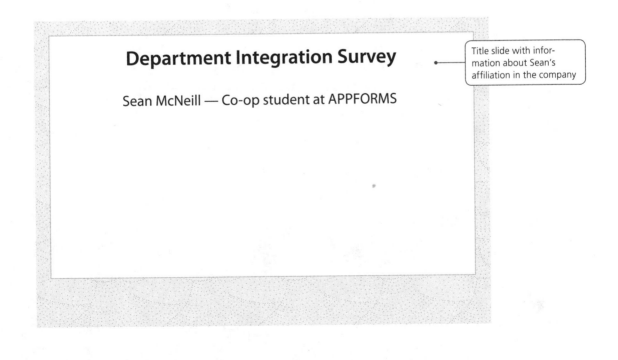

Department Integration Survey

Sean McNeill — Co-op student at APPFORMS

Title slide with information about Sean's affiliation in the company

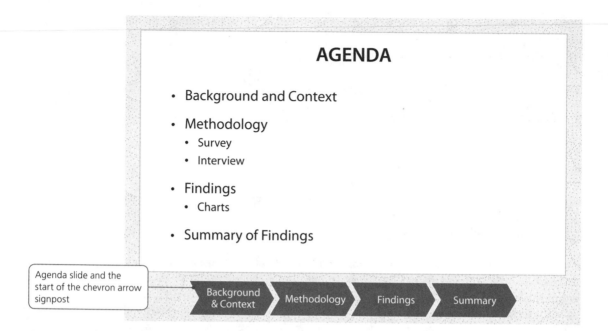

Agenda slide and the start of the chevron arrow signpost

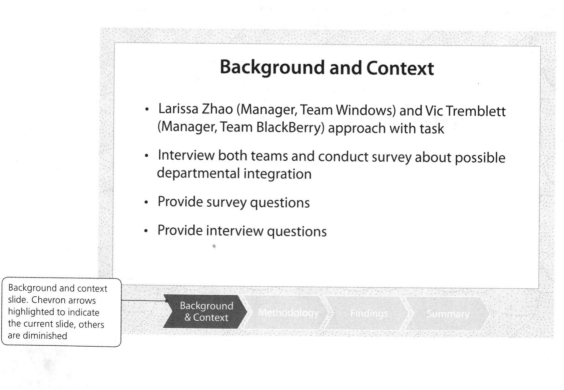

Background and context slide. Chevron arrows highlighted to indicate the current slide, others are diminished

Survey—Importance—5-point Scale

Rate the Following on Importance	Not Important		Neutral		Very Important
Maintaining an independent identity	1	2	3	4	5
Leveraging best skill sets	1	2	3	4	5
Increasing profitability	1	2	3	4	5
Increasing productivity	1	2	3	4	5
Maintaining team dynamics	1	2	3	4	5
Maintaining company culture	1	2	3	4	5
Keeping the same roles and positions	1	2	3	4	5
Exploring new avenues for collaboration	1	2	3	4	5

Background & Context | **Methodology** | Findings | Summary

> Slide listing the first set of survey questions on Importance. Chevron arrows highlighting the methodology section

Survey—Agreement—5-point Scale

> Second slide for the survey questions on Agreement

Rate the Following on Agreement	Completely Disagree		Neither Agree nor Disagree		Completely Agree
My current role is challenging	1	2	3	4	5
My current role is rewarding	1	2	3	4	5
I am able to produce high-quality work	1	2	3	4	5
I would like to work with other platforms	1	2	3	4	5
I would like to work with other people in the company	1	2	3	4	5
I am happy with the money I make in this company	1	2	3	4	5
I am happy with the recognition I get in the company	1	2	3	4	5
I see prospects for growth in this company	1	2	3	4	5

Background & Context | **Methodology** | Findings | Summary

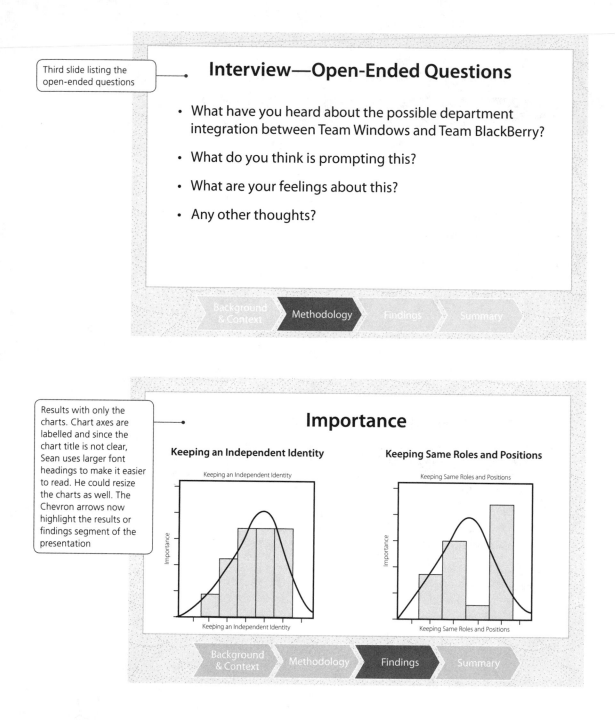

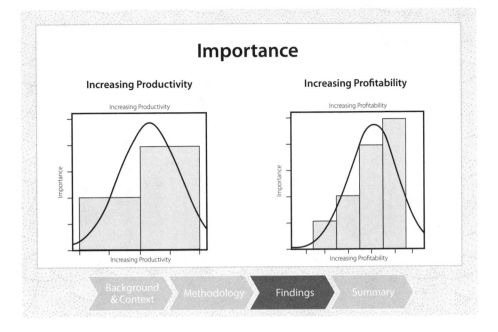

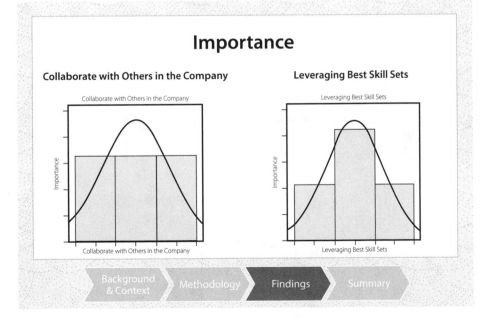

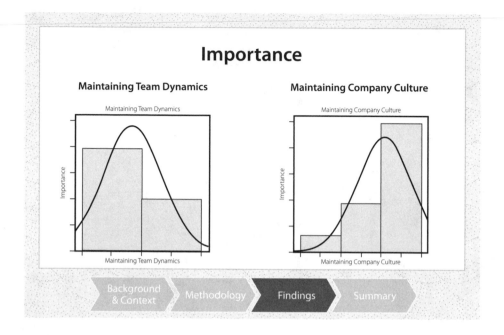

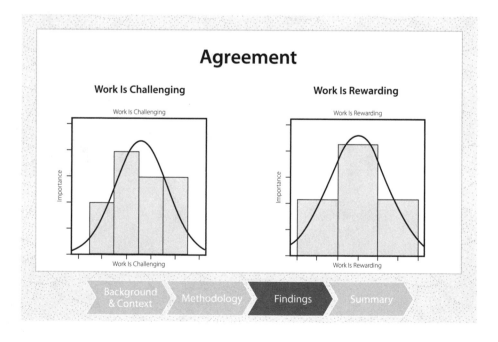

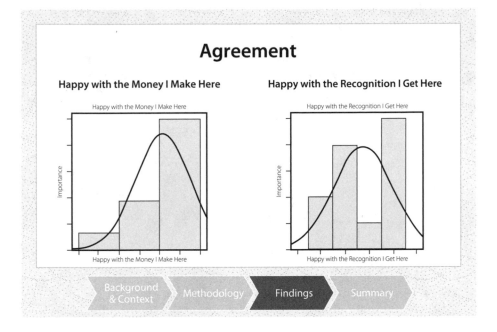

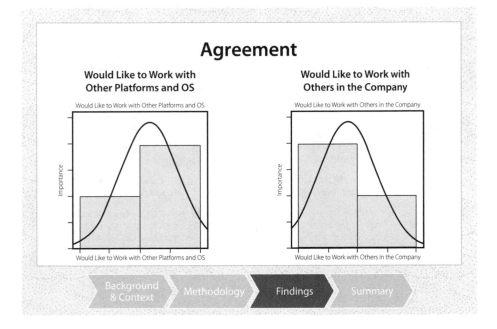

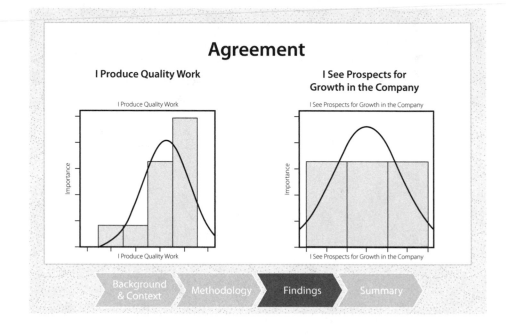

He now summarizes the findings in a Comparison Layout Slide. Sean realizes that this is a rather text heavy slide. He has kept each line to about 5–7 words, but feels it may still be too much. He adds white space between the bullet points to improve readability. The font size initially is at 18 points, but he feels he may need to increase that a bit and increases it to 20. The chevron arrows now indicate the summary segment of the presentation.

Summary of Findings

From Survey—Importance

- Mixed feelings about keeping an independent identity and staying in current roles

- Unanimous feeling for the need to increase productivity, but mixed feelings about increasing profitability

- Most would like to collaborate with others in the company and also leverage best skill sets

- Most feel strongly about the importance of maintaining team dynamics and company culture

From Survey—Agreement

- Most would like to work with other operating systems and development platforms and with others in the company

- Almost all feel their work is challenging and rewarding

- Almost all are happy with their salaries and the recognition they get here

- Mixed feelings about producing quality work and about growth prospects for themselves in the company

Background & Context ⟩ Methodology ⟩ Findings ⟩ Summary

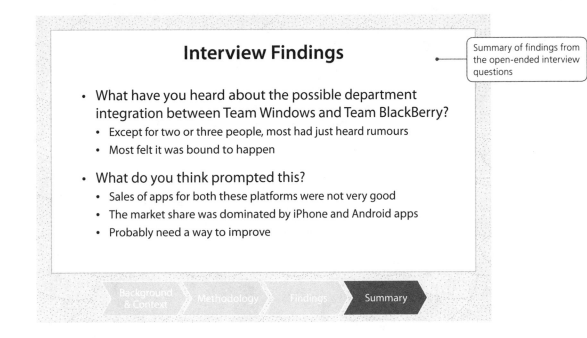

Interview Findings

Summary of findings from the open-ended interview questions

- What have you heard about the possible department integration between Team Windows and Team BlackBerry?
  - Except for two or three people, most had just heard rumours
  - Most felt it was bound to happen

- What do you think prompted this?
  - Sales of apps for both these platforms were not very good
  - The market share was dominated by iPhone and Android apps
  - Probably need a way to improve

Background & Context | Methodology | Findings | Summary

Interview Findings

Second slide with findings from the open ended interview questions. These summary slides are important as they speak directly to the business needs of Sean's audience. They are business decision makers and need to take certain actions regarding integrating two departments. The management is showing sensitivity by trying to ascertain the moods and feelings of their employees and the summary slides are crucial in helping them in this process.

- What are your feelings about this?
  - Nervous
  - Not sure if their jobs will exist
  - Teams will be bigger—maybe duplication

- Other thoughts
  - Integration can be exciting
  - May need ramp-up time
  - Challenges of coding in new operating systems

Background & Context | Methodology | Findings | Summary

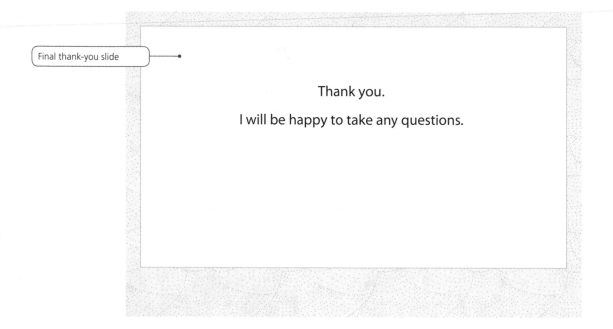

Final thank-you slide

Thank you.

I will be happy to take any questions.

Sean has 18 slides in his presentation deck, and thinks he will be speaking for about a minute per slide. However, he may not need to spend a minute on the title slide or the final slide or some of the other slides. He will have ample time to go over some of the slides in a little more detail, especially the summary slides. He begins to practise and time himself and feels confident and ready. On the day of the presentation, he presents with ease. Despite speaking quickly a couple of times, he manages to control himself, and completes his presentation successfully. He is also able to handle questions comfortably. Since he is not required to make recommendations, he only needs to answer questions related to the methodology and the meaning of some of the charts.

Presenting in Teams

The above discussion on presentations and the two scenarios are all oriented toward individual presenters. Most students and even professionals have to present in teams at some point or another. While most features of presentations hold true both for individuals and for team presentations, a few additional factors come into play when teams of two to four people are presenting. The team presentation is similar to a relay race in that the team with the best presentation has a strong starter, good solid speakers in the middle, and a strong finisher. Each team member is crucial to the effective performance of the whole team. While the slides need to be organized and seamless, so do the speakers. The handoffs and transitions between slides prepared by different team members should be smooth and so should the transitions between speakers. The team also needs to be seen working effectively. Even if only one speaker appears unprepared, it affects the performance and effectiveness of the entire team presentation. To summarize, the various elements of a team presentation are listed below.

Organization

- Use an effective introduction that develops context appropriately, identifies a clear main idea, and provides a specific overview
- Apply appropriate organizational strategy; structure is explicit throughout
- Include a meaningful conclusion with effective summary and strong take-away statement
- Effectively use time provided, adhering to time limit. No one speaker dominates the presentation
- The transitions between the different speakers are smooth

Content

- Clearly identify why this issue was chosen
- Identify criteria for or features of a possible solution
- Explain how the solution meets criteria
  - Provide detailed analysis of the problem and solution
  - Make a clear claim; provide evidence from research and proper warranting to back up the claim

Delivery Style

- Speak clearly, at an audible volume and adequate pace
- Use an engaging vocal delivery with a natural speaking rhythm and control over vocal tics
- Maintain eye contact with audience throughout by the speaker; other team members to alternately look at audience and speaker
- Use controlled and purposeful gestures, without distracting physical tics

Use of Visuals

- Effectively integrate slides into presentation content through gestures and by making explicit references in speech
- Seamlessly present slides even though they may be prepared by different team members
- Use slides with a clear and specific purpose to support content
- Use a design with clearly legible fonts
- Effectively frame slides titles and figure headings

◉ SCOPE

Strategy in presentations is extremely important, particularly because most presentations have a set time limit, ranging from 2 or 5 minutes to 45 minutes or longer in some cases. As always, the presenter needs to have a clear awareness of the audience. In most cases, audiences are not hostile, but every so often, presenters may encounter hostile sections in an audience. Whether the audience comprises lay people or business decision-makers or experts, the presenter needs to employ a strategy in organizing the information appropriately and developing a narrative that will engage the audience. Carrie du Plessis had only five minutes to present. While recommending icebreaker and team-building activities appears to be a trivial task, the fact that the entire senior management of APPFORMS was in the audience was enough to convey to Carrie the importance of her task. The senior management of APPFORMS took their retreat and team morale seriously and wished to make decisions that would benefit the entire organization. Carrie's diligence to the task assigned to her was well appreciated. Sean's presentation involved a serious business situation and his diligence with how he approached his task was also appreciated. Since he was not required to make recommendations, his strategy was to focus on his findings and the summary of his findings.

Content for presentations originate from work done prior to the presentation. They can be reports or even informational presentations. Regardless of the nature of the presentation, the content has to be thoroughly researched and analyzed, and sources need to be cited. Carrie had one source, while Sean had none because his information came from his primary data collection. Both Carrie and Sean employed certain techniques and methodologies that had to be explained in their reports and presentations. This provided the evidence for their recommendations, findings, and interpretations. The reason the methodologies needed to be explained was so they could be replicated by others and, if done correctly, have similar results. This approach also helps document the methodologies

for future use and ensures fairly similar content across time.

The *outcome* of successful presentations is often what the audience takes away at the end of the presentation. If the audience stays engaged throughout, follows the speaker as she or he talks to the slides and guides the audience, then the audience is more likely to recollect key points from the presentation. If the audience enjoyed the presentation and had a good laugh, but did not receive relevant information from the presentation, then the outcome would be negligible. Thus, the summary slides are key to ensuring the audience gets the main point of the presentation and is able to take the necessary business decisions. Both Carrie and Sean had clear summary slides that summarized either the recommendations or the findings, allowing the senior management of APPFORMS to take the appropriate business decisions.

Presentation brings us back to the form and design aspects. Although Carrie and Sean used different presentation applications, they used standard forms to create their presentations. This would allow their managers to quickly follow the line of thought and focus on parts that were relevant to their decision-making processes. Carrie and Sean used clear structures, informative headings, bullet points and numbered lists, figures and tables, and referred to the figures and tables and provided signposts and roadmaps to allow the audience to absorb the material quickly. Because managers and business leaders may not have the time to read full-length reports, effective presentations that have summaries and clear take-aways in the conclusions are critical in aiding business leaders in their decision-making processes.

Ethics is central to the presentation of ideas and opinions in a report or a presentation. While care must be taken to organize and present content in a structured manner, extra care needs to be taken to ensure that the content is free of misleading interpretations, erroneous conclusions, and false data. Making up data only leads to problems. Citing credible and verifiable sources ensures that the data presented is valid and real. Presenting clear evidence of the type of research or analysis undertaken further helps ensure the methodology is sound, verifiable, and replicable. Carrie cited the one source she drew her list of activities from, and clearly explained her method of categorizing and ranking criteria. Sean reported the results of the survey and outlined his techniques of analysis. Both Carrie and Sean understood the serious nature of the tasks they were assigned and approached them with due diligence. They were rewarded with appreciation for their work.

Chapter Summary

This chapter presented various aspects of creating and delivering effective presentations. These aspects included the organization and design of presentation slides using two common presentation applications, Prezi and Microsoft PowerPoint. The first part of the chapter provided conceptual and practical aspects of the design, style, and delivery of presentations, and the last part of the chapter followed the specific business tasks of Carrie du Plessis and Sean McNeill as they prepared, practiced, and delivered their presentations. The chapter ended with a brief discussion of team presentations.

Discussion Questions

The discussion questions in this chapter involve the scenario presented below. Read the scenario and discuss the questions based on the events described in the scenario.

The Case of James Patel: New Business Opportunity

James Patel has been asked by Pierce Sanchez, manager of Team Android, to conduct a market analysis of the demand of smartphone apps that would perform business data analytics and aid in business decision-making as people are moving about. James needs to make his recommendations in a report. It is a rather lengthy report so Pierce asks him to present his findings and recommendations to APPFORMS's senior management.

1. Once James knows who the audience is going to be for his presentation, what should his first question to Pierce be before he starts preparing?
2. Refer to James's report in Chapter 7 and list which elements he should include in his presentation.
3. What key design choices would he need to make as he prepares his presentation?
4. What should be the focus of his presentation be: his methodology, his findings, or his recommendations? Why?
5. How and where should James cite his sources?

Exercises

1. Identify the best fonts and point sizes to use in an effective presentation.
2. What should be the first question you ask before you start to prepare any presentation using Microsoft PowerPoint, Keynote, Google Presentations, or Prezi?
3. What are the different ways a presenter can guide the audience through a presentation?

4. What are the most critical aspects of vocal delivery that make a presentation effective?

5. What is meant by the phrase "embrace the pause"?

Good Advice or Bad?

1. You have to prepare slides for a two-minute presentation on the global oil market. You decide to talk about oil-price fluctuations, supply and demand, and dependence on fossil fuels. You friend suggests you use graphics showing sea creatures that died because of oil spills and a GIF image of oil gushing from an offshore oil well. Good advice or bad? Why?

2. For your five-minute presentation on investing in the stock market, you choose a dark background with bright 16-point font across all six slides, because there is a lot of information you want to cover. Your classmate suggests you increase the point size to between 18 and 20, omit a fair bit of the information, and cover only some key aspects. Good advice or bad? Why?

3. As you practise your presentation, you are not sure if you will be able to look at all parts of the audience. Your friend suggests that you use three people in the audience, one in the centre and one on each side, as markers and look at each of these three people in turn. That would give the audience the impression that you are looking at all parts of the audience. Good advice or bad? Why?

4. Because you are nervous about presenting, you are not sure what to do and decide that you will stay close to the podium where your laptop will be and you will read from your slides. Your friend suggests that you should put some notes on a few index cards and look at them instead. Good advice or bad? Why?

Strategic Language: Effective Messaging Strategies for Presentations

Whether you are preparing a short or long presentation, the writing is often different than the writing in reports or memos or letters. The one place where presenters can take liberties with sentence structure is in presentations. While typographical, grammar, editing, and spelling errors need to be fixed, sentences in presentations need not always be complete. That is, the bullet points can be short, incomplete sentences, parts of clauses, subordinate clauses, or just words and phrases. Long sentences in presentation slides cause the audience to read the presentation, rather than listen to the presenter. Extremely text-heavy slides are hard to read. A few things to keep in mind when using text in presentations include the following:

1. Use words or phrases to lead you to tell a story or explain a concept.
2. Use known words and concepts to get to the point quickly.
3. Use words and phrases that are relevant to the topic being discussed.
4. Ensure there are no grammar mistakes such as *your* vs. *you're*, *its* vs. *it's*, *then* vs. *than*, *lose* vs. *loose*, etc.
5. Pay attention to redundancies.

Dave Paradis (2013) provides good tips about grammar for presentation slides. The following three paragraphs are taken from his blog post. The link to the blog post is provided in the Bibliography of this book.

> I probably get more questions about how to format bullet points than I do about any other text on a slide. I want to start by addressing whether text points on a slide need a bullet point or not. A bullet point indicates a hierarchical relationship, with each level of bullet points breaking down the higher level point above it. In many slides I see, there is no hierarchical relationship in the list of points. In this case, I suggest you remove the bullet point character and use a simple list of text points. Use extra line spacing after each point to make the points properly separated on the slide. If you are using bullet points, use a filled bullet character that has enough presence to be seen and will indicate to the audience where each point starts.

> When formatting points on a slide, make sure the indentation is correct. For bullet points, the bullet character should sit to the left of the text with the lines of text starting at the same spot on each line. Using the default bullet point content placeholder sets this up for you automatically. If you are creating bullet points in a text box, set the hanging indent properly in the ruler. If you are not using bullet points, each text point should be left-aligned and start in the same spot on each line. If you have removed the bullet formatting from the default content placeholder, you will need to correct the hanging indent in the ruler to properly align the text points.

> The final tip about text or bullet points on a slide is to remember that they are supposed to be brief points to give the audience context for what you are about to say. Text or bullet points are not supposed to be a transcript of what you will say, so they should not be formatted like the sentences in a report. There should be no period at the end of a text or bullet point because it is not a proper sentence. The points should be written using sentence case instead of Title Case because they are not titles.*

Convert the three paragraphs quoted from the blog post into three PowerPoint slides that contain only bullet points and short sentences.

*Reprinted with permission from Dave Paradi http://www.thinkoutsidetheslide.com/issue-293-august-20-2013/

Additional Resources

Additional Internet Resources

Dlugan, A. (2013, August 27). Toastmaster's Speech 2: Organize your speech. *Six Minutes: Speaking and Presentation Skills*. Retrieved from http://sixminutes.dlugan.com/toastmasters-speech-2-organize-your-speech/

Duarte, N. (2012a). Structure your presentation like a story. *HBR Blog Network*. Retrieved from http://blogs.hbr.org/2012/10/structure-your-presentation-li/

Jeff, P. (2009). 10 ways to end your speech with a bang. *Six Minutes*. Retrieved from http://sixminutes.dlugan.com/10-ways-to-end-your-speech/

McMahon, G. (2016). What to do with charts [Blog post]. Retrieved from http://makeapowerfulpoint.com/2013/04/22/what-to-do-with-charts/

Reiffenstein, K. (2014, May 30). Using story in presentations [Blog post]. Retrieved from http://andnowpresenting.typepad.com/professionally_speaking/using-story-in-presentations/

Theriault, M. (2013, November 4). 9 tips for more powerful business presentations. *Forbes*. Retrieved from http://www.forbes.com/sites/allbusiness/2013/11/04/9-tips-for-more-powerful-business-presentations/

Video Resources

Cuddy, A. (2012). Your body language shapes who you are. *TED*. Retrieved from http://www.ted.com/talks/amy_cuddy_your_body_language_shapes_who_you_are

Duarte, N. (2012b). The secret structure of great talks. *TEDxEast*. Retrieved from http://www.ted.com/talks/nancy_duarte_the_secret_structure_of_great_talks.html

History Channel. (2012). *The Secrets of Body Language*. Retrieved from https://youtu.be/8Zv5dc-nnug

Pease, A. (2013). Body language, the power is in the palm of your hands. *TEDxMacquarie University*. Retrieved from https://www.youtube.com/watch?v=ZZZ7k8cMA-4

CHAPTER NINE

Managing Individual and Corporate Identities on Social Media, Web 2.x, and Beyond

© iStock/mihailomilovanovic

PART IV · THE INDIVIDUAL, THE ORGANIZATION, AND SOCIAL MEDIA

Learning Objectives

A. **Understand** communication on social media and the Web 2.x.
B. **Understand** the differences and similarities between individual and corporate identities.
C. **Understand** the concepts of identity, image, brand, and reputation.
D. **Recognize** the differences and similarities between social media and professional networks.
E. **Develop** skills and strategies to present and manage individual and corporate online identities.
F. **Incorporate** techniques of argumentation, persuasion, and presentation effectively when managing individual and/or corporate identities.
G. **Present** oneself and one's organization more favourably by using evidence, rhetorical tools, and ethics with a view to maintaining or enhancing the image and reputation of both.

The Story So Far

Chapter 8, which deals with creating effective presentations, discussed the design elements, form, and content of business presentations, as well as style and delivery aspects of the effective presenter. We did this by following the cases of Carrie du Plessis and Sean McNeill. Carrie used Prezi to present her recommendations for icebreakers and team-building activities for the company retreat. Sean used Microsoft PowerPoint to present his findings about a survey he conducted regarding a departmental merger at APPFORMS. The chapter concluded with a brief discussion of presenting in teams.

Chapter 9 looks at how individuals and organizations can manage their identities on social media. Once students leave their relatively sheltered lives on university and college campuses, and enter the workplace, their individual identities become intertwined with the identities of the organizations for which they work. This chapter will show a few examples of how to best manage individual and organizational identities on social and professional media sites.

Introduction

As you read these words, the world is standing at the threshold of the next generation of web and mobile tools, applications, and services—possibly Web 3.0. It has been argued that it takes about seven years for any technology to completely move from one generational suite of offerings to the next. The phrase "social media" has come to stand for the entire collection of online and mobile applications and networks that allow people to create and share content. Communication is now about conversations between people and organizations, although participants were mainly people, with organizations wanting to participate. Honesty and transparency were at the core of the content distribution, and this communication is about pulling people into the conversations and not just pushing out centralized information.

Internet usage of the mid- to late 1990s typically revolved around static content and unidirectional communication from the creators of content to the consumers of the content. Around the year 2002, a year after Wikipedia was started, the Internet changed from static web pages to more dynamic sites, with developers writing applications that allowed users to connect to one another, and write to the content creators (often organizations) about their likes, dislikes, and preferences, and even produce content themselves. Blogging by individuals and eventually organizations began in earnest, with everyone wanting to reach readers. All of this was named the Web 2.0. It took a while for Web 2.0 to firmly be established with an array of web-based applications and services that address dynamic content and increasing levels of user engagement. Communication became bidirectional with users adding content and engaging with, not just one another, but with organizations and governments.

Online social networking sites had their roots in Internet relay chats (IRCs) and an assortment of chat rooms. They evolved into more standalone and sought-after entities.

Technologies to connect users to one another existed prior to this time, such as Usenet, Geocities, AOL, electronic bulletin boards and even some early blogging. But it was Friendster, which later gave way to **Orkut** (from Google) and MySpace, that created a momentum toward the establishment of Web 2.0. These three websites held interest for many millions of individuals. In 2004, considered the official beginning of Web 2.0, Facebook appeared, to be followed by Flickr, Digg, and podcasting. By 2005, Rosenbush (2005) reported that MySpace was getting more page views than Google, Twitter was launched, and YouTube was gaining in popularity. By 2009, Facebook had become the most used social networking site with more than 200 million users, the likes of which had never been seen before (and it was not going to slow down any time soon). Words like *googling* and *unfriend* have become common usage, enough to warrant their own dictionary entries. Search became a key feature that users sought, and as Google remained the most popular search engine, Yahoo (an early search provider) and Microsoft and a host of other organizations began to realize the importance of having superior searching and indexing capabilities as a competitive advantage in this fickle and transient business.

In 2015, Facebook had about 1.59 billion users, YouTube had over 1 billion users, WhatsApp had over 900 million users, QQ had over 800 million users, Twitter had over 500 million registered users (over 307 million of them active), Google+ had over 350 million users, LinkedIn had over 225 million users, Tumblr (purchased by Yahoo) had over 555 million users and over 100 million blogs, **Baidu Tieba** and Skype had about 300 million users, Snapchat and **Sina Weibo** had over 200 million users each, Instagram had over 100 million users, Flickr had over 90 million users, and a host of other sites such as Pinterest and Reddit all boasted over 100 million users and counting (Statista. com). Organizations; governments (from municipal to federal); community groups; and interest, self-help, and support groups all have a presence in at least one, if not several, social networking sites. A large percentage of users access the online world using their mobile devices (smartphones, tablets, etc.). Furthermore, a substantial percentage of users have friended a brand on Facebook. This is the connection between the individual and the organization, where individual identities are linked to organizational identities, for one purpose or another, in a public space. By using Twitter and Facebook updates, citizen journalism provides real-time news and alerts about natural or human-caused events.

While North Americans are familiar with the above-mentioned social networking sites, many of which were developed in North America, other parts of the world have also created popular online applications and social media networks. Baidu, created in 2000 in China, offers several services including an online encyclopedia, search capabilities, and a searchable keyword-based discussion forum. In November 2014, Baidu ranked fifth worldwide (after Google, Facebook, YouTube, and Yahoo) in Alexa Internet rankings and currently provides over 740 million indexed web pages, over 80 million images, and over 10 million media files. China's Taobao Marketplace, an online shopping destination, and QQ, which has games, instant messenger, mail, search engines, and so on were at ninth and tenth places on the Alexa Internet rankings. Sixth on the list was Wikipedia, seventh was Amazon, and Twitter was eight (Alexa, 2016). In other words, the top ten online websites in the world are either search engines or portals like Google, Yahoo, and Baidu, which lead and point users to content or social media networking sites like Facebook, QQ, and Twitter; online marketplaces like Amazon or Taobao; or entertainment sites like YouTube or Baidu. It appears that people want to search for information (Wikipedia or Baidu), find content (text, images, or media), connect with one another, and shop online. The top 25 sites on the Alexa rankings included several more search engines (Ask, Bing, Google India and Google Germany, and Yahoo Japan), online shopping destinations, and a few blogging and microblogging sites like Blogspot (owned by Google) and Weibo (China's version of Twitter and Facebook) and auction sites like eBay. On 11 November 2014, Alibaba, the Chinese e-commerce portal, was poised to generate about $8.17 billion in one-day sales/transactions, booking an increase of about 40% from its one-day sales for 11 November 2013, which was about $5.8 billion (Harjani & Min, 2014).

All of these rankings and statistics show that users wish to maintain an online presence, connect with friends and family and even organizations, want access to information, and would like to use this information for personal consumption (news, entertainment, and shopping). Organizations need to be in this online space to engage with individual users, especially B2C (business to consumer) companies, so that users can talk about the organizations' products and services, which will lead to increased sales. It is said that the focus of Web 3.0 (or whatever version it will be called) will be how to increase these connections between users and organizations, but with more specificity. The increasing use of mobile apps is an indication of the users' need for access to information, news, entertainment, and shopping as they are moving about. Already, organizations gather information about users' preferences, which is used to target the advertisements they see. Every time a user searches for something online or sends a message with a certain subject line, the email, messenger, microblogging, or networking application they are using tracks the content of the message and responds with a personalized advertisement, whether it is for a baby stroller, medical remedy, car, or movie. By using GPS and other geo-location services collected from cellphone towers, Web 3.0 tools would provide locations to online users so that they can find outlets for purchasing a product or service. Although there are hundreds of thousands of mobile apps available online, viewing and downloading all of them will be impossible.

Web 3.0 will likely provide customized flashcards that will either recap the message of an email or a series of tweets, show only pictures similar to those the user has typically viewed in the past, direct users to news or entertainment or games that the users have viewed or played in the past, and make things easier for users to access what they want. While users want their preferences to be recognized by the organizations, organizations want users to talk about the organizations' products and services. The organization wants its identity and image to be transmitted to the users' networks, bearing the users' individual identities and image in their networks. To ensure this happens, organizations strive to create content that makes their products and services appealing to targeted consumers. One other key feature that Web 3.0 applications aim to capitalize on is trust. This does not refer only to users trusting organizations, but also to users trusting sources of information, verifying the credibility of ratings on shopping sites, and trusting people in their personal and professional networks. This will be a significant requirement from users who are never sure whom to trust when viewing news or entertainment online or buying things online based on ratings they see. A host of new applications will provide enhanced trusting mechanisms to provide validity for product or service ratings and direct users to trusted products and services.

Throughout the evolution of the Internet, two things have been common to all users, whether individual or organizational: identity and content. Every time an individual creates an online profile on a site or produces a blog or wiki, they are creating and establishing their identity. As the quality of their content improves, so does their credibility, identity, image, and reputation. This is also the case for organizations. Organizations are constantly trying to maintain and/or enhance their image, credibility, and reputation, which requires constant work. While individuals, especially young adults, are skillful at managing their online profiles and social identities, often they are unable to manage both their social identities and professional identities. For example, many are unaware that a LinkedIn profile requires a different approach from their Facebook, Twitter, or Instagram profile. This lack of awareness has led to much grief and frustration for individuals who have said something inappropriate on a social networking site. The inappropriate comment may become public through their professional networks and affect their current or future career prospects. Organizations also struggle to manage their corporate identities on social media, mainly when they view it only as another marketing channel and not as a channel of engagement. Such an approach has led to many organizations having their image and reputation damaged because of what was said on their behalf on a social networking site. In most cases, users immediately draw attention to the organization's mistake.

Identity and content are intertwined, and will continue to be so as long as individuals and organizations want to engage with one another. Chapter 9 specifically addresses how effective communication on social media will help both individuals and organizations manage their identities, image, and reputation. This long introduction provides a context for the rest of the chapter. The chapter will give you an overview of the world beyond the university. In the previous chapters, you learned how to create and nurture your individual identities (by creating résumés), present yourselves to external audiences (by writing persuasive cover letters, and short and long speeches), communicate with external organizational stakeholders (by writing traditional letters and/or emails), and analyze business problems and present them in various formats to business audiences (by creating short and long reports and presentations). Many of you may soon be looking for co-op work-term placements or internships. As co-op students or interns, you will become part of an organization, although only for a short time, and you will likely embrace the organizational culture. You will soon realize that your individual identities will become associated with the organization's identity, and this will become even more apparent when you join the work force as part- or full-time employees after you graduate. If individuals stay employed in an organization for long periods, individual identities often become aligned with or inseparable from their organization's identity. Managing the two can be quite a burdensome task. However, with clear priorities and effective communication strategies, the task can be managed quite well.

Chapter 9 follows a slightly different approach at the start. We present a few more theoretical concepts than in other chapters because they are necessary and useful to know and understand when going through the scenarios presented later in the chapter. We discuss some rhetorical concepts, such as tropes and memes, that play a key role in content creation, especially on the Internet and social media. This will bring us to the discussion of some communication strategies that are particularly relevant when using modern communication channels, and we will talk about concepts such as presence, reach, frequency, and push and pull. All this will set the context for some scenarios that involve co-op students and other APPFORMS's employees as they manage some workplace situations.

Identity, Image, Brand, and Reputation

We used the terms *identity, image,* and *reputation* in the introduction without defining them. Table 9.1 lists the definitions for these terms, and the term *brand*. The definitions come from the *Oxford Dictionaries* and *Corporate Communication* (Cornelissen, 2014).

Table 9.1 Identity, Image, Brand, and Reputation

	Individual (*Oxford Dictionaries*)	Organization/Corporate (Cornelissen, 2014)
Identity	The fact of being who or what a person or thing is This is typically conveyed by what people do or how they behave or, in the case of a thing, what it does and how it performs. It can be self-identity or whether one identifies with someone or something other than one's self.	The profile and values of an organization conveyed through symbolism, communication, and behaviour
Image	A representation of the external form of a person or a thing It is also a representation of an idea, and can be self-image or a projected one.	An individual's perception of an organization, product, or service at a certain point in time
Brand	A particular identity or image regarded as an asset For an individual seeking a particular job or career, developing a unique brand can be an advantage and let the individual stand out from the crowd.	The set of physical attributes of a product or service, together with the beliefs and expectations surrounding it; a unique combination that the name or logo of the product or service should evoke in the mind of the audience
Reputation	The beliefs or opinions that are generally held about someone or something An individual's actions can lead to increasing either his or her reputation and credibility or notoriety. A reputation of having integrity is good, while being known to be chronically late can be bad.	An individual's collective representation of past images of an organization (induced through either communication or past experiences) established over time; the general evaluation of an organization (compared to its rivals), leading to likeability and preference

Table 9.1 presents the definitions of the words *identity*, *image*, *brand*, and *reputation* in both individual and corporate contexts. With respect to social media, we need to look at one more concept, *presence*, and more specifically, *online* or *social presence*. The *Oxford Dictionaries* define *presence* as "the state or fact of existing, occurring, or being present." Other definitions include "the sense of being with another" (Biocca, Harms & Burgoon, 2003); "the degree to which a person is perceived as a real person" (Gunawardena, 1995); "a student's sense of being in and belonging in a course and the ability to interact with other students and the instructor" (Picciano, 2002). Lowenthal (2009) presents the idea that social presence is the sum total of an individual's affective responses (emotions, humour, and self-disclosure), cohesive responses (vocatives, use of inclusive pronouns, and social task-oriented communication or salutations) and interactive responses (continuing a thread, quoting or referring to other messages, asking questions, and expressing agreement or appreciation).

While social presence has all these definitions, it is mainly used in the context of social learning and social interactions, particularly in technology-mediated and online environments and specifically with reference to individuals present in these environments. The organizational version of this would then be "online corporate presence." A corporation can very well use emotions, humour, and self-disclosure to connect with its key users or stakeholders to establish its identity and create an image or brand. A corporation can also use inclusive pronouns and salutations to directly address its key stakeholders and likewise use interactive responses to engage with its users. When a corporation does all of this online, it begins to establish an online corporate presence to the extent that it becomes a significant presence in its stakeholders' personal or professional networks. Just as individuals need to maintain their singular identities and image, create brand awareness (being smart, informative, funny, silly, etc.) and enhance their reputations, so too do corporations strive to enhance their corporate identities, image, brand awareness, and reputations. Regardless of whether it is the individual or an organization, the image, credibility, and reputation of the identity or brand depends wholly on how consistently individuals or organizations are able to demonstrate quality of work or product/service, and how ethical they are when producing the work, product, or service.

Individual, Marketing, and Corporate Communication

Everyone communicates. However, the continued effectiveness of the communication depends not only on hard work, but also on the creation of useful communication strategies that are relevant, timely, and always evolving and adapting to the context and the communication channel. Both individuals and organizations are constantly marketing themselves to acquire readership and patronage. These can be measured at the lower level by the number of likes for a post or a picture, the number of followers on a Twitter account and, specifically, the number of retweets for an original tweet or the number of views or downloads for a YouTube video or an Instagram photograph. Often defined as **reach**, it is the ability to be read or seen by a maximum possible number of people and includes number of friends on Facebook and the followers of a Twitter account, as well as those in the extended networks of the posters or tweeters. Additionally, the number of reposts or retweets increases the **frequency** of the original post, tweet, or video being seen, read, or heard. Once something crosses a certain threshold of views, reads, retweets, reposts, and downloads, then that online message (post, tweet, video, or photo) is said to have **gone viral**—that is, the message has spread rapidly across many networks in a short period of time. The number of views or reposts are often counted in the hundreds of thousands or more.

Measures used to confirm the popularity or notoriety of an online message, such as the Alexa Internet ranking system, often use detailed analytics and rating indices to generate rankings. They use complex algorithms to detect and measure page views to see whether a particular tweet or post **pulled** people to a certain website, or **pushed** people to go searching for a product, service, or information. The measures look at downloads and views of software, games, videos, songs, photos, and even the duration of time a Snapchat picture is allowed to stay at a receiver's device before becoming invisible to the receiver. Table 9.2 presents individual, marketing, and corporate communication in the context of some of these measures.

Table 9.2 Individual, Marketing, and Corporate Communication

Considerations	Individual Communication	Marketing Communication	Corporate Communication
Audience	Friends, family, and potential employers	Customer	Multiple internal and external stakeholders
Channel	Email, texts, phone calls, social media	TV, radio, print, social media	Memos, letters, reports, traditional media, social media
Identity	Self, perceived self	Product or service	Entire organization
Image	Self, projected image	Key feature of product or service	Entire organization
Brand	Self, perceived as an asset	Beliefs and expectations surrounding the name or logo of the product or service that are evoked in the mind of the audience	Beliefs and expectations surrounding the name or logo of the organization that are evoked in the mind of the audience
Reputation	Individual credibility	Brand credibility	Organizational credibility
Reach	Individual's personal or professional network	Number of people who read news, watch TV, listen to the radio, follow or like on social media	Internal and external stakeholders, including the general public

Frequency	Number of times the individual's comments or posts or photos are responded to or reposted, liked, or retweeted	Number of times the brand is talked about or discussed on posts/reposts, tweets/retweets in the brand's direct and extended viewership/target audience	Number of times the organization is talked about or discussed among its internal and external stakeholders and the general public
Creative Freedom	A lot of creative freedom for self-expression; sometimes this can lead to unwanted fame or notoriety	More room for creativity, when using messages to target and attract patronage of the product or service	Less room for creativity, considering long-term reputation, longevity of the organization, and the need to be accountable to shareholders, boards, employees, and the supply chain
Consistency	Need to be consistent with self-image and portrayed image	Need to be consistent with products and services	Need to be consistent with corporate identity, image, reputation, and organizational values, objectives, mission, and vision
Push and Pull	Needing validation from others in their networks; creating and sending messages that enhance image, brand, and reputation; and drawing others in the network into conversations is essentially a pull function	Organizations tend to push information about their products and services and tailor messages to drive traffic (pull) to their websites, have engaged conversations with users and potential users, and want to be more effective	Communication is more controlled and is typically push to maintain image and reputation and avoid public relations disasters

The concepts presented in Table 9.2 are fairly self-explanatory, but it is worthwhile noting the range and complexity of the communication required for individuals and organizations in maintaining their identities, image, brand, and reputations. They need to have clear, relevant, and effective strategies to manage them online. We will now explore some of those strategies.

Strategies for Managing Individual and Corporate Identities Online

For any strategy to be effective, it must be dynamic by design. This means that it should be relevant and adaptable to different contexts and it must evolve. It must also be designed honestly, without overestimating the strengths and abilities of the individual or organization, or underestimating the power of the channel through which the strategy will be deployed or the ability of the stakeholders to perceive or detect dishonesty. The way any technique or strategy can be dynamic is to incorporate feedback in the design stage itself. Any situation or event will present moments from which the individual or organization can learn and then incorporate the learning into the strategy and thus be prepared for the next occurrence of the same or similar event. Communication is strategic when it aligns consistently with the individual or corporate goals, image, values, and existing reputation, and works to maintain or enhance that reputation. This communication strategy has clarity, is understandable to a wide audience, is truthful, is repeated, is consistent in the messaging, and is communicated passionately. It is in this context we introduce tropes and memes, two rhetorical concepts often associated with online communication, and the Internet troll. In order to devise a good set of strategies for effectively managing individual and organizational online identities, it is necessary to understand how these rhetorical concepts play a role in determining how dynamic and adaptable communication strategies are.

The *Oxford Dictionaries* define **trope** as "a figurative or metaphorical use of a word or expression." It is often seen used as a significant or recurrent theme. The word itself is of Greek origin and means "to turn." For example, consider the word *blog*. It is a shortened form of *web log*, which is an online journal where an individual posts their thoughts or feelings about themselves or a topic they are interested in (a love interest, a poem, a brand, or a cause). Web log has thus morphed into blog and is used frequently enough to have its own dictionary entry as both a noun and verb. It also is the root word for other words such as *blogosphere*. Another trope is **flog**, which is a combination of *fake* and *blog*. However, it also can mean "to flog" a product or service, as in a sales pitch. Flogs are usually generated by vectors or "sock puppets." The sock puppet is a fake online identity created by an individual or an organization. It acts as an independent third-party to praise or defend the individual, organization, product, or service. Many online communities try to block sock puppets and view their use as unethical.

The *Oxford Dictionaries* define **meme** as "an element of a culture or system of behaviour passed from one individual to another by imitation or other non-genetic means." In the context of the Internet, it defines *meme* as "an image, video, piece of text, etc., typically humorous in nature that is copied and spread rapidly by Internet users, often with slight variations." The origin of the word is Greek from the word **mimēma**, which means "that which is imitated." Internet memes are copied from person to person, like mimicry. It can thus be seen as a virally transmitted cultural symbol or social idea (Gil, n.d.). Most Internet memes involve either humour or shock value and often consist of a picture or video. "A link to a YouTube video of Rick Astley, a file attachment with a Stars Wars Kid movie, an email signature with a Chuck Norris quote . . . these are a few examples of modern meme symbols and culture spreading through online media" (Gil, n.d.). What is important to remember is that a photo taken at a party can end up as an Internet meme, especially if an individual is photographed doing something inappropriate or in an awkward pose. The same can happen to organizational images, especially when organizations hastily try to promote a product or service without doing diligent research about the target audience or by making unsubstantiated claims. The individual or organization's post, photo, or video becomes fodder for everyone to copy and redistribute with variations, all of which are aimed at mocking the original poster (individual or organization).

Finally, there is the **Internet troll**, typically someone who posts inflammatory messages to provoke emotional responses from users or communities. The sole purpose is to disrupt normal discussions. Internet trolls appear to wait for people or organizations who are careless with their online posts, and seize the opportunity to bombard the site with a barrage of messages aimed at causing angry and emotional responses from the users.

Identity Management Strategies

Keeping in mind that effective identity management communication strategies need to be clear, honest, aligned with individual and/or corporate goals and vision, and dynamic, we present in Table 9.3 strategies with reference to some of the more popular social and professional network sites. We cannot list every popular website, so we have placed them into the broader categories taken from the Alexa Internet ranking's top 25 most popular websites. These categories are social networking, professional networking, information sharing (blogs and Wikis), entertainment (media and gaming), and shopping (sales and auction sites). Furthermore, we use the considerations identified in Table 9.2 to provide specific context for these strategies. We begin with one clear statement that should frame the rest of the discussion: never post, tweet, say, or upload anything that can or will come back to haunt you. This applies equally to individuals and organizations.

As you will see from the following strategies and scenarios, many appear intuitive, but some are not and require thinking and processing. Often the root causes of conflict or problems with any communication, including online, is the urge to interpret the comment or message according to one's bias and respond immediately. It is always better to take the time to process the received information to prevent an impulsive response. Impulsive responses often contain errors in writing and poorly conceived and ill-informed ideas. The responder allows emotions to dictate the message. While emotions play an important role in our lives and our communications, taking the time to process information reduces conflict and embarrassment caused by hastily communicating poorly conceived or underdeveloped ideas. This applies equally to individual responses to social media content and organizational responses to user comments.

Corporations do not seem to learn from their mistakes. Many are still attempting to implement ill-conceived or poorly executed marketing campaigns on social media and quickly learn how such approaches can go wrong (Sundararajan & Sundararajan, 2012). Social Driver, a digital agency that provides solutions and services for clients to connect with technology, also has a blog called *Get with the Future* that discusses social technology and digital trends. The blog has chronicled some historic corporate social media campaign failures and the lessons learned from these failures (Social Driver, 2013). These include famous names such as McDonald's (customers of the fast-food company pointing out bad service and contaminated food experiences), Poland Springs (a bottled water company missing an opportunity to capitalize on a public event), KitchenAid (an employee of the home-appliances company mistakenly posting an offensive tweet about American president Barack Obama to the KitchenAid official Twitter account, instead of to a personal account), Caribou Coffee (the coffee company only using a traditional press release instead of social media to lay off employees), Tesco (the grocery company using Hootsuite to schedule a tweet about sleep and hay after horsemeat was found in their burger patties) and Taco Bell (a fast-food company using social media twice to inform patrons about a product that was not yet available at their outlets, giving patrons the opportunity to complain about stores that did not have these products).

There are many lessons to be learned, but the main lesson is to think through the reason why a post or a comment needs to be made. Once a real need (not a perceived need) is determined, then a good deal of thought can be put into designing the appropriate response or campaign, always with a view to engage, be relevant, provide evidence-backed information, and provide support. However, crises do occur and both individuals and corporations must be prepared to respond to them. It is always better to assume a high level of responsibility for one's actions, however far in the past these actions may have occurred. While public memory can fade, with everything being retrievable once posted to the Internet, it does not take long for someone to dig up events from the past. It is always a good strategy to own up and take responsibility for the actions, even if they are committed by a disgruntled employee, a former associate, or a romantic partner. "Fess up if you mess up" is a great approach to have. People will forgive if the individual or organization is seen as genuinely repentant for their actions.

We will now discuss the frameworks for managing individual and corporate online identities with specific emphasis on certain types of online social media channels. Once we present the strategies, we will work through scenarios that involve the use of that strategy.

Maintaining Individual Identity on Social Media

While all the channels discussed in this chapter are social networking sites, some are specifically meant only for socializing and connecting with friends and family, and as a way to extend one's circle of friends. Most people use the sites to catch up with classmates, current friends and acquaintances, and even co-workers. They also share their likes, dislikes, and preferences for events, humour, and a range of topics. Nothing is considered taboo, although friends and family members often chide their connections for inappropriate behaviour or posts. Since so many people, especially young adults and teenagers, are on these sites, many teachers in high schools, colleges, and universities have resorted to engaging their students directly through these sites, particularly Facebook, Twitter, Tumblr, and Instagram (which is owned by Facebook).

While students need to keep and maintain their personal identities on these sites, so too do teachers, educators, and corporations. Most people are associated with either a school or college or an organization (private or government). It would be inappropriate for a teacher to teach professionalism in their face-to-face or online classes and then post silly comments or pictures of themselves or others to their social media accounts. They will soon be exposed and will likely harm their reputation and credibility. They could also be fired from their jobs (Huffington Post, 2015). Organizations also need to be wary of how they represent themselves and how their employees represent themselves as individuals and as representatives of the organization. A misstep by one invariably affects the image and reputation of the other, such as the blackface controversy at Mayfield Secondary School in Caledon, Ontario (Karstens-Smith & Rushowy, 2013).

Table 9.3 presents some strategies that will help individuals and organizations (private or government) better manage their online presence and identities. In the first column, we list a few of the social networking sites. The next two columns list the strategies and approaches with specific attention to audiences, image, identity, brand, reputation, reach, frequency, and whether the strategy is push or pull. The last column lists ways to track the impact of the activities of these entities (individuals or corporations). The strategies and approaches and strategies listed in Table 9.3 are not meant to be exhaustive, but they do cover a broad set of actions and, hold true regardless of the channel.

Table 9.3 Managing Individual and Corporate Identities on Social Networking Sites

Channel (Social Network)	Individual	Corporate	Impact
Facebook Baidu/Weibo, Twitter, MySpace, Foursquare, Snapchat	• Audience is friends and family. • Maintain self-identity and enhance self-image. • Individual is the brand. • Individual has full creative freedom. • Actions impact reputation. • Individuals are tempted to write, say, or upload anything. • Individuals typically reach almost everyone in the network. • Frequent posts or comments can be considered a nuisance, unless content is really funny, useful, or relevant and appropriate. • It may work as a pull strategy for a while until people get tired. • Most network friends/family are forgiving. • Try to avoid getting tagged too often. • Definitely use emotional messages, but try never to insult, flame, or shame anyone. • Never bully or tease anyone; watch out for cyberbullies in your network and if necessary take action to stop such activities.	• Audience is current and potential stakeholders. • Creative freedom needs to be exercised with caution. • Never make claims based on assumed superiority of product or service. • Do not take brand loyalty for granted. • Use emotional messages appropriately. • Make only claims that can be supported by real and verifiable evidence. • Participate with the intent to engage followers and interested patrons. • To extend reach, users need to repost or retweet about the brand or company. • Be consistent in the messaging. • Do not try to push too much marketing information. • Create policies for online behaviour of employees both as individuals and as representatives of the organization.	• Create social and cultural change. • Track number who repeat behaviour. • Track number who behave as desired. • Track number who change attitudes. • Track number who change opinions. • Track number who learn message content. • Track number who repost/retweet messages. • Track number who receive messages.

The Case of Kailee Pereira: Snapchat and Twitter

Kailee Pereira is an administrative assistant at APPFORMS who works with Bernard Ramdin, director of communications. Kailee is in charge of creating and managing documentation related to internal and external communication. She is quite efficient at her work and also has a good working relationship with Bernard and with her co-workers. She is well liked by everyone at APPFORMS, especially for her quirky sense of humour. Kailee has an active presence on several social media platforms, including Facebook, Twitter, Instagram, Pinterest, and Reddit, where she posts comments, updates, and photos.

One morning, Kailee comes out of a rather frustrating meeting with Bernard. He wanted some archived communication items and could not find them on his computer. He expected Kailee to have them. She did, but he was not specific in his request and made vague references to an event that had occurred several months ago. He insists that Kailee finds the information as he needs it for an upcoming meeting with the managing partners. She sets aside the important task that Bernard had requested of her earlier and begins a thorough search of her computer. She successfully finds the information and forwards it to Bernard.

Frustrated at having to suspend her regular tasks, Kailee spends some time fuming quietly. Then, in order to relieve some tension, she opens up a paint program and doodles a caricature of Bernard. Happy with her art work, she wants to share it, but decides it would not be wise to send it to anyone in her workplace. She gets on Snapchat, a messaging application that allows users to set time limits from 0 to 10 seconds for any message with or without an attachment. Kailee uses Snapchat to message her close circle of friends with whom she has created a "by invitation only" group. She sets a time limit of 6 seconds for this particular message and sends out her newly created graphic with a quip: "The ogre was particularly irritating this morning." Kailee and her friends have a humorous exchange about their supervisors, all with the knowledge that the conversations soon disappear.

My boss b4 his cup of joe. ROTFL

Unfortunately for Kailee, one of her Snapchat friends thought her image was really funny and grabbed it (without notifying Kailee that she was doing so) and pushed it out to her network on Twitter, with the hashtag #badbosses, tagging Kailee as she did so. Kailee Pereira's Twitter handle is @kaiper and her friend sends out the following tweet.

@**shainews**
Shaina Newstace

#badbosses Yo, yo, yo, check out
@kaiper cute graphic of her silly boss.

Although Kailee's original image and conversation have disappeared from Snapchat, it comes to life on Twitter when many Twitter users pick up the meme and begin extended conversations about bad bosses. Twitterbots, used by companies and individuals to tweet and retweet messages, picks up the meme and the hashtag #badbosses soon begins trending on Twitter with many users adding to the image or creating their own memes and pushing it further. By afternoon, APPFORMS's employees begin to pick up the tweets, particularly because it has Kailee's Twitter handle, which she also uses in official APPFORMS's tweets. When Kailee returns from lunch, she is surprised to see her co-workers giggle as she passes their cubicles on her way to her office. She picks up her phone and to her horror finds the inbox of her personal email account filled with comments about her image. She will talk to her Snapchat group about this, but she realizes that the damage has been done, as a serious looking Bernard, accompanied by Juanita Olson, director of human resources, motions to Kailee to join them for a conversation in Bernard's office. A red-faced Kailee slowly follows them. Behind closed doors, Bernard, Juanita, and Kailee discuss the sequence of events that day. The image was particularly funny and Bernard takes it in good spirit and laughs about it. Kailee apologizes profusely and he sportingly accepts her apology. Juanita and Bernard also recognize the experience as an opportunity for APPFORMS, and will look at some sensitivity training for everyone, including the managers and directors.

Fortunately for Kailee, the day ends without too many negative consequences. Bernard decides to use the meme to begin a broader discussion on supervisors and managers with difficult personalities. He decides a blog post on the topic will serve people well and provide a platform for people to talk about their workplace experiences. APPFORMS is able to turn this potentially damaging incident into a platform for discussion about good and bad management practices.

Let us now look at the sequence of events that led to the bad boss meme going viral and the lessons that can be learned from this incident.

1. Kailee should never have sent the image to anyone. Working for a tech firm as she does, especially one that specializes in the mobile phone business, Kailee should have known the possible outcomes of her actions. While she most certainly needed to vent her frustration and doodling the caricature may have helped, she should have stopped there. As well, at the next available opportunity, she should have discussed this situation with Bernard himself and resolved it with him. He was not a bad supervisor. He just had a bad moment and Kailee knows that most of us have those at some time or the other.

2. Having decided to send the image to her friends on Snapchat, Kailee should have prefaced it with a warning to her friends not to grab the image or forward it anywhere.

3. Alternatively, Kailee should have at least created different Twitter handles for her personal tweets and for her professional tweets. The fact that Kailee uses the same Twitter handle for both allowed people at APPFORMS to connect Kailee to the image. Her individual identity and her professional identity were linked.

4. There is no guarantee that Snapchat or any other online service or application will keep messages and images private. It has been found that the Snapchat app does not delete images or messages, but instead stores them deep inside the sender's device (Shontell, 2013). There are also third-party apps that allow users to grab images or conversations without sending notifications to the sender.

5. Bernard's idea to create a blog post would allow them use the event to shed light on a common workplace issue of how to deal with bad managers and bad employees. This way, he would prevent the corporate identity of APPFORMS from becoming tarnished and present the organization in a good light.

6. Inadvertently, Kailee helped start the conversation and in the process realized it is never a good idea to shame or defame anyone, no matter how innocuous the words or how funny the image. Fortunately for her she did not have a bad boss. If she really did, she might be looking for a new job.

7. The event also allowed Juanita Olson to think about creating a program on sensitivity training and discussion of other workplace issues in her organization. A new set of policies could emerge from such a program or workshop that will allow employees to have freedom of expression, an open-door policy to talk about workplace issues, and be respectful of one another.

LinkedIn and Other Professional Networking Sites

LinkedIn is probably the most popular networking site for organizations and individuals to connect to one another in a professional environment. A high level of professionalism is expected from everyone on the site. Information about previous work experiences, education, skills, and achievements need to be accurate and verifiable. Other professional networking sites, such as Plaxo, Zerply, Branchout, and Meetup, require similar levels of professionalism and accuracy in profile descriptions. Although the other sites work a little differently than LinkedIn, all the sites allow professionals and organizations to connect to one another in order to facilitate recruitment of talent and vendors, provide referrals for projects, promote products and services, and enhance individual and organizational profiles and image. We explored the referral side of LinkedIn in Chapter 2. The focus here will be on the managing of individual and organizational identity in a professional networking environment.

Table 9.4 Managing Individual and Corporate Identities on Professional Networking Sites

Channel (Professional Network)	Individual	Corporate	Impact
LinkedIn, Meetup, Branchout, Zerply, Plaxo	• Audience is typically professionals, other network contacts, and potential employers. • Maintain a professional appearance. • Only contact others through network introductions. • Research well before contacting network members. • Do not make your connections do extra work. • Ensure that network members trust you enough so that they can introduce you to their contacts. • Do not misuse or abuse network relationships. • Check with network members if they are willing to help before introducing new contacts. • New contacts you introduce will either enhance or damage your reputation. • Do not overuse network contacts. • Return favours. • Write clearly and promptly to thank network contacts for their introductions.	• Audience is typically other organizations, competition, vendors, potential employees, and new business connections. • Ensure professionalism and consistency in messaging. • Use clear, evidence-based information to support claims about organizational achievements. • Cultivate and nurture network contacts by responding quickly to queries. • Employ people skilled in writing to manage the profile page and produce content. • Ensure all links to company website work. • Feel free to engage with network participants. • Ensure that hiring firms do not convey false or misleading information. • Use community networks to establish community relations. • Use product and service user groups to provide support.	• Track number of new introductions. • Track number of résumé submissions for posted jobs. • Track number hired through applications from these sites. • Track number of people discussing the company. • Track number of interview calls received. • Track number of new business opportunities. • Track number of new contacts into community networks. • Track impact of community relations on community and on the employee morale. • After product launch, track visits to profile.

Managing Corporate Identity on Social Media

Blogs and Wikis allow individuals to write in detail about themselves, ideas, and themes, and invite responses from other who may either be following the blogs or Wikis or come across the websites while searching for something. In the case of organizations and corporations, blogs and Wikis provide a platform for promoting products or services, and invite user groups to generate ideas and debate the perceived or real qualities of products or services. They also allow organizations to connect to the communities where they operate their businesses and other stakeholder groups. Organizations and sometimes even individuals try to increase traffic to their sites by using sock puppets. However, if they are found out, the blogger loses credibility. Table 9.5 presents some strategies for managing identities on blog and wiki sites.

Table 9.5 Managing Individual and Corporate Identities on Blogging Sites

Channel (Blogs and Wikis)	Individual	Corporate	Impact
Blogger, Tumblr, Wordpress, Wikipedia, WikiTravel	• Audience can be anyone. • Ensure consistency of style, accuracy, and credibility of information. • Write in an engaging and compelling style. • Always cite your sources. • Pay attention to subscriber comments. • Do not use unreadable fonts. • Use transitions in paragraphs. • Ensure length is appropriate. • Watch out for Internet trolls. • Do not use sock puppets.	• Audience is internal and external stakeholders. • Ensure consistency of style, narrative, accuracy, and credibility of information. • Pay attention to subscriber comments. • Respond with corrections or positive affirmations. • If customers are complaining, try and attend to them quickly. • Try not to get trapped into arguments with Internet trolls. • Do not use vectors or bots to produce spam comments; there is no faster way to lose credibility.	• Track number of subscribers. • Track frequency of reader comments and responses to each blog post. • Track how deep discussion threads get before the discussions dry up. • Keep discussions positive but track negative comments to check validity. • Be prepared to adapt, modify, and change.

The Case of James Patel: Blog

Bernard Ramdin approaches James Patel, who has gained a reputation at APPFORMS as a co-op student with great potential and a possible permanent hire after he graduates. From conversations with James's supervisor, Pierce Sanchez, Bernard learns that James is good at writing blog content. Bernard discusses his idea about creating a new blog under the APPFORMS name that deals with workplace issues and suggests that James can start with the topic of bad bosses at the workplace. James is surprised, especially after the recent incident with Kailee on Twitter. But he realizes that Bernard is serious and, after all, this is something that James loves to do. James is impressed by Bernard's proactive approach.

While James has experience writing his own blog, he realizes that the audience for his blog is primarily college and university students looking for information about the latest technological trends. The audience for this new APPFORMS blog will be broader. It will include employees from organizations, private or government, large or small, and will likely include team leaders, managers, and business leaders. James then thinks about the image and identity that APPFORMS has as a tech company that produces apps. It is a respected company and has the image and reputation of being a diverse, adaptive, entrepreneurial organization with a decentralized decision-making structure. It also has the reputation of producing useful, high-quality apps for a variety of mobile and computer platforms. The users who have downloaded and used apps produced by APPFORMS are the existing user base that the blog will reach. Depending on the success of the first blog post, James feels that he can recommend the frequency of each new post to be once a week or once a month. He turns his attention to the actual topic and the content.

James knows that a blog post needs to be compelling and easy to consume. Before people will read the content, they need to be pulled in with a title and a hook that will make them curious. He understands that the title and the content (both text and images) must be searchable. Search engines typically work by looking for a close fit of the search terms. When organizations and individuals post content on the Internet, they employ search engine optimization or SEO. This refers to designing content so that it is visible to different search engines (based on keywords and indexing activities). Having written his own blog posts, James understands that in order for the new APPFORMS blog to be successful, he needs to write compelling content, and use words and images that reflect typical search terms and keywords. He decides on a title for his first blog post that is simple, yet poses a question: "Bad Bosses: Myth or Reality?" James feels his title will attract people who have had experiences with bad supervisor or managers. It will also attract those who have never experienced bad bosses and probably think that bad bosses are a myth. This allows for at least two sides and provide a platform for a healthy debate among readers. James knows that the APPFORMS's vetting process for user posts will reject content intended to flame or shame other posters and keep the debate as civil as possible. Of course, he also knows that he will not know how his post is received until some time has passed.

He decides to keep his first blog post reasonably short, about three or four short paragraphs. To provide contrast, he chooses Georgia and Verdana (one serif and one sans serif font), a fairly standard font pair for web content. Font pairs provide good contrast for the text. Good designs use one font for headings and a different one for the text. James begins writing his draft, which he will later show to Bernard and others at APPFORMS before he actually posts it. He wants confirmation from others that his blog post reflects both the workplace culture at APPFORMS and the image and reputation of APPFORMS in the tech community. James uses his first sentence as a hook to draw in the reader. He ensures the rest of the content is interesting to hold the readers' attention and have them read all the way till the end of the post.

This part of the sentence is also written as a pronouncement. But it is something that many readers are likely to identify with. Many people may feel that they know someone who is occupying a leadership position that they are not qualified to hold.

Georgia font for title; Verdana for the rest of the post

Bad Bosses: Myth or Reality

First hook. Not necessarily a shocking statement, but one that will definitely cause a reader to read on. This sentence is written as a grand claim. Readers will expect that the rest of the post may contain support for this claim and will likely be compelled to read further.

There are no bad bosses—only people who have, either by accident or by connections, reached positions of leadership that is way beyond their individual capabilities. To compensate for their lack of training or abilities, such people tend to shout louder, blame others for their own mediocrity, pass the buck, take credit for others' work, and generally behave badly at the workplace. Co-workers or subordinates working with such leaders will definitely label such leaders or managers as "bad bosses."

Here James is highlighting behaviours seen in "bad bosses" as well as other employees.

Here he addresses the title again and sets up the pivot.

The myth about bad bosses stems from the fact that they are always mean, intent on harassing their subordinates, and are not good people to work with. However, this need not always be the case. Bosses too are people who have certain abilities, and are probably really good at certain things, though leadership or managing may not be one of them. With proper training in leadership, sensitivity, and empathy, they can be made into good managers and leaders, and may even become fantastic bosses.

The pivot

James moves on to a more positive and constructive approach to the workplace situation involving a bad boss or manager.

This is back to empathizing with a section of the targeted readership/audience.

Here the sentences seek to give readers a different perspective and have them consider the motivation behind a boss's bad behaviour.

Most people will be able to narrate first-hand or second-hand accounts of their experiences with bad bosses. There are likely to be some really mean people out there and it may seem that nothing can be done about such people. But, for the most part, if people stop to think about the bad actions or bad behaviour of these bosses, then maybe they can get an idea why these people were behaving badly. Often, some deep-seated insecurity or a personal problem could manifest itself as bad workplace behaviour. Senior leaders in an organization must be tuned in to all their employees so that they can detect signs of bad behaviour early, and provide intervention in the form of training. Of course, at no time should harassment and bullying be condoned. If we teach our children to talk to their teachers about class bullies, employees should also be emboldened to record, for evidence, bullying and harassment by bosses or even co-workers, and report them to the human resources department for further follow up and action.

An analogy to encourage employees to report bad behaviour, especially if it involves harassment or bullying

Returning to the title and closing

Bad behaviour is a reality and bad bosses are somewhat real and somewhat of a myth. We invite comments on this from all our patrons, and others who may stumble upon this blog and look forward to a healthy and respectful debate on this important issue.

A request to the readership for a healthy and respectful debate, indicating professionalism and concern

A caution to not condone bullying or harassment at the workplace

Here James projects the image and culture at APPFORMS without explicitly stating so.

James rereads what he has written as a first draft and feels fairly satisfied at what he has said. He heads to Bernard's office to show him the draft.

Entertainment, Media, and Gaming Sites

Entertainment sites such as YouTube, Flickr, Vimeo, and Vevo allow people to upload, download, and watch videos, short movies, photos, and so on. Most of these sites try to ensure that material in violation of copyright laws is not uploaded and, if they are, the site administration deletes the content quickly. Users upload home videos of themselves or family members or pets (such as cats and dogs) doing antics. The aim is to get as many views as possible (similar to the likes on Facebook or follows or retweets on Twitter). Mashups of popular videos or photos are also popular, as are music tunes providing background scores for photo slideshows.

The key thing to be aware of when using these sites is to check whether the material has copyright protection and whether it is real or a hoax (Clifford, 2009). In one hoax, two employees of a Domino's Pizza franchise filmed themselves soiling the pizza and posted it to YouTube. The news spread on social media and it was soon discovered to be hoax. People alerted Domino's about the hoax and the location of the franchise and the employees were fired. The CEO of Domino's Pizza filmed a video to thank the supporters and posted it on YouTube. Other instances of CEOs and senior leaders of organizations posting apologies or messages thanking their supporters include the CEO of BlackBerry (then Research in Motion or RIM) apologizing for a worldwide BlackBerry outage and the CEO of Maple Leaf Foods apologizing for listeria contamination at one of their meat plants that led to the deaths of some consumers. The speed with which an organization responds to requests by users or stakeholders, especially during crises, determines whether the organization's image and reputation are enhanced or tarnished.

Gaming sites have their own rules and etiquette, which, if not followed properly, can cause people to get evicted from these sites. While a lot of friendly banter is expected when gamers compete against one another in various online games, some of it can get quite heated. However, most gamers respect one another's gaming skills and look for healthy competition. Often, flaming is frowned upon. Although winners may gloat, overt shaming of losers is not received well. Gamers want both winners and losers to exhibit grace and respect. Table 9.6 presents some strategies for managing identities on entertainment and gaming sites.

Table 9.6 Managing Individual and Corporate Identities on Entertainment and Gaming Sites

Channel (Entertainment, Media, and Gaming)	Individual	Corporate	Impact
YouTube Flickr, Vimeo, Vevo, IGN, Dailymotion, Game FAQs	• Audience can be other media users or gamers. • Be careful not to upload copyrighted material • Do not violate copyright laws. • Be careful when uploading mashups. • Try not to infringe on others' rights to privacy. Always seek permission before uploading photos or videos. • Do not treat others' material as your own. That is plagiarism. • Respect network members and other gamers. • Follow the rules of etiquette laid out in the gaming site. • Avoid flaming or shaming anyone; it is not worth it. • Report suspicious behaviour to the appropriate authorities.	• Audience is internal and external stakeholders. • Beware of hoaxes such as fake videos or altered images. • Be alert to the possibility of copyright infringement. • Respond immediately when users or viewers detect issues with your product or service. • Respond with a video message. • Use emotionally themed messages carefully. • Provide evidence of change or action, especially during times of corporate crisis. • Do not deny culpability if the organization is in some way responsible for a mishap.	• Track increased viewership. • Track number of times video or image is distributed in viewer networks. • Track and respond to viewer comments immediately. • Provide updates quickly and respond quickly in times of corporate crisis. • Delegate skilled people to produce content or images.

Shopping Sites

An increasing number of people are making many of their purchases online. These range from groceries to electronics, clothes, baby items, automobiles, and even industrial goods. Shopping sites are growing with many offering better deals than storefront retail outlets. Many traditional bricks-and-mortar retail outlets have a significant online presence and account for a substantial amount of quarterly, seasonal, or yearly sales for their products or services. They compete on price and quality and most of all they rely on user experience and satisfaction ratings to enhance their image and reputation. Organizations seek to "friend" users on social media sites and increasing numbers of users have "friended" or follow a brand on social media sites.

Users should always protect themselves from identity theft and only use secure payment systems. Corporations have set up many easy payment methods to allow users to shop from their smartphones. However, identity theft is always a concern and hackers are always looking to steal credit card and personal information, as happened recently with

Target Corporation (Chapman, 2014). Individuals should also provide truthful accounts of their shopping experiences and try not to mislead other patrons. If they feel they have not received the goods or services they paid for, they should report to the appropriate consumer protection bureau. Nothing will prompt an organization to respond to genuine customer complaints faster than the fear of their brand or image being tarnished, especially considering how quickly bad reputations spread on social media. Corporations that assume a high level of responsibility for their products, services, and actions typically respond faster to consumer complaints and try to rectify the situation or provide an alternative (or a replacement if the product is defective or a refund if the service was not satisfactory). Table 9.7 presents some strategies for managing identities on shopping sites.

Table 9.7 Managing Individual and Corporate Identities on Online Shopping Sites

Channel (Shopping)	Individual	Corporate	Impact
Amazon, Alibaba, Flipkart, Taobao, eBay	• Ensure payment is through secure channels only. • Be wary of identity theft. • Provide satisfaction ratings soon after receiving the product or service. • To ensure prompt delivery of product or service, provide correct mailing address and track package or performance of service. • Be fair in your ratings of the quality of the product or service, timely delivery, and overall shopping experience. • Your comments will be useful to other potential shoppers.	• Audience is anyone who needs to buy the products and services offered. • Provide secure payment channels for patrons. • Ensure prompt payment confirmation, delivery information, and an ability to track packages for products and performance for services provided. • Give comparisons on price, performance, availability. • Deploy people on chat clients to help shoppers find what they are looking for. • Follow up after the purchase to gauge satisfaction with the shopping experience. • Deploy people on chat clients to help solve problems involving bad quality, poor performance, returns, etc. • Setup BOPUS (buy online and pick up in store) and BORIS (buy online and return in store) options for customers.	• Track buyer satisfaction ratings. • Track sales. • Track purchases. • Protect purchaser identity and credit card information. • Track repeat purchases from same shopper. • Track repeat visits to same site. • Track time spent on various product or service pages. If someone leaves without buying, make efforts to find out why.

◉ SCOPE

Strategy is the essence of this chapter, particularly in the context of managing individual and organizational identities in online social media environments. Whenever individuals and organizations assume a high level of responsibility for their actions, they are automatically adopting a strategy that will allow them to reflect carefully on every action they perform. Social media sites, particularly the social networking sites, are all channels of engagement and pull, where users (individual or organizational) seek to connect with one another and engage in meaningful and mutually beneficial conversations. In such environments, the strategy should always be that of accountability for deeds or actions. Since nothing will ever go away from the Internet and every thought, deed, or action is recorded and can be retrieved, the key strategy for managing identities in these environments is always one that is cautious, inclusive, sensitive, and ethical. Even when laws are being enacted that allow individuals to be "not remembered," (so that search engines do not bring up murky pasts of individuals or organizations), such information is still available and can be found by persistent people with technical skills.

Content is the factor that establishes what an individual or organization's brand or image is likely to be. While repentance for poorly conceived actions is good, it is always better to think several times before posting or uploading questionable content or unsupported or unverifiable claims. Plagiarism is always discovered, as are instances of presenting false information. These instantly damage the credibility of the individual or the organization. Malicious use of information to shame or defame others can damage the source, as can the use of fake accounts, flaming, or vectors to generate content or buy followers and likes.

The *outcome* for any communication event or episode is to further the relationship between the sender and the intended receiver. Every effort must be made by the sender to verify the statements or information and ensure their credibility. The short-term outcome will strengthen the relationship between the sender and the intended receivers and the long-term outcome will be the establishment of the credibility, image, and brand of the sender. For every update that is liked by one's followers on Facebook—whether a humorous update, a family picture, or support for a cause or charitable action by the individual or organization—the outcome will lead to the enhancement of the reputation of the individual or organization.

Presentation is key to successful social media strategies for maintaining online identities, image, and reputation for both individuals and organizations. Writing and producing content for each social media site involves thought and strategy. The effective presentation of an individual or corporate brand requires a clear understanding of the audience, its needs, and how presenting content that engages the audience in meaningful conversation is far better than thrusting information in forms often suited to traditional channels like print or television. The individual or organization should be able to adapt the presentation of the content to suit the social media channel and the audiences consuming these channels.

Ethics and ethical behaviour are crucial to establishing the integrity of the individual or organizational brand. The longevity of any brand depends on the quality of the brand (individual actions or performance of the product or service) and how truthfully the brand is consistently presented. Unethical actions or behaviour will be found out quickly through online social media sites. People are constantly looking for forgeries, false information, false representation, and patterns of behaviour that indicate attempts to mislead network members or consumers. Public memory fades, but even when unethical behaviour occurred a while ago, people find ways to bring up past unethical actions. Individuals and organizations have to answer to social media justice (notoriety and public vilification) and, if they are not repentant, they suffer a loss of reputation.

Chapter Summary

This chapter differs from the rest of the chapters in this textbook because it has more theoretical concepts presented explicitly. Such an approach was necessary to clearly make the connection between the individual and the organization. We have used the words *organization* and *corporation* interchangeably as in essence both mean the same, although corporation tends to denote a private entity. Regardless of the chapter's structure, the key theme has been to highlight the critical need for individuals and organizations to successfully manage their online presence and identities in various social media outlets. We looked at the importance of maintaining an online presence and how the online

actions of individuals and organizations affect and impact their image and reputation. We looked at some specific scenarios involving popular social media sites. Scenarios involving other sites are presented in the exercises that follow. Two important points to remember from this chapter, which apply equally to individuals and organizations, are the following:

1. Never post, say, or upload anything that can come back to haunt you.
2. It is easier to repair your image and reputation if you assume a high level of responsibility for your actions.

Discussion Questions

1. As a marketing co-op intern for a company that produces athletic and fashion wear, you are asked to take charge of the social media marketing of the company's products and services. How will you proceed? Who will your target audience be? Which channels will you start with? Why?
2. Using the strategies presented in the chapter, describe possible steps in a marketing campaign that uses LinkedIn and YouTube.
3. Akira Montoya is a manager at a small technology firm dealing with software automation for business processes. His clients are typically other businesses. How can he use social media

to improve the sales of his company's products? How can he use social media to establish his company's brand and image and differentiate his company from the competition?
4. You are a co-op intern in the buying department at a manufacturing company that makes industrial parts and tools. One of the tasks you are assigned is to source a new set of suppliers for office supplies (stationery, etc.). How will you proceed? How will you use social media to help you in this process? Will you make your purchases online or at bricks-and-mortar stores?

Exercises

The exercises in this chapter involve the scenario presented below. Read this scenario and answer the questions based on the events described in the scenario.

The Case of Eric Jamal: LinkedIn and Windows App Store

Eric Jamal is a developer on Team Windows at APPFORMS. Eric and his fellow developer Allia

Naqvi have recently developed a set of new apps based on location-based services that allow users to receive alerts, navigate to the physical locations of restaurants and retail outlets, and even receive health care when needed. Once apps are tested and approved, Larissa Zhao, manager of Team Windows, authorizes the release of the apps to the Windows App Store. They then hand the management of the apps to the business analyst on the team, Maria Andretti. Ben Membertou, the finance and accounting person on the team, begins to track downloads of new apps and the revenue generated. The other teams at APPFORMS follow a similar process, with some variations.

Eric feels they need to do something different for this new set of apps. In addition to promoting the description of the apps on the Windows App Store, he is convinced that they can use LinkedIn to promote the apps. The others in the team are not so sure.

1. Why is Eric Jamal convinced that LinkedIn would serve them best in promoting this new set of apps?
2. Why are the others in the team not so sure?
3. What are the alternatives? Why? How can these alternatives be used effectively?
4. Once apps are developed for a particular smartphone platform (for example, Windows), they are then modified so they work on the other platforms. If you were a member of Team Android, how would you proceed to market this new set of apps using social media? What would you do differently from what Eric Jamal suggested?

Good Advice or Bad?

1. You are at an office party and you take several photos of your co-workers. You are also in many of the photos. The next day as you are looking at the photos with a friend who is not a co-worker, the friend suggests you upload the photos to Instagram. Good advice or bad? Why?
2. You are an assistant manager at a microbrewery. You have new Facebook and Twitter pages. After inviting people to stop by and sample your product, you ask them to comment about it on your social media pages. One of your friends suggests that you can also employ an Internet marketing firm that will pay people to like your products on Facebook and add followers to your Twitter page. Good advice or bad? Why?
3. You are a co-op intern at a beverage company that produces and sells carbonated drinks. You have been asked to come up with some catchy memes to promote your product. Your friend from another country recommends you look at content in Spanish and Italian for similar products and simply translate them into English. He says no one will know if you use them. Good advice or bad? Why?
4. You are following an online news article about the quality of restaurants in your neighbourhood. A version of it appears on Reddit and users begin posting various comments about the neighbourhood and the restaurants. Some of these comments are offensive and you share them with some friends. One of them suggests that you too go on the offensive and "take down these trolls." Good advice or bad. Why?
5. You own a fast-food restaurant and take pride in the quality of the food and the service you offer. However, you recently came across a review on Yelp that was quite unfavourable to you and your restaurant. Your restaurant manager suggests you sue the people who made the comments. Good advice or bad? Why?

Strategic Language: Using Optimal Language for Writing Online

Hoa Loranger, writing on the Nielsen Norman Group (Loranger, 2014), says, "Web writing differs from print writing to emphasize scannability. Some grammar rules are worth breaking if they improve fast comprehension." He states that writing online is different from writing for print because web users are often action-oriented, read very few words, and can be confused when a search leads them to something they were not seeking. Also, web content is delivered to users in multiple platforms (computers, smartphones, etc.). Loranger states that while some grammar rules should never be broken, web content is more readable using flexible style guidelines:

1. Use sentence fragments.
2. Use numerals for all numbers.
3. Paragraphs may can contain fewer than three sentences.

Consider the writing in the following paragraph. Rewrite the message so that you use sentence fragments and numerals for small numbers, and decide on the number of sentences so that the message can be posted on Facebook, Twitter, and Reddit. Choose an appropriate title for the post that would appear on Facebook and Reddit.

> In recent years, there has been a slow increase in the popularity of alternative sources of energy, particularly solar and wind. While the costs of setting up solar panels and windmill grids are high, increased demand and long-term returns will make these systems cost effective and sustainable. Many locations where sunshine is plentiful year round have seen the slow, but steady rise of rooftop solar panels. Homeowners have been able to generate enough electricity from rooftop solar panels to power their homes and put energy back into the city grids at market rates. Utility companies want to buy the energy at a lower rate because they feel they are shortchanging those who get their supply directly from the utilities. Alternatively, utility companies want to raise the rates to direct energy consumers to offset utility company costs of buying energy at the market rate from rooftop solar panel users. The case of wind farms is completely different, however. Homeowners cannot afford to set up their own windmill. The location of wind farms near residential areas seems to be causing some health risks and high rates of annoyance from the noise generated from the windmills. Four families in London, ON, are looking at legal recourses to have the wind farms moved from near residential areas, but appear to be blocked by complex laws. The move to sustainable energy sources is fraught with new and unanticipated issues that governments, environmental bodies, and citizens need to work together to resolve.

Additional Resources

Additional Internet Resources

Best practices for attribution [Blog post]. (n.d.). Retrieved from https://wiki.creativecommons.org/wiki/Best_practices_for_attribution

Cooper, B. (2015, January 8). Write the perfect blog post: 4 tips from 24 months of content marketing [Blog post]. Retrieved from https://zapier.com/blog/how-to-write-a-blog-post/

Hoelzel, M. (2015). A breakdown of the demographics for each of the different social networks [Blog post]. Retrieved from http://www.businessinsider.com/update-a-breakdown-of-the-demographics-for-each-of-the-different-social-networks-2015-6

Lin, A. (n.d.) Write like a pro: 5 techniques top bloggers use to write successful blog posts. Retrieved from http//:www.convinceandconvert.com/content-marketing/write-like-a-pro-5-techniques-top-bloggers-use-to-write-successful-blog-posts/

Rampton, J. (2015, April 13). 20 free images for your blog or social media posts [Blog post]. Retrieved from http://www.inc.com/john-rampton/20-sites-with-free-images-for-your-blog-or-social-media-posts.html

Rotolo, A. (2012, January 23). How to write an effective blog post [Blog post]. Retrieved from http://infospace.ischool.syr.edu/2012/01/23/how-to-write-an-effective-blog-post/

Bibliography

eBiz MBA Guide (2016). The top 500 sites on the web. Retrieved from http://www.ebizmba.com/articles/social-networking-websites.

Alexa (2016). The top 500 sites on the web. Retrieved from http://www.alexa.com/topsites/global.

Amin (2012, December 5). Learn from yammer and become an adaptive tech company [Blog post]. Retrieved from https://7geese.com/learn-from-yammer-and-become-an-adaptive-tech-company/.

Biocca, F., Harms, C., & Burgoon, J. (2003). Towards a more robust theory and measure of social presence: Review and suggested criteria. *Presence: Teleoperators and Virtual environments, 12* (5), 456–480. doi: 10.1162/105474603322761270.

Bradt, G. (2011, April 27). Top executives agree there are only three key job interview questions. *Forbes.* Retrieved from http://www.forbes.com/sites/georgebradt/2011/04/27/top-executive-recruiters-agree-there-are-only-three-key-job-interview-questions/.

Chaffey, D. (2011). Mobile usage statistics 2010–2015, *Smart Insights.* Retrieved from http://www.smartinsights.com/mobile-marketing/mobile-marketing-analytics/mobile-usage-statistics-2010-2015/.

Chapman, M. (2014, January 10). Target Corp reveals full scale of payment card theft: 70 million customers' data stolen. *Financial Post.* Retrieved from http://business.financialpost.com/2014/01/10/target-corp-credit-card-breach/.

China-Japan "Voldemort" attacks up ante in propaganda war. (2014, January 8). *Reuters.* Retrieved from http://uk.reuters.com/article/2014/01/08/uk-china-japan-idUKBREA0704620140108.

Clifford, S. (2009, April 15). Video prank at Domino's taints brand. *The New York Times.* Retrieved from http://www.nytimes.com/2009/04/16/business/media/16dominos.html?_r=0 –.

Cornelissen, J. (2014). *Corporate communication: A guide to theory and practice* (4th ed.). London: SAGE.

Cuddy, A. (2012, June). *Amy Cuddy: Your body language shapes who you are.* [Video file]. Retrieved from http://www.ted.com/talks/amy_cuddy_your_body_language_shapes_who_you_are.

Doyle, A. (2015, January 11). College job interview questions and answers. *About Careers.* Retrieved from http://jobsearch.about.com/od/interviewquestions answers/a/collegegrad.htm.

Gartner. (2013, December 16). Gartner predicts business intelligence and analytics will remain top focus for CIOs through 2017. Retrieved from http://www.gartner.com/newsroom/id/2637615.

Gil, P. (n.d.). What is a "meme"? What are examples of modern internet memes? *About Tech.* Retrieved from http://netforbeginners.about.com/od/weird webculture/f/What-Is-an-Internet-Meme.htm.

Glassdoor. (2015, March 25). 50 most common interview questions. Retrieved from http://www.glassdoor.com/blog/common-interview-questions/.

Gunawardena, C.N. (1995). Social presence theory and implications for interaction collaborative learning in computer conferences. *International Journal of Education Telecommunications, 1* (2/3), 147–166.

Harjani, A. & Min, W. (2014, November 9). Alibaba to smash single's day sales record. Retrieved from https://ca.finance.yahoo.com/news/alibaba-smash-singles-day-sales-record-223605524.html.

HBS Elevator Pitch Builder. (2007). Harvard Business School.

Helpguide.org (n.d.) Retrieved from http://www.helpguide.org/life/job_networking_how_to_find_job.htm.

Henschen, D. (2014, January 30). 16 Top big data analytics platforms. *Information Week.* Retrieved from http://www.informationweek.com/big-data/big-data-analytics/16-top-big-data-analytics-platforms/d/d-id/1113609.

Stempel, J. (2015). Teacher fired. *Huffpost Politics.* Retrieved from http://www.huffingtonpost.com/entry/court-rules-teacher-cant-sue-after-being-fired-for-blogging-about-her-students_us_55e9bddce4b002d5c075d722/.

Irish, R. & Weiss, P. E. (2013). *Engineering communication: From principles to practice* (2nd ed.). Toronto, ON: Oxford University Press.

Karstens-Smith, G. & Rushowy, K. (2013, November 13). "Blackface" controversy at Mayfield Secondary School in Caledon not the first. *Toronto Star.* Retrieved from http://www.thestar.com/news/gta/2013/11/12/black face_controversy_at_mayfield_secondary_school_in_caledon_not_the_first.html.

Lions Club (n.d.). Icebreakers, team building activities, and energizers. Retrieved from www.lionsclubs.org/EN/common/pdfs/icebreakers.pdf.

Loranger, H. (2014, March 23). Break grammar rules on websites for clarity. *Nielsen Norman Group.* Retrieved from http://www.nngroup.com/articles/break-grammar-rules/.

Lowenthal, P. (2009, February 22). Social presence: What is it? And why does it matter? Retrieved from http://www.slideshare.net/plowenthal/social-presence-what-is-it-and-why-does-it-matter.

Marshall, R. (2014, July 2). How to estimate ROI for customer-facing mobile apps. *Gartner.* https://www.gartner.com/doc/2789317?ref=SiteSearch&sthkw=customer%20usage%20of%20data%20analytics&fnl=search&srcId=1-3478922254.

NSBI (n.d.). Invest in Nova Scotia, Growth Sectors, Information and Communication Technology. Retrieved from http://www.novascotiabusiness.com/en/home/invest/sectorinfo/technology/default.aspx.

OECD. (2005). Glossary of statistical terms. Retrieved from http://stats.oecd.org/glossary/detail.asp?ID=6864.

OECD. (2001). STI scoreboard. Retrieved from http://www.oecd.org/sti/sci-tech/1900544.pdf.

Paradis, D. (2013, August 20). Presentation tip: The grammar of text on slides [Blog post]. Retrieved from http://pptideas.blogspot.ca/2013/08/presentation-tip-grammar-of-text-on.html.

Picciano, A.G. (2002). Beyond student perceptions: Issues of interaction, presence, and performance in an online course. *Journal of Asynchronous Learning Networks, 6*(1). 21–40.

Robison, Jennifer (2006, June 8). Too many interruptions at work? *Gallup Business Journal.* Retrieved from http://businessjournal.gallup.com/content/23146/too-many-interruptions-at-work.aspx#2.

Rosenbush, S. (2005, July 19). News Corp.'s place in MySpace. *Bloomberg BusinessWeek.* Retrieved from www.businessweek.com/technology/content/jul2005/tc20050719_5427_tc119.htm.

Shontell, A. (2013). Actually, Snapchat doesn't delete your private pictures and someone found a way to resurface them. *Business Insider.* Retrieved from http://www.businessinsider.com/snapchat-doesnt-delete-your-private-pictures-2013-5.

Social Driver. (2013, July 9). 6 biggest social media fails (and what you can learn from them) [Blog post]. *Get with the Future.* Retrieved from http://socialdriver.com/2013/07/09/6-biggest-social-media-fails-and-what-you-can-learn-from-them/.

The Statistics Portal (n.d.). Transitional words & phrases. Retrieved from http://www.statista.com/.

Sundararajan, B. & Sundararajan, M. (2012). Like us on Facebook and follow us on Twitter: Corporate identity management across social media platforms. In C. Cunningham (Ed.), *Social networking and impression management* (pp. 129–146) Toronto, ON: Lexington.

Sword, H. (2012, July 23). Zombie nouns. *The New York Times.* Retrieved from http://opinionator.blogs.nytimes.com/2012/07/23/zombie-nouns/.

Tennant, D. (2016, March 11). Smartphones review. *Top Ten Reviews.* http://cell-phones.toptenreviews.com/smartphones/.

Verkooij, Kim. (2012, June 29). Mobile business intelligence: Key considerations for implementation projects. *Journal of Computer Information Systems, 54* (1), 23–33.

Wilson, K.G. (1993). *The Columbia guide to standard American English.* New York: Columbia University Press.

Writing Center at UNC-Chapel Hill (2014). Transitions. Retrieved from http://writingcenter.unc.edu/handouts/transitions/.

Glossary

agenda a list of meeting activities in the order of importance

analysis to break up or loosen; to understand individual components of a project, process, event, or activity in order to learn how things work, what did not work, and what can be done to improve the process

apps smartphone or computer applications

argumentation a process of reasoning by providing supporting evidence to any claims or counter-claims, using rebuttals appropriately

attributes characteristics or traits of an individual or thing

Baidu Tieba Chinese text, video, photo posting site

behavioural question a standard job interview question where the candidate is asked to give an example of a particular behaviour or trait, such as levelheadedness, initiative, and so on

business intelligence (BI) update statistics about how a business is doing, based on the various aspects of that business, i.e., sales, production, supply, accounts receivables, payables, hiring, payroll, client management, etc.

BI dashboard a business intelligence snapshot providing highlights of the key performance indicators of a business

block style all the elements of the letter are aligned on the left

brand a product, service, individual, group, organization, or even idea that is clearly distinguishable from other similar entities

business process analysis analysis of various main and sub-processes in any business

chronological résumés résumés that provide education and experience history in chronological order (usually in reverse)

cloud-based servers maintained by a third-party company used to manage the IT needs of an organization

clustering a grouping of items in certain categories or themes

cover letter a letter that accompanies a résumé and highlights how a candidate fits the job being applied for

cross-functional team a team with experts in multiple disciplines often brought together to complete a specific task or project

data analytics the analytical processes and software used to provide intelligent information to businesses by analyzing volumes of business data

decision matrix a matrix that allocates weights to attributes or options for an event or set of choices, based on predetermined criteria

diversity having variety in thought, action, team, or organizational composition to allow for cross-pollination of different perspectives. There are many types of diversity including cultural, ethnic, gender, sexual orientation, age, and subcultural

elevator pitch a series of short statements that highlight the achievements of individuals, products, or organizations, so that individuals can get job interviews, products can be purchased, or ideas can be funded

enumeration using numbered lists

ethics the possession of a set of high moral standards

ethos Greek for ethics

explain the background provide information on the context and frames of reference for an event

Facebook the most popular social media site at present

faux pas a social error

feasibility analysis a report that analyzes the feasibility of a project or endeavour

flog a fake blog

form how something appears or is expected to appear; its shape, structure, etc.

frequency the number of times a message is seen or heard

functional résumés résumés that focus on specific job experiences, rather than the chronology of the experiences; used particularly when there are gaps in the work or education history

gone viral when information or message spreads rapidly across many networks in a short period of time

icebreakers activities that can help people getting to know one another

informational report a report that provides particular information about an event or project or business activity

Internet troll typically a person (or assumed to be a person) who posts inflammatory messages to provoke emotional responses from users or communities

knowledge-based economy an economy where information and data hold the key to many successful businesses, and directly affects the gross domestic product (GDP) of that economy

lean a way of thinking in business that sheds complicated processes, and adopts simple ways and means to achieve business goals

LinkedIn a professional networking site

logos Greek for logic; logical reasoning

meme an image, video, piece of text, etc., typically humorous in nature that is copied and spread rapidly by Internet users, often with slight variations

memo short for memorandum, the standard form for sending intra-organizational messages, both vertical and horizontal

mimēma that which is imitated

MOST analysis Mission, Objectives, Strategies, and Tactics analysis

networking the process of identifying individuals or groups to whom one can be of service and, in return, benefit from

Orkut A social networking site started by Google that is quite popular in Brazil and India

pathos Greek for emotion

PESTLE analysis Political, Economic, Sociological, Technological, Legal, and Environmental analysis

progress report a report that updates management about how a project is progressing and what the timelines for completion are likely to be

pulled messages that draw people to a particular product, service, or website

pushed messages that push the target audience via a variety of communication channels to search for a product, service, or information

QQ Chinese instant messaging application

reach the ability to be read or seen by a maximum possible number of people

résumé a short one- or two-page summary of a job seeker's work experience, education, and activity history

rhetoric the art of effective speaking or writing—according to Isocrates, also the art of ethical choice in human affairs

roadmaps signs to indicate to the audience or reader where in the narrative they are at that present time

root cause analysis a type of investigative analysis process conducted to identify the main cause of a particular event

SCOPE Strategy, Content, Outcome, Presentation, and Ethics

signposts signs to indicate to the audience or reader where in the narrative they are at that present time

Sina Weibo Chinese microblogging site

situational question a standard job interview question where the candidate is asked to explain how he or she would respond when facing a particular workplace situation such as conflict with a co-worker or client, an ethical dilemma, and so on

Skype a video conferencing application

Snapchat an instant messaging application where message contents are supposed to disappear after a very short time

solicited something specifically requested, such as a job advertisement seeking candidates

specific request what the asker or sender wants the receiver to do or provide

stakeholders key constituents for an organization who are directly or indirectly benefited by the organization

STAR a process of answering behavioural questions in a job interview that describe situation, task, action, and results

state the purpose clear mention of what is required of the receiver or audience

status report a report that provides the current status of an event, project, or business activity

style how something is presented; how it looks and feels, the way a presentation is delivered, the way a narrative is able to captivate a reader or audience

substantive important matter

SWOT Analysis Strengths, Weaknesses, Opportunities, Threats analysis, often conducted about a particular organization

synthesis to place together; the process or putting things together in a manner easily consumed by the targeted audience

template a pre-formatted, ready-to-use document that can be customized

text any written, spoken, acted, created product including video, report, graphic, song, picture, etc.

the "get" what one can expect to get from an individual or organization in exchange for the "give"

the "give" what one should expect to give to an individual or organization in exchange for the "get"

timeline a series of dates with times of completion for each part or phase of a project, event, or business activity

trope a figurative or metaphorical use of a word or expression. It is often seen used as a significant or recurrent theme

Twitter A popular microblogging site

unsolicited something not specifically requested

uptake making use of something readily available

Vostu A social games developer in Brazil

work ethic a value based on hard work, attention to detail, professionalism, and high ethical standards

Xing European social networking site for business professionals

Index